MW00826844

# CONCEPTIONS OF HAPPINESS

## REVISED EDITION

## Ignacio L. Götz

University Press of America,® Inc.
Lanham · Boulder · New York · Toronto · Plymouth, UK

Library of Congress Control Number: 2009938915
ISBN: 978-0-7618-4995-7 (paperback : alk. paper)
eISBN: 978-0-7618-4996-4

♾™ The paper used in this publication meets the minimum
requirements of American National Standard for Information
Sciences—Permanence of Paper for Printed Library Materials,
ANSI Z39.48-1992

To those who have enriched their lives with joy

*Deine erste Pflicht ist, dich selbst glücklich zu machen.*
*Bist du glücklich, so machst du auch andere glüchlich.*
*Der Glückliche kann nur Glückliche um sich sehen.*

Ludwig Feuerbach

# TABLE OF CONTENTS

# PREFACE TO THE REVISED EDITION

It is, perhaps, inappropriate to write a Preface to a book on happiness; the matter should disclose itself to the reader directly, without intermediaries. One might even wonder why there should be need for a book on happiness, it being clear, as Skinner maintained, that we just "know" when we are happy without anyone having to instruct us. But human experience is very rich and varied and the circumstances attending it equally diverse, so that it is proper to ask if we mean the same thing when we, dwellers of such multifarious cultures, call ourselves happy. To be happy, claimed Fuentelapeña, is to be "flooded by a deep sea of sweetness"; but who would claim that the waters of the many seas are all the same? Does not the sky have different hues of blue in different places and at different altitudes?

It takes time to be happy, and it takes experience. But our experiences are filtered through the nurturing we have received and the biases of our cultures. To these must be added the hype of business and entertainment staking exclusive claims to their own brands of happiness. There is need, then, to discriminate, to be clever money changers capable of discerning true coinage from the counterfeit. "Pleasure," as Chamfort said, "can rest on illusion, but happiness only on truth." It is the purpose of this book to help sift the gold from the rubbish.

This book is a comprehensive study of conceptions of happiness spanning the centuries as well as various world cultures. It contains an introduction to the idea of happiness and a detailed analysis and categorization of various points of view.

After the Introduction, there is an anthology comprising twenty-six of the great statements on the subject by the great representatives of the traditions, classical as well as contemporary. Each section or chapter includes a brief sketch of the life of the author in question; a general introduction to the particular philosophy or point of view of the writer or tradition; and a brief summary of the theory of happiness espoused. The section closes with a succinct bibliography of primary as well as secondary sources. The book concludes with an Epilogue and an Index. This Revised Edition includes suggestions made by friends and colleagues regarding omissions in the previous edition.

The writing of this book has been a long, but never a tedious, journey spanning some forty years. I have found happiness in the writing of it very much as one finds a joy of sorts in a pilgrimage. Also, over the years, I taught a course on conceptions of happiness. To my students from thirty-three countries who have joined me in this inquiry I owe a debt of gratitude impossible to repay; I hope they, too, found happiness in the classroom prodding and, lately, have experienced fulfillment in their lives. May they have learned to carry a portable paradise in their hearts.

Ignacio L. Götz
Point Harbor, NC
August, 2009

# INTRODUCTION

1.  There was recently a report that claimed that in the 1960s women felt happier than men, while now the reverse was true. The report did not specify what women and men considered happiness to be in the 1960s, and what they considered it to be now. In other words, the report assumed that all people at all times in all places have the same view of what happiness is, so that all one has to do is ask whether or not they are happy, whatever that mean. This book is devoted to the proposition that this is not so. Different people at different times and in different places and climes have had different views of happiness, and these conceptions should be taken into account when asking (and answering) the question whether or not one is happy. Moreover, individuals may consider themselves happy differently at different times in their lives. This is the reason why this book deals with *conceptions* of happiness, and not with happiness in general. Happiness "in general" does not exist.

It is the same with unhappiness. Lord Russell lists several reasons why people live with a sense of foreboding, if not with actual unhappiness. Many have, he writes, a sense that we are born to fight, to suffer, and never really to enjoy ourselves or be happy. They are pessimists, or fatalists, who believe that a dark destiny is the lot of all people on earth. Others are the victims of the competitive world many nations have created for themselves and their citizens. They feel they must always be ahead of the others, and if they are not at the top, they feel defeated, unworthy, failures; or they are consumed by a corroding envy and jealousy of the successful ones. Still others are the victims of boredom, that monster who, in Camus's apt simile, haunts the labyrinthine streets of our metropolises like a minotaur, seeking whom it may devour. Others are trapped by a feeling of worthlessness, guilt, and sin, and consider themselves unworthy of such a state as happiness, or even of the fleeting excitements of joy. They live in a vale of tears, and their expectations are projected unto a heaven where, they believe, they will be eventually happy. Finally, there are those who do not seem to know what happiness is, and who therefore may pass it by whenever it crosses their path, or may turn it out whenever it knocks at their door. For all we know, they may have been happy—they may still be happy—but they do not know it, do not have the words to describe it, or the conceptual framework to understand what they feel. Some may have grown to identify happiness with only one type of experience, and when this eludes their grasp, they deem themselves unhappy when, in fact, they could count themselves among the blest. It is as if one had forever identified a good car ride with being driven in a Cadillac, and therefore could not enjoy a ride in a Chevy, or a Ford, or a Toyota. This is one major reason why this book deals with *conceptions* of happiness; that is, with different ways in which happiness has been both lived and defined by human beings on this earth.[1]

**2.**   All the theories of happiness that have been proposed agree that we aim at some kind of "good," the possession of which makes us happy. Then a further step is taken. A particular view of happiness is identified as this good. Many argue, then, that human nature is so constituted that all humans aim at *this particular good*; that is, at *this particular happiness*. This good becomes the criterion for judging the morality of actions; they are moral if they tend to, facilitate, or obtain the good, or if the good results from them; they are immoral if the consequence is otherwise. Finally, a "system" of dos and don'ts is constructed, sometimes even legally, for the guidance and evaluation of human behavior. In this way a marriage is effected between happiness and morality. Happiness and "the good life" become indistinguishable, and one may even seem to speak reasonably of an inalienable "*right* to the pursuit of happiness."

**3.**   Let us begin. In ordinary usage, happiness often means *temperament*; that is, a disposition to be cheerful, and, generally, to be unmoved or greatly disturbed by reverses of fortune. It also connotes *mood*, or frame of mind, as when we say we are "feeling happy," or "feeling good," where the antonym is "sad." While temperament connotes a certain stability of character ("he/she has a happy disposition"), mood conveys a peculiar note of fleetingness: moods come and go, and "feeling happy" may soon give way to "feeling sad." There is a third usage, though, that in some ways encompasses both the temporality of mood and the stability of temperament in some kind of *life long* characterization of a person's life. When we say, "he/she has found happiness," or "he/she led a happy life," we seem to have in mind some kind of overall preponderance of happiness over unhappiness, such as would allow us truthfully to label a person's life "happy."[2]

**4.**   It is primarily this third version of ordinary usage that is up here for discussion. But some further clarifications are necessary. It is customary to distinguish between the *definition* or the *meaning* of happiness, and the *reality* of happiness; between what the term happiness *means* in particular circumstances, and what counts as an *experience* of happiness. Not that the two are entirely disconnected, for obviously, we often signify by *happiness* what we have experienced as happiness; but since experiences vary and linguistic connotations change, the distinction is not entirely inappropriate.[3] Further, there are also *conditions* of happiness, circumstances that will determine whether or not one will experience it, whatever it be. Thus we have chance factors, such as winning the lottery; dispositional factors, such as health, moods, and the like; and human agency factors, such as the steps we take (or fail to take) to render happiness possible for us.[4]

5.    Etymologically, the definition of happiness presents certain problems, for the denotation is different in different languages, and many languages employ several terms to denote facets and nuances of the experience.

In English, *happiness* comes from the root *hap*, meaning chance, good luck or fortune. The connection with chance is clear when one thinks of words such as per-*haps*, and its synonym per-*chance*. The closest definition can be given in John Fowler's words: "Happiness is that it happens to me."[5] In this sense, happiness is akin to German *Glück*, luck; to Sanskrit *sukha*; and to Latin *felix* (and Spanish *feliz*).

Other languages have words (some of them imported into English) which emphasize other aspects of the experience of happiness: *blessedness*, and *rapture* convey the sense that the lucky one has been chosen by the gods; *bliss* (*blith, blithe*) express the feeling of kind-heartedness and joy, which *joy* itself, and *glad* convey; *enjoyment, pleasure* (Sanskrit *bhoga*), *relish* convey a feeling of earthy abandon; the Greek *eudaimonia*, good spirits, expresses geniality, high spirits, merriment, well-being, inner comfort, ease; in many languages, the predominant character is visual: *beatitude* (Latin *beare*, to see), *enchantment, beatific*; the unending character of happiness is conveyed by the Sanskrit *ânand* (= a[n]ant= no-end); *playfulness* is expressed in such terms as frolicsome, funny, cheerful; and finally, the inebriating tone of the experience is kept in terms such as *ecstasy, trance*, and *fascination*.

6.    Beyond etymology, one might define happiness generally as *a certain kind of relationship between a person and his/her own existence.* This is, essentially, the definition given by Camus. The relation grounds a judgment, often implicit, about the value of the relation.[6]   The judgment asserts, first, that the relationship lacks dissatisfactions that are lasting, preponderant, and considered serious by the judge; second, that most of the judge's most important wants or desires are satisfied most exquisitely. Thus, the judgment regards both quantity and quality of satisfaction; third, that there is balance of positive feeling over negative; that is, happiness is not merely not being unhappy; rather, it is positively "being happy."[7] Briefly, one might say that a statement about one's happiness involves a judgment of *the balance of satisfaction over desires.* It is as if the essence of happiness could be expressed by an equation:

$$\text{Happiness} = \frac{\text{satisfaction}}{\text{desires}}$$

Typically, approaches to and definitions of happiness will vary as they emphasize an increase in the *numerator* or a decrease in the *denominator*. For example, if to be happy *all* of one's desires must be satisfied, happiness is relegated to a transcendent stage, as in a heaven. This is the position of Christianity, Vedanta, Islam. If, on the other hand, the amount of satisfaction is considered finite, then one's desires must be curtailed. This is the view of Stoicism, Hedonism, and, generally, of contentment.

Typically, again, views of happiness that emphasize the numerator tend to be *elitist*; that is, open only to the few: the contemplative, the pessimists, the heroes. On the other hand, emphasis on the denominator characterizes *populist* positions, such as those of hedonism, stoicism, and the followers of Dionysus.

Again, numerator-based views tend to be *individualistic*, or to see happiness primarily in terms of individual achievement, while denominator-based views tend to be social, or *universalistic*; that is, they see happiness as available to everybody.[8]

7.   But it may be that the answer to the question, "What is happiness?" cannot be ratiocinated. It may be that we all come to know what happiness is through some experience, intuition, or direct awareness. Skinner has certainly maintained this, and one can easily see how G.E. Moore, too, might argue a similar position. Happiness, he might say, is undefinable, just as "good" is, and "yellow," and "blue." We *know* what yellow is, and we understand what anyone talking about yellow means, only because we have had a direct, experiential knowledge of it. It would be impossible to communicate what yellow is to someone who had never experienced it, such as someone blind from birth. Similarly, one could argue that we all know what happiness is, and we understand what someone talking about happiness means, because we have experienced happiness ourselves.

The matter becomes more complicated if one considers that people's experiences are extraordinarily varied. In consequence, some people may have come to experience what they call happiness only in certain circumstances, at certain times, or in connection with certain objects. On being asked, "What is happiness?" they might be expected to respond exclusively by reference to their experience, which may not at all match that of the questioner, who might then conclude that the person queried did not know what happiness is. This is possible because happiness, unlike yellow, is not defined within very clear and fixed parameters, as vibrations of a certain wavelength within the color spectrum. Asking someone, "What is happiness?" is, rather, like asking someone, "What is color?" If the respondent answered based on his/her experience of red, while the questioner had in mind his/her *own* experience of blue, the questioner might reasonably conclude that the answerer did not know what color was. But obviously, this conclusion is only partly correct.

8.   Similarly, it might be possible to maintain generally that someone asserting, "I

am happy," cannot be mistaken, in the same way as someone asserting, "I am thinking," or "I have a pain in the head," cannot be mistaken. Such statements are incorrigible if made while the subject is undergoing the experience in question. On the other hand, the fact that experiences of happiness are polymorphous renders the statement, "I am happy," questionable so long as no agreement on a definition of happiness has been reached beforehand. It is this polymorphous nature of the experience of happiness that allows us to raise legitimate questions about statements, such as "I am happy," which otherwise would be deemed incorrigible.[9]

9.    Finally, in some traditions, such as Buddhism, happiness consists in the total annihilation of the denominator ("desires"). But when such a negation takes place, the desiring self is thereby eliminated, so that the resulting equation, "Happiness = satisfaction" is meaningless because there is nothing to which it might be referred.

According to the Buddha, happiness is the name of a state in which there is no desire, not even the desire for the self to exist so as to enjoy happiness. It is a state of pure cessation, and this, logically, entails the cessation of the self. But we are incapable of conceiving what a state without a self might be, or what it might mean to be without a self. If happiness is this being without a self, then, indeed, it is *nirvâna,* that is, unutterable, unspeakable, ineffable; not because it is exalted and beyond description but because we truly have no idea what it could mean. Happiness, therefore, may ultimately exist, but it is ultimately indescribable.

10.    The different views of happiness presented here follow a chronological order, for they are centered on their original or most representative proponents. But it is possible to view the human pursuit of happiness from a different perspective. Stephan Strasser, in *Das Gemüt,* has given us a phenomenological typology that can be used as a base for a description of the various ways in which human beings have thought of, as well as pursued, happiness. *Happiness as chance,* of which we spoke already, is one of them, and I will say nothing more about it here, but I would like to comment on the others by way of introducing this matter of conceptions of happiness. I shall begin with those views that generally enlarge the numerator of the equation *satisfaction/desires.*

11.    *Happiness as transcendence.* To wish for a happiness without end; to desire an absolute satisfaction of one's desires; to want to be freed from temporality and short-comings is to make the experience of happiness so perfect that it cannot be had fully in this life, or in this place. Glimpses of it, perhaps, may be caught here, but the fullness of the experience must wait for our delivery from this earth. Vedanta, Christianity, Islam: all proclaim a happiness so ineffable that it can exist only in heaven. St. Augustine, al-Ghazâli, St. Thomas Aquinas, as well as Teilhard de Chardin and Hermann Hesse—their happiness is a *non plus ultra* of heavenly bliss. Even the Marxist notion of happiness is transcendent; for although Marx rejects heaven as an illusion, we are promised heaven on earth after the revolution; that is,

after the elimination of the present conditions that engender illusion.

**12.** *Happiness as ecstasy*. For Strasser, the term is *rapture* (*entzücken*):

> The enraptured one . . . will be drawn out of himself and, what is more, drawn by a power that is "other than himself"—in the present case by the power of an experience of happiness. Happiness as rapture will assume the forms of enthusiasm, trance, ecstasy, that is, of conditions in which the subject forgets his being-a-subject; (whence the impression of being driven out of oneself by foreign powers, forces, spirits). The man who enters into rapture gives himself over to a "foreign" life which enchants, inspires, and sweeps him away.[10]

This kind of happiness has existed in all cultures and times, though it has always been frowned upon by those in control, for it is a happiness of excess, of letting go. Dionysus is the patron of ecstatic happiness, and his worship is maintained in the various *tantric* movements of eastern cultures. In the West, the exhilaration of masquerades, still preserved in Mardi Gras and Carnival and in "Freak Formals" and Halloween celebrations, bears witness to this ecstatic happiness in which we transcend ourselves yet remain on earth. The masks help, for they conceal identity; so does the drink, for it dissolves the Ego's boundaries and creates the new, temporary identity of the group. "Forget the difference," Dionysus says, "and you will find a new identity, larger than your self."[11]

Besides the drink, dance has been a major tool of ecstatic happiness, because its means of transcending the ego, its tool of intoxication, is none other than the body of the dancer. All of this is communal, and where the dance has degenerated into duet, it is difficult to appreciate the ecstatic nature of dancing. Not without significance, an old Chinese proverb remarked that one can judge a king by the state of dancing during his reign, and Plato, with the rest of his countrymen, believed that one mark of an educated person was the ability to take part in the choral dances of a play (*agoreutos apaideutos*).[12]

The pursuit of ecstatic happiness has declined *pari passu* with the rise of rationalism in society. The barometer for this decline is the presence or absence of choral dancing in a culture, and the judgments we make of its significance. Champagne bashes for the winners at the end of a sports season, cast parties at the end of a play, dancing the *hora* during weddings, are celebrative affirmations of life that remind us of what once was prevalent, but has now ceased to be the rule.

**13.** *Happiness as rational harmony*. Ecstatic and heavenly views of happiness place the experience in a moment which transcends time. Rational harmony (*eudaimonia*) concentrates on an experience of happiness that is *this*-worldly and, consequently, immersed in time. It is something we can achieve while alive and can enjoy over a reasonably lengthy period of time. This is Apollonian happiness, the happiness of the Golden Mean. It implies the rejection of disorder as "barbaric," and the triumph of *logos* over *pathos*.

This form of happiness received its fullest expression in Plato's conception, but it can be found, too, in Stoicism and Epicureanism, as well as in the philosophies of the Buddha and of Lao-tzu. It is, undoubtedly, a difficult thing to achieve, and therefore it has always been the province of an elite, admired by the populace, but never truly popular.

**14**. *Happiness as contemplation*. The idea that happiness consists primarily in the exercise of the mind can be traced to Aristotle. For him, it is a happiness to be had here, on this earth. Christianity turned Greek *eudaimonia* into heavenly beatitude, the beatific vision, which is the overwhelming contemplation of the Divine Essence. Aquinas's statement, "The essence of happiness consists in an act of the intellect,"[13] is basically Aristotelian; but for Aristotle, such an experience takes place here on earth, among one's friends, while for Aquinas, it takes place in heaven, and is essentially individualistic.

The pursuit of happiness as contemplation became the ideal of the Western tradition, though it obviously was restricted to an elite. Efforts to make the ideal accessible to the populace have always misfired, and now more than ever the ideal remains unattainable by the multitude. In fact, democracy has always been inimical to contemplation, for democracies want equality, not justice, yet the truth of contemplation is esoteric and not determinable by majority vote. For the democrat, as Norman O. Brown put it years ago, truth is what any fool can see.

A life constantly overshadowed by the exercise of the mind is a contemplative life (*bios theoretikos*); such a life is supremely happy because it drinks from the deepest springs of what makes us human *par excellence*, our rational minds. Thomas Jefferson sipping sherry with his friends in the rotunda of his house at Monticello, and pondering the questions raised by the philosophers of the Enlightenment, is as true and perfect a picture of contemplative happiness as has ever been painted.

**15**. *Happiness as contentment*. Some approaches to happiness concentrate on a *decrease* of the denominator in the equation *satisfaction/desires*. That is, they place the emphasis on a "containment" of desires, on not letting desires exceed the amount of satisfaction available. When a fit is achieved between what one wants and what one gets *because one wants only what one can get*, one is happy. This is contentment.

Contentment is essentially the approach of Stoicism, Hedonism (including Bentham and Mill), the Qôhéleth, Lao-tzu, the Buddha, Schopenhauer, and Freud. For all of these, though in different ways, happiness consists in knowing how to adjust oneself and one's desires to the circumstances of time, place, persons, working conditions, and the like, in which one happens to find oneself. One knows one's way around. One knows how to accommodate oneself to one's environment, and out of this adjustment is born a certain sense of happiness, namely, contentment. The containment necessary for this kind of happiness is achieved in either of two ways, by checking desires in oneself (*enkrateia*), or by redefining certain things as *not desirable* (*sophrosyne*). Either way the fit of contentment is achieved, and happiness ensues.

**16.** *Happiness as possession.* Many people find their happiness in material possessions. "Possession" here may mean *consumption*, the acquisition of material goods; thus we have "consumer happiness," which has a certain active ring to it. It may also mean, simply, *possession*, in a static sense; the experience of joy at being surrounded by things. The phenomenon is too common to require much elaboration.

No one, to my knowledge, with the exception of Ayn Rand, has made sheer possession a virtue. Feuerbach, it is true, expressed the view that people are what they eat ("*der Mensch is was er isst*"[14]), but he did not elaborate. The Roman Emperors understood this, and therefore they made sure that they provided for the people "*panem et circenses*"—"bread and circus"; that is, mouth-watering victuals and entertainment to be consumed, a strategy well known to governments ever since.

The rationale for the connection between happiness and things is easy to see: if one *has* everything one's heart desires (and money can buy), is not one satisfied? and is not one thereby happy?

From another perspective, happiness as possession is the unique experience of beings who are both subjects and objects in the world; it is the happiness of those who, at least momentarily, reap the benefit of a habitual synthesis of subjectivity and objectivity (of the for-itself and the in-itself); it is the happiness of experiencing what one lacks as subjectivity, namely, objectivity, not statically, but dynamically, in the process of possessing. Therefore, in a very true and perfectly orthodox sense, it is an experience of fulfillment, of fullness, of completeness.

**17.** *Happiness as striving.* Can one claim realistically that the sum of happiness experienced through a life time is, for all and sundry, greater than the sum of unhappiness? The answer is probably No. Can we, then, measure the general value of life primarily in terms of happiness? The answer, again, is No. Moreover, being happy is not something that depends on us alone, since so many fortuitous circumstances attend its acquisition. Happiness, thus, is only conditionally good (that is, conditioned on circumstances outside our control). Accordingly, Kant did not consider happiness as *the* primary goal of life. For him, the goal was *to become worthy* of happiness.

For Nietzsche, similarly, the goal was not happiness, but power; that is, self-overcoming. And for Camus, the goal was revolt. Thus we have the emergence of a point of view that makes happiness a concomitant or accompaniment of striving. It is as if for Kant, Nietzsche, and Camus (though in different ways), the traditional equation *satisfaction/desires* were discarded in favor of another one, *achievement/potential*. The question for them is not, how much enjoyment, pleasure, etc., one has experienced, but how much *overcoming* one has achieved.

The result here is a view that, basically, ties happiness to heroism. In fact, Nietzsche himself uses the words: "A happy life is impossible: the highest obtainable by man is a *heroic* life."[15] Even though the context for the utterance is the somewhat pessimistic philosophy of Schopenhauer, the meaning is unmistakable. True happiness accrues only to the strong, to the heroic; for the mediocre or contented, "being mediocre is their happiness."[16] That this is a highly elitist view of happiness goes without saying. The contented may number in the billions, but of heroes there is a paucity, despite the loose use of the term in contemporary parlance. And yet, who can deny that, in their own way, they were happy?

**18**. *Happiness as egoism*. Many of the views of happiness presented above suggest or imply that happiness is to be pursued and found in isolation. More narrowly, Stirner and Ayn Rand maintain that the individual's only concern must be his/her happiness, and nobody else's.

Stoicism and Epicureanism, in their different ways, argue that the way to happiness is through a certain indifference as well as a withdrawal, so that one will not suffer pain and vexation and thereby be unhappy. This kind of withdrawal is found, too, in Hinduism, Buddhism, and in the Christian monastic tradition. Contemplative views of happiness also tend to promote isolation, since contemplation cannot be carried out properly in the hustle and bustle of daily life or amidst the noise of groups. Self-development, too, implies that one is developing *oneself*, something that can be done only by the self. Kierkegaard echoed this self-centered trend, when he wrote:

> A "crowd" is the untruth. . . this means that every man should be chary about having to do with "the others," and essentially should talk only with God and with himself—for only one attains the goal.[17]

All these views are, truly, antisocial.[18] At bottom they hearken to the essential incommunicability of the experience of happiness, as Fowler has pointed out.[19] But while it is difficult to deny the existence of a certain insularity in the experience of happiness, this does not seem to necessitate or justify a pursuit of enjoyment *at the expense of others*, as egoism recommends.

**19**. But is there happiness at all? Schopenhauer has denied it, making the goal of life the extinction of desire, and Freud, in an equally pessimistic vein, has seen civilized life, the brief flicker between nothingness and nothingness, as dominated by discontent. Earlier (No. 1) we saw Lord Russell refer to the happiness of animals, and Schopenhauer, too, thought that "the lower animals appear to enjoy a happier destiny than man."[20] This thought has ancient roots. Odysseus's mates, turned to animals by Circe, were sad to see their animal existence ended; even Circe pitied them![21] Literally, they preferred to remain satisfied as pigs than to live unsatisfied as humans. It is not difficult to see the origin of the contrast between pigs satisfied and Socrates *dis*satisfied!

I suppose there is something to be said for this view, and all the conceptions of happiness have had to deal with the presence, and even, all too often, the great amount of unhappiness in the world. As a feeling, pessimism is understandable. As a philosophy, it is self-contradictory. On the other hand, the quest for happiness, however defined, and in whatever circumstances, has been extraordinarily persistent.

**20.** Can one be truly happy before thirty? In order to prepare an answer to the question, one must first make a distinction between *product* goals and *process* goals. *Product* goals are goals which are achieved with the creation or acquisition of a product or thing. The means to this end are usually clear and well defined. All one needs to do is apply the means and the product follows. Once the product or thing has been manufactured or acquired, activity ceases. For example, wanting a table is a specific goal. We know the materials, means, and procedures needed to construct one. Once the table is produced, the activity of construction ceases, for the goal, the table, has been produced.

*Process* goals, on the other hand, are goals one aims at without ever being really certain how to acquire them. They are generally goals that are not tangible, like a chair, but are, rather, somewhat fuzzy, like being healthy, being well educated, and so forth. Again, they are goals, to obtain which, we cannot prescribe means that would be certain of obtaining the desired results. Thus, for example, we cannot say that dieting will certainly make one healthy, or that exercise will, or that taking vitamins will help, or that all of these combined will surely produce health. Further, being healthy is not something that one can stop aiming at once one is healthy; on the contrary, it is something that must be desired constantly, and must be procured indefinitely, or at least as long as one intends or desires to be healthy. Being healthy is not something that can be bottled and placed on the shelf of a medicine cabinet for use at a later time. No; it is something that must be constantly aimed at, and that exists only as a process. Therefore it can be aimed at only as a process.

Happiness is a process goal. If one wants to be happy, then being happy is something one must want to be throughout a life time; and no recipe, or set of instructions, or particulars of living will guarantee that one will be happy, either today, or tomorrow, or in twenty years. And when one is once happy, one cannot stop aiming at happiness, neither can one "save" the experience for future use during bad times. Happiness is something that exists only while one is happy; that is, while one is in the process of being happy. Therefore it is something that can be pursued only as a process.

If being happy, then, is a process; and if becoming happy is something one must achieve progressively, then it is easy to understand that certain types of experiences may be helpful at some stages and not others, and that one may experience oneself as happy in certain circumstances, at one time, and in different ones, at another.

**21.** Can one be happy in the presence of so much evil and suffering as exists in the world? Can one be happy when all around beggars beg, the homeless dwell in hovels, refugees dot the countrysides of warring countries, hospitals are full of human misery, women are raped, and innocent children are betrayed and abused?

The question is old, having been raised by Gilgamesh at the death of his friend

Enkidu. As if the spectacle of human suffering here were not sufficient, theologians have asked the question with regard to the blessed in heaven: can the saints be happy while aware of the suffering of the damned in hell? Can God himself be happy while contemplating the mess this world, which he created, is in?

Here, the Stoic answer seems insufficient. It is not enough to inure oneself against externals by the achievement of an unassailable serenity: one may counter that one *ought* to be moved by the sufferings of the world. One may claim, too, that this is one time when happiness must be sought in the experience of striving to overcome or alleviate the evil of the world in some sort of Nietzschean battle against all odds. But the *Übermensch*, after all, is not a machine; feelings are engaged even while people fight.

Optimists through the centuries have tried to reassure the troubled sentiment with rational arguments about ours being "the best of all possible worlds." Leibnitz has been made the butt of jokes about this supposedly naive optimism

Theological lore is full of answers, none of them satisfactory, considering that even God, when challenged by Job to provide one, could only grumble and hurrumph. Therefore, one can do worse than to call upon mystery here; or, perhaps, with a touch of optimism, to suggest with von Hügel, that "evil and its effects are not as fully and concentratedly evil, as good and its effects are full and concentrated."[22] If this were so, one could live with the hope that, when the world's sadness and joy are weighed, the scales will tilt toward joy. But such a thought, appropriate for quiet contemplation in the sanctuary of one's mind, is almost obscene in the real world of Auschwitz, Central Park, Bosnia, Rwanda, Darfur and Kurdistan.

There is no answer—no overall, general answer. We all must frame our own within the circumstances in which we live. The only thing to add is that for nothing in the world is the pursuit of happiness to be given up.

22. The U.S. "Declaration of Independence" affirms the existence of an inalienable right to the pursuit of happiness, and many courts in the U.S. have adjudicated cases in favor of plaintiff because they considered plaintiff's "right to the pursuit of happiness" to have been violated. But what meaning can this "right to happiness" have when both operative terms, *right* and *happiness* can mean any number of things? The Founding Fathers never defined strictly what they meant by happiness. Additionally, how is 'men' to be understood?[23]

The Declaration is more concerned with historical grievances than philosophical statements of rights.[24] The Founding Fathers were *not* egalitarians in our sense of the term, though the Declaration explicitly states that all are created "equal." They were aware that people were unequal in virtue, accomplishments, and judgment, and did not bother about socio-economic inequality as much as we do today,[25] though they understood that "everyone may equally aspire to happiness"[26] and not just the few landed aristocrats or the traditional nobility. While equal rights under the law was almost taken for granted, it would not have occurred to them that people were equal in dignity, manners, and sound moral character.[27] The American Revolution was not undertaken as a social revolution, though it eventually achieved one.[28]

Many years ago, in an article for LIFE, C. S. Lewis stated succinctly that the Declaration simply demands "that whatever means of pursuing happiness are lawful for any should be lawful for all." Beyond that, he claimed, given the ambiguities of meaning, the affirmation of a "right to happiness" does not mean anything at all. He may be correct, for beyond the generalities of seeking to actualize one's potential while respecting others' rights, it is impossible to determine, at least at a theoretical level, what means are necessary for anyone's pursuit of happiness, and which ones should be declared lawful or unlawful.

This also is true, that the Declaration affirms simply a right *to pursue* happiness, not to *be* happy. The latter would be a nonsensical affirmation, for it is ludicrous to affirm a right to be what one can never guarantee, such as a right to be ten feet tall, or to have naturally blue eyes. The actual attainment of happiness, as Kant emphasized, is contingent on a number of factors beyond our control. The acquisition of happiness, therefore, can never be a categorical duty, nor can we credit ourselves with a right to it; for it is nonsensical to require us without exception to pursue something it is not in our power alone to obtain. Similarly, what could it mean to have a right to be something we do not even know how to define, or how to obtain?

We have a right *to pursue*, that is, to strive to be whatever we want to be, as long as we respect the same right in others, and as long as our pursuit does not interfere or curtail the same right in them. We may even have the right to ask others if they are sure they know what they mean by happiness, or if what they are striving to become is worth pursuing, so long as we acknowledge *their* right equally to question us.

It also appears to be the case that the phrase meant that though the government was not the origin of it, it would *protect* equally the people's pursuit of happiness, though there was also a concern for *aiding* it. Thus Madison wrote in *The Federalist*, No. 62: "A good government implies two things: first, fidelity to the object of government, which is the happiness of the people; secondly, a knowledge of the means by which that object can be best attained." Thus, that the government would protect, and even seek to ensure the people's right to pursue their happiness was deemed obvious and natural, a matter of course. Writing to George Wythe in 1776, John Adams could state that the happiness of society is the end of government in the same way as the happiness of the individual is the ultimate human goal. It would have been as contradictory to imagine a government not seeking the happiness of its people as it would have been to conceive of an individual not pursuing happiness.

The importance of the "right to happiness," therefore, is not that it guarantees happiness, but that it guarantees equal access to its pursuit. In the best of all possible worlds, it would also guarantee that government has at heart, really, enabling all citizens to engage in the pursuit of their own happiness, a point admirably argued by Murray in his book, *In Pursuit of Happiness and Good Government*. But we are far from this, even though already Aristotle, at the beginning of political theorizing, had declared the citizens' happiness to be the goal and justification of all legitimate government.

**23.** This concludes the general introduction. With sober minds, we now pass on to the consideration of specific conceptions of happiness. These, like waters from an endless spring, have flowed on through the centuries to cool our ardors and enhance our ease. They are a testimony to the human quest for happiness in which we all, still, are engaged.

> And we will lave
> Us deep in human waters, till the mind
> Grows wise and kindly, and we haply steal
> A paradise from Nature!
> (James Stephens, "Optimist")

.oOo.

# Bibliography

Allport, Gordon. *Becoming.* New Haven: Yale University Press, 1955.

Annas, Julia. *The Morality of Happiness.* New York: Oxford University Press, 1993.

Bailyn, Bernard. *The Ideological Origins of the American Revolution.* Cambridge: Harvard University Press, 1967.

Barrow, Robin. *Happiness and Schooling.* New York: St. Martin's Press, 1980.

Bronowski, Jacob, and Bruce Mazlish, *The Western Intellectual Tradition.* New York: Harper Torchbooks, 1960.

Brown, Norman O., "Apocalypse: The place of Mystery in the Life of the Mind," in *The Movement toward a New America,* ed. Mitchell Goodman. New York: Knopf, 1970.

Camus, Albert. *The Myth of Sisyphus.* New York: Vintage, 1955.

Collard, Edgar Andrew, ed. *The Art of Contentment.* New York: Doubleday, 1974.

Csikszentmihaly, Mihaly. *Flow: The Psychology of Optimal Experience.* New York: Harper & Row, 1990.

———. *Finding Flow.* New York: Basic Books, 1997.

Delgado, José M. *Emotions.* Dubuque: Wm. C. Brown & Co., 1966.

Dodds, E. R. *The Greeks and the Irrational.* Berkeley: University of California Press, 1971.

Durant, Will and Ariel. *The Age of Voltaire.* New York: Simon & Schuster, 1965.

Durkheim, Émile. *Suicide.* Glencoe: Free Press, 1951.

Ellsberg, Robert. *The Saint's Guide to Happiness.* New York: Northpoint Press, 2003.

Erikson, Erik. *Childhood and Society.* New York: W. W. Noron & Co., 1963.

Feuerbach, Ludwig. *Briefwechsel und Nachlass,* ed. K. Grün. 2 vols. Leipzig/Heidelberg, 1874.

Fowler, James W. *Stages of Faith.* New York: Harper & Row, 1981.

Fowler, John. *The Aristos.* Boston: Little, Brown & Co., 1964.

Fromm, Erich. The Sane Society. New York: Fawcett Books, 1967.

Gelven, Michael. *Winter, Friendship, and Guilt.* New York: Harper Torchbooks, 1972.

Gibran, Kahlil. *The Prophet.* New York: Knopf, 1964.

Graves, Robert. *The Greek Myths.* 2 vols. New York: Braziller, 1955.

Gunaratana, Bhante Henepola. *Eight Mindful Steps to Happiness.* Boston: Wisdom Publications, 2001.

Hare, Richard. *Freedom and Reason.* New York: Oxford University Press, 1969.

Heidegger, Martin. *What is Called Thinking?* New York: Harper Torchbooks, 1968.

Higgs, Eric, *et al.*, eds., *Technology and the Good Life?* Chicago: The University of Chicago Press, 2000.

Hudson, Deal W. *Happiness and the Limits of Satisfaction.* Lanham, MD: Rowman & Littlefield Publishers, Inc., 1996.

Hügel, Baron Friedrich von. *Essays and Addresses on the Philosophy of Religion,* First Series. New York: Dutton, 1921.

Jaspers, Karl. *Philosophy.* 3 vols. Chicago: The University o Chicago Press, 1969.

Jones, Howard Mumford. *The Pursuit of Happiness.* Cambridg: Harvard University Press, 1953.

Kendall, Elaine. *The Happy Mediocrity.* New York: G.P. Putnam'sSons, 1971.

Kierkegaard, Søren. *The Point of View of my work as an Author.* New York: Harper Torchbooks, 1962.

Kingwell, Mark. *In Pursuit of Happiness.* New York: Crown Publishers,1998.

Lane, Robert E. *The Loss of Happiness in Market Democracies.* New Haven: Yale University Press, 2000.

Levinson, Daniel J. *The Seasons of a Man's Life.* New York: Knopf, 1978.

Luper, Steven. *Invulnerability: On Securing Happiness.* Chicago: Open Court, 1996.

Marcel, Gabriel. *Being and Having.* London: Collins, 1965.

Marcuse, Herbert. *Negations.* Boston: Beacon Press, 1968.

———. *One-Dimensional Man.* Boston: Beacon Press, 1968.

McGill, Vivian. *The Idea of Happiness.* New York: Praeger, 1947.

Mauzi, Robert. *L'idée du bonheur dans la littérature et la pensée françaises au XVIII siécle.* Paris: A. Colin, 1969.

Merleau-Ponty, Maurice. *The Phenomenology of Perception.* New York: Humanities Press, 1962.

Montague, Roger Montague, "Happiness," *Proceedings of the Aristotelian Society* ,67 (1966-1967): 87-102.

Murray, Charles. *In Pursuit of Happiness and Good Government.* New York: Simon & Schuster, 1988.

Nietzsche, Friedrich. *Thus Spoke Zarathustra.* New York: The Viking Press, 1966.

———. *Schopenhauer as Educator.* Chicago: Henry Regnery Co., 1965.

———. *The Antichrist,* in *The Portable Nietzsche,* ed. Walter Kaufmann. New York: The VikingPress, 1968.

——— *Twilight of the Gods,* in *The Portable Nietzsche,* ed. Walter Kaufmann. New York: The Viking Press, 1968.

Ortega y Gasset, José. *Obras Completas.* Madrid: Revista de Occidente, 1966 —.

Pieper, Josef. *Happiness and Contemplation.* New York: Pantheon, 1958.

Plutchik, Robert. *The Emotions.* New York: Random House, 1962.

Pontifex, M., "The Doctrine of Hell," *Downside Review* 1 (1953): 135-152.

Rouner, Leroy S., ed., *In Pursuit of Happiness.* Notre Dame, IN: Notre Dame University Press, 1995.

Rousseau, Jean-Jacques. *Émile.* New York: Teachers College Pess, 1962.

Russell, Bertrand. *The Conquest of Happiness.* New York: Bantam Books, 1958.

Sartre, Jean-Paul. *Being and Nothingness.* New York: Washingon Square Press, 1966.

Saint-Exupéry, Antoine de. *The Little Prince.* New York: Harcourt, Brace & World, 1971.

Schopenhauer, Arthur. *Studies in Pessimism*. New York:Boni & Liveright, Inc., s.a.
Strasser, Stephan. *Das Gemüt*. Utrecht: Spectrum, 1956.
————. "The experience of happiness: a phenomenological typology," in *Readings in Existential Phenomenology*, ed. Nathaniel Lawrence and Daniel O'Connor. Englewood Cliffs: Prentice-Hall, Inc., 1967.
Sumner, L. W. *Welfare Happiness and Ethics*. Oxford: Oxford University Press, 1996.
Telfer, Elizabeth. *Happiness*. New York: St. Martin's Press, 1980.
Unamuno, Miguel de. *The Tragic Sense of Life*. New York: Dover Publications, 1954.
Von Wright, G. H. *Varieties of Goodness*. London: Routledge & Kegan Paul, 1963.
Zweig, Paul. *The Heresy of Self-love*. Princeton: Princeton University Press, 1980.

.oOo.

# Notes

1. Bertrand Russell, *The Conquest of Happiness* (New York: Bantam Books, 1958), 3.
2. Elizabeth Telfer, *Happiness* (New York: St. Martin's Press, 1980), 2-3.
3. Robin Barrow, *Happiness and Schooling* (New York: St. Martin's Press, 1980), 44.
4. Ibid., 131.
5. John Fowler, *The Aristos* (Boston: Little, Brown & Co., 1964), IV.36, 72.
6. G. H. Von Wright, *Varieties of Goodness* (London: Routledge & Kegan Paul, 1963), 98; Barrow, *Happiness and Schooling*, 45.
7. Barrow, *Happiness and Schooling*, 47; Roger Montague, "Happiness." *Proceedings of the Aristotelian Society*, 67 (1966-1967), 98.
8. Herbert Marcuse, *Negations* (Boston: Beacon Press, 1968), 175-178; Paul Zweig, *The Heresy of Self-love* (Princeton: Princeton University Press, 1980), *passim*.
9. Richard Hare, *Freedom and Reason* (New York: Oxford University Press, 1969), 127-129.
10. Stephan Strasser, "The experience of happiness: a phenomenological typology," in *Readings in Existential Phenomenology*, ed. Nathaniel Lawrence and Daniel O'Connor (Englewood Cliffs: Prentice-Hall, Inc., 1967), 293.
11. E. R. Dodds, *The Greeks and the Irrational* (Berkeley: University of California Press, 1971), 76.
12. Plato *Laws* II. 654.
13. *Summa Theologiae* 1-2, 3, 4.
14. Ludwig Feuerbach, *Briefwechsel und Nachlass*, ed. K. Grün (2 vols. Leipzig/ Heidelberg, 1874), II. 90.
15. Friedrich Nietzsche, *Schopenhauer as Educator* (Chicago: Henry Regnery Co., 1965), 44-45.
16. Friedrich Nietzsche, *The Antichrist*, in *The Portable Nietzsche*, ed. Walter Kaufmann (New York: The Viking Press, 1968), 57.
17. Søren Kierkegaard, *The Point of View of My Work as an Author* (New York: Harper Torchbooks, 1962), 110-111.
18. Fowler, *The Aristos* IV.35, 72.
19. Ibid., IV.32-33.

20. Arthur Schopenhauer, *Studies in Pessimism* (New York:Boni & Liveright, Inc., s.a.), 17.

21. Homer *Odyssey* X. 388.

22. Baron Friedrich von Hügel, *Essays and Addresses on the Philosophy of Religion*, First Series (New York: Dutton, 1921), 214-215; M. Pontifex, "The Doctrine of Hell," *Downside Review* 1 (1953): 135-152.

23. Howard Mumford Jones, *The Pursuit of Happiness* (Cambridge: Harvard University Press, 1953), 99-100.

24. Jacob Bronowski and Bruce Mazlish, *The Western Intellectual Tradition*. New York: Harper Torchbooks, 1960), 380.

25. Charles Murray, *In Pursuit of Happiness and Good Government* (New York: Simon & Schuster, 1988), 168.

26. Ibid., 169.

27. Bernard Bailyn, *The Ideological Origins of the American Revolution* (Cambridge, MA: Harvard University Press, 1967), 307-308.

28. Ibid., 302.

# 1

# HINDUISM

## (With special reference to Vedanta)

Hinduism denotes the way of life of the Hindus, that is, the inhabitants of Sindh, the ancient land east of the mighty river Indus. Hinduism is not, strictly speaking, a religion as Westerners understand it. Rather, it is *dharma*, a holding together, a cohesion, what makes a thing hold up and be itself. As *dharma*, Hinduism is what most essentially holds together the human existence of the people of Sindh.

But what is this *dharma* that holds a people together and differentiates them from all other peoples? It is the power of becoming divine—rather, the power of realizing that we are divine already, that divinity is our inmost nature, that we are "It." At twenty-four, and after twelve years of study, the young man Svetaketu Aruneya still had this lesson to learn. His father explained it to him:

"Bring me a fruit from this banyan tree."
"Here it is, father."
"Break it up."
"It is broken, Sir."
"What do you see in it?"
"Very small seeds, Sir."
"Break one of them, my son."
"It is broken, Sir."
"What do you see in it?"
"Nothing at all, Sir."

Then his father said to him, "My son, from the very essence in the seed which you cannot see comes in truth this vast banyan tree. Believe me, my son, the Spirit of the whole universe is an invisible and subtle essence. That is reality. That is Atman. YOU ARE THAT [*tat-tvam asi*]."

"Explain this again to me, father," said Svetaketu.
"So be it my son. Place this salt in water and come to me tomorrow morning."

Svetaketu did as he was told, and in the morning his father said to him, "Bring me the salt you put into the water last night."

Svetaketu looked into the water, but could not find the salt, for it had dissolved. His father then said, "Taste the water from this side. How is it?"
"It is salt."
"Taste it from the middle. How is it?"
"It is salt."
"Taste it from that side. How is it?"
"It is salt."
"Look for the salt again and then come to me."

The son did so, saying, "I cannot see the salt. I only see water."

His father then said, "In the same way, O my son, you cannot see the Spirit. But in truth it is here. The Spirit of the whole universe is an invisible and subtle essence. That is reality. That is truth. You are that."[1]

This is one of the key texts in the entire Hindu tradition. To realize one's oneness with the divine is the quest of all Hindus. It is a quest for "home,"[2] and the roads (*marga*) that lead to it are many and diverse. That is why Hinduism gives the impression of being complex and manifold. It is, for it is the holding together of the many paths toward self-(Self)-realization. Hinduism is an organic whole. As Sen puts it, "Hinduism is more like a tree that has grown gradually than like a building that has been erected by some great architect."[3]

Hinduism is best exemplified in the lives and experiences of the people. These experiences have roots in the very ancient past. They are also recorded in some of the most beautiful, varied, and profound literature the world treasures.

Hindustan (India) was peopled by the Dravidians, the builders of Mohenjo-daro and Harappa, the great Indus Valley civilization that predates the invasion of the Indo-Europeans by more than a thousand years. The Indo-Europeans (2,000–1,000 B.C.E.) settled in India as they settled in Europe, but their culture flourished here sooner. The early hymns of the Vedas predate Homer by some 700 years (1,500–800 B.C.E.). They are beautiful songs of praise to the gods and exaltations of life. Later (800–300 B.C.E.) come the Brahmanas, incipient commentaries, prayers, the rites that consecrate daily living. These are followed by the Upanishads, the profound speculative treatises on which the later bulk of historical commentaries are based. During this time, too (ca. 700 B.C.E.–400 C.E.), the "Six Systems" of Indian philosophy developed, each claiming a legendary founder or compiler. They are Sâmkhya, Yoga, Mimânsâ, Vedanta, Vaisesika, and Nyâya. The two monumental epics, the *Râmâyana* and the *Mahâbhârata* appear between 400 B.C.E. and 400 C.E., with the *Bhagavadgîtâ* standing out as a precious meditative jewel in the midst of feats of heroism. Later still (350 C.E.) come the Puranas, ancient stories of an ancient people, and eventually the Tantras (400–600 C.E.). The basic texts, like luminaries in an endless sky, are each surrounded by a plethora of commentaries, each profound and beautiful in its own right.

.oOo.

One of the fundamental notions that concern us here is that of *karma*. *Karma* (act, or action) meant, during the Vedic age, essential ritualistic activity, the rites of propitiatory worship of the various gods and goddesses. But during the Upanishadic era that followed, knowledge (*jñâna*) was introduced as a better path to salvation than praying to the gods, and even though the traditional religious observances were not eliminated (they are still found wherever Hindus live, all over the world), the Upanishads clearly proclaimed enlightenment as the goal, and the cessation of action (to be achieved through yoga) as the practical means thereto.

When the notion of *karma* first appeared in the Upanishads it was presented as a secret.[4] Religiously, the term connotes the universal association between action and consequence, cause and effect. Every action has a consequence or fruit (*karma-phala*) in the temporal realm of existence. Some consequences are good, some are evil. Like evil and good seeds, the seeds of weeds or flowers, these consequences are "stored up," or sown in the fertile earth of the life of the sower. Some of them lie waiting to sprout and bear fruit (*sâncita-karma*); some are ready to germinate only if one's life remains unchanged (*âgâmi-karma*); some, having been sown in previous existences, have already germinated and borne fruit in our present lives—they are our misfortunes, our current fate (*prârabda-karma*). The more one continues to act, the more seeds are sown, and they wait their turn to germinate, in this life or in the next.

> According as people act and walk in the path of life, so they become. Those who do good become good; those who do evil become evil. By pure actions they becomes pure; by evil actions they become evil.
>
> And they say in truth that one is made of desire. As one's desire is, so is one's faith, and so are one's works. As one's works are, so one becomes. It was said: "One comes with one's actions to the end of one's determination."
>
> Reaching the end of the journey begun by one's works on earth, from that world one returns to one's world of human action.[5]

As long as a human being continues to act in the world the law of *karma* binds him/her to unceasing cycles of death and rebirth. Every seed sown must germinate, and if this cannot happen in one life-time, it must needs happen in another one. But this ineluctable association between sowing and reaping obtains only in the phenomenal world, or at the phenomenal level of existence. Essentially, the human spirit (*atman*) is identical with Brahman (the divine substratum), and therefore it is not subject to change. It is only its empirical or phenomenal part that is subject to the law of *karma* and consequently to the process of death and rebirth. If this fundamental distinction is realized, the chain of reincarnations is broken.

.oOo.

Despite its connection with ultra mundane merit, the doctrine of *karma* does not necessarily entail the withdrawal from action in some kind of detachment achieved through ascetical and purificatory techniques. This latter view of *karma* owes its origin to Sâmkhya philosophy, while the asceticism connected with it derives from the *Yogasûtra* of Patañjali. Both are pre-Vedic, and their points of view are some of the doctrines that the *Bhagavadgîtâ* mixes with later Vedic and Upanishadic lore. In the *Gîtâ*'s sense, however, *karma*, as the realm of action and consequences, merely represents a dimension of the world which is "inherent in the very nature of things."[6] The point is to realize this and to keep this dimension in its place, as it were. In other words, the point is to understand that while one must live in a world in which there are actions and consequences, this does not necessarily mean that one is *really* acting in the world. We humans are "trapped in action," as Nicolás puts it.[7] In an existentialist sense, acting is one of the "conditions of existence," and in a pessimistic frame of mind one might even say that we are condemned to act. The thrust of Krshna's speech to Arjuna is that karmic acting can lead to karmic thinking: "Karmic thinking in this case consists in Arjuna or anyone thinking that he is the agent; that is, he deludes himself into thinking linearly by casually uniting action after action and ontologically linking them with himself."[8] When this happens, confusion ensues, as well as anxiety, agitation, despair, and inaction.

But the *Gîtâ* 18:16 says, "Those who think they are the sole agents of their actions miss the truth." Two reasons are given. First, because thinking oneself the agent obscures the real, transcendental nature of the self (*âtman*), which is inactive. Second, because the transcendental self is unreachable by the consequences of karmic action and is, therefore, truly immutable and unalterable:

> That Brahman [-âtman] .... is unseen but seeing, unheard but hearing, unper-
> ceived but perceiving, unknown but knowing. There is nothing that sees but It,
> that hears but It, that perceives but It, that knows but It.[9]

This Self (*âtman*) pervades all things and yet it is not perishable like them.[10] Those who understand this remain unmoved by the activities of the world and can engage in action without apprehension. It is this Self we must seek to know: "The Self which is free from sin, free from old age, from death and grief, from hunger and thirst, which desires nothing but what it ought to desire and imagines nothing but what it ought to imagine, this it is that must be sought, this it is we must try to understand."[11]

The realization that the phenomenal self is identical with the transcendental Self grounds an understanding of the world of action different from our usual Western view. While the normal (to us)—but "deluded"—*karmic* state of mind perceives the phenomenal self as causally connected with the consequences of the self's presumed actions, and the whole of living as the interconnection of actions and consequences, the *dharmic* state of mind ignores or glosses over causal and linear connections and apprehends, instead, connections that arise purely from the fact that actions flow out of a sense of duty (*dharma*). Acting out of a sense of duty imposes a different perspective on the whole realm of action, one in which the agent is, in some sense, detached from the causal flow, and yet immersed in it, but only as a spectator.[12] An example may make this clear:

> A potter creates dishes, bowls, and other utensils for use in everyday life. All of the elements are used: the earthen clay, water, heat produced from friction, air for drying, with space being filled by each. The first task for the potter is to center all the elements and confine the clay on the rotating wheel. In order for this to take place, the mind has to be stilled. The hands do the work; if a thought enters such as "I am going to make a perfect pot," the process is ruined and the pot is knocked off center. Hence, a steady detachment must be maintained: the action is performed, but the doer does not claim its fruits. Sitting above the spinning wheel, distanced and yet intimately involved, the witness silently watches the pot grow and take shape. There is reciprocity between the stillness and the activity.[13]

The thing is to act without desire for results and only out of a sense of duty.[14] When this happens, involvement in the very pleasure one does not desire occurs, but without staining the soul. "He who has searched out that Self and understands It, obtains all worlds and all desires."[15] In this state, the enlightened self "moves about laughing, playing, and rejoicing, be it with women, carriages, or relatives, never minding the body into which it was born."[16]

Similarly, according to Krshna, acting out of a sense of duty (*dharma*) means that the action happens, as it were, by itself. Action (*karma*) is the dimension in which material and formal causes form themselves in specific ways according to their laws. The fact that our bodies are involved does not change this perspective, since our bodies are material and, as such, subject to the laws of *karma* just like everything else. No efficient causality is needed; therefore, no agent.[17]

The crisis of Arjuna in the Bhagavadgîtâ consists in his thinking he is a real agent in his world, as if his phenomenal self, immersed in the flux of actions and consequences, were ontologically united with it and were not, in truth, identical with the transcendental Self. This is the classic error described in the Sâmkhya system, according to which the transcendental Self (*purusha, âtman*), though essentially inactive and uninvolved in the world of matter (*prakrti*), is deluded into thinking it is involved. According to Zimmer, the error "is precisely as though an unmoving personage, reflected in a moving mirror, should be thought to move"[18]—rather, should think that it moves. To think that the Self (*purusha*) acts in the material world (*prakrti*) because it is surrounded by it, is as erroneous as thinking that one is in a mirror because one is reflected in it.[19]

> Ahankâra, the ego-function, causes us to believe that we feel like acting, that we are suffering, etc.; whereas actually our real being, the purusha, is devoid of such modifications. Ahankâra is the center and prime motivating force of "delusion" (*abhimâna*). Ahankâra is the misconception, conceit, supposition, or belief that refers all objects and acts of consciousness to an "I" (*aham*).[20]

In this way is formed what Sri Aurobindo terms "this poor trepidant braggart egoistic condition of consciousness, *ahamkrta bhâva*, the crippling narrowness of this little helpless separative personality according to whose viewpoint we ordinarily think and act, feel and respond to the touches of existence.[21]

How are we to escape this bind? The *Gîtâ* introduces the idea of *karmayoga*, the yoga of detachment in action: all actions, even seemingly holy ones (such as the offering of sacrifices and the performance of rituals) are to be performed without attachment to the fruits of the action (*Gîtâ* 18:6). As was mentioned above, we cannot avoid action; we are "condemned to act"; action is a primary component of our circumstance in the world, of our human condition. This determinism, however, this enslavement is escaped or transcended through unattachment to the results of action. The enlightened spirit disassociates itself from its empirical self and thus attains liberation (*mukti*) from the flux of life. It continues living, but "it/It" sows no more seeds, since at bottom, in very truth, "it/It" is totally inactive. The fruits of the germinating seeds (*prârabda-karma*) eventually exhaust themselves, and with their cessation all phenomenal existence ceases for good. The *Kaushitaki Upanishad* I,2-6, describes the scene as the souls of the dead are questioned as to their identity. If they do not know their identity with Brahman, they are ordered to be reborn in whatever shape—bird, reptile, human—their karma requires. If, on the other hand, on being questioned they answer, "I am a season . . . I am Thou," they enter bliss.

.oOo.

Hinduism distinguishes between the immortal spirit, which is eternal and identical with "us," and the phenomenal self (*ahamkâra*) that is immersed in time, and which acts through the body. It is the Spirit which is identified with Brahman.

> Know that when the eye looks into space it is the Spirit of man that sees, the eye is only the organ of sight. When one says, "I feel this perfume," it is the Spirit

that feels, it uses the organ of smell. When one says "I am speaking" it is the Spirit that speaks, the voice is the organ of speech. When one says, "I am hearing," it is the Spirit that hears; the ear is the organ of hearing. And when one says, "I think," it is the Spirit that thinks, the mind is the organ of thought. It is because of the light of the Spirit that the human mind can see, and can think, and enjoy this world.

All the gods of the heaven of Brahman adore in contemplation their Infinite Spirit Supreme. This is why they have all joy, and all the worlds and all desires. And those who on this earth find and know *atman*, their own Self, have all their holy desires and all the worlds and all joy.[22]

Hence, the search for liberation and salvation (*mukti* and *moksha*) involves escape from the body and the phenomenal world (*samsâra*), release from the karmic obligations that bind the spirit to the Wheel, the cycle of death and rebirth. Reincarnation is needed as long as evil effects outbalance good effects, as long as the spirit is not wholly pure. When the spirit is finally pure, freedom ensues, and with it, the fullness of happiness.

The experience of happiness as transcendent (re-)union with the One is not understood, much less pursued, by all. The *Bhagavadgîtâ* clearly distinguishes three kinds of happiness, and three kinds of pursuits associated with them.

And now hear from Me, [Arjuna] O Best of the Bharatas, the three kinds of happiness . . . .

That happiness which is like poison at first and like nectar at the end, which springs from a clear understanding of the Self is said to be of the nature of "goodness."

That happiness which arises from the contact of the senses and their objects and which is like nectar at first but like poison at the end—such happiness is recorded to be "passionate."

That happiness which deludes the soul both at the beginning and at the end and which arises from sleep, sloth, and negligence—that is declared to be of the nature of "dullness."[23]

Radhakrishnan's comment is enlightening, "Happiness is the universal aim of life. Only it is of different kinds according to the modes which dominate our nature. If the *tamas* [inertia] predominates in us, we are satisfied with violence and inertia, blindness and error. If *rajas* [passion] prevails, wealth and power, pride and glory give us happiness. True happiness of human beings lies not in the possession of outward things but in the fulfillment of the higher mind and spirit, in the development of what is most inward in us [*sattva*]. It may mean pain and restraint but it will lead us to joy and freedom. We can pass from the happiness of knowledge and virtue to the eternal calm and joy, *ânanda* [bliss] of the spirit, when we become one with the Highest Self and one with all beings."[24] The way to union is through yoga, that is, through the yoking or linking of the soul to the One.

The *Gîtâ* describes various methods or yogas to achieve this linking, the method of work (*karma yoga*), the method of knowledge (*jñâna yoga*), and the method of devotion (*bhakti yoga*), and other methods or yogas, and *marga* (ways) have been described in the Scriptures, such as "the yoga of the feminine power" (*kundalini yoga*), and the way of renunciation (*nivriti mârg*). The purpose is union. This state of union is detailed in the *Gîtâ*:

> Endowed with a pure understanding, firmly restraining oneself, turning away from sound and other objects of sense and casting aside attraction and aversion;
> Dwelling in solitude, eating but little, controlling speech, body and mind, and ever engaged in meditation and concentration and taking refuge in dispassion;
> And casting aside self-sense, force, arrogance, desire, anger, possession, egoless and tranquil in mind, he becomes worthy of becoming one with Brahman.
> Having become one with Brahman, and being tranquil in spirit, he neither grieves nor desires. Regarding all beings as alike he attains supreme devotion to Me [Krishna].
> Through devotion he comes to know Me, what My measure is and who I am in truth. Then, having known Me in truth, he forthwith enters into Me.
> Doing continually all action whatsoever, taking refuge in Me, he reaches by My grace the eternal undying abode.[25]

It is clear that this state of union is to be achieved here on earth, struggling against the assaults of illusion (*mâyâ*), of pain and suffering. Eternity confers the security of possession, but the possession has to be reestablished here, in the world of *samsâra*, of change, of illusion (*mâyâ*). And there is no other way. As the *Brihad-Aranyaka Upanishad* says, "this is the path supreme; this is the supreme treasure; this is the world supreme; this is the supreme joy!"[26]

> Supreme happiness comes to the yogin whose mind is peaceful, whose passions are at rest, who is stainless and has become one with God.[27]
> Joy comes from God. Who could breathe, and who could live if the joy of Brahman filled not the universe?[28]
> For from joy all beings have come, by joy they all live, and unto joy they will all return.[29]

# Additional Readings

## Sources

*The Vedanta Sutra*, ed. G. Thibaut. 2 vols.; Oxford: Oxford University Press, 1890-1896.
*The Bhagavadgîtâ*, ed. and transl by S. Radhakrishnan. London: George Allen & Unwin,

1960.

*The Upanishads*, transl. Juán Mascaró. Baltimore: Penguin Books, 1970.
*Eight Upanishads*, transl. Sri Aurobindo. Pondichery: Sri Aurobindo Ashram, 1965.
*The Thirteen Principal Upanishads*, ed. R.E. Hume. Oxford: Oxford University Press, 1934.

## Commentaries

Sri Aurobindo, *Essays on the Gîtâ*. Pondichery: Sri Aurobindo Ashram, 1966.
Chapple,Christopher. *Karma and Creativity*. Albany, State University of New York Press, 1986.
Klostermaier, Klaus K. *A Survey of Hinduism*. Albany: State University of New York Press, 1989.
Nicolás, Antonio T. de. *Avatâra*. New York: Nicolas Hays, Ltd., 1976.
Nirvedananda, Swami. *Hinduism at a Glance*. Calcutta: Ramakrishna Mission, 1963.
Radhakrishnan, Servapalli. *The Hindu View of Life*. New York: Macmillan, s.a..
Sen, Chad Mohan. *Hinduism*. Baltimore: Penguin Books, 1972.
Sharma, I. C. *Ethical Philosophies of India*. New York: HarperTorchbooks, 1970.
Zaehner, Richard C. *Hinduism*. New York: Oxford University Press, 1966.
Zimmer, Heinrich. *Philosophies of India*. New York: Meridian Books, 1964.

## Notes

1. *Chandogya Upanishad* vii.6.
2. *Chandogya Upanishad* vi.l4.
3. Chad Mohan Sen, *Hinduism* (Baltimore: Penguin Books, 1972), 14.
4. *Brihad-Aranyaka Upanishad* 3, 2, 13.
5. *Brihad-Aranyaka Upanishad* 4, 3-4.
6. Richard C. Zaehner, *Hinduism* (New York: Oxford University Press, 1966), 102.
7. Antonio T. de Nicolás, *Avatâra* (New York: Nicolas Hays, Ltd., 1976), 180.
8. Ibid.
9. *Brihadâranyaka Upanishad* III,8,11.
10. *Bhagavadgîtâ* 2:17-25.
11. *Chândogya Upanishad* VIII,7,1.
12. Christopher Chapple, *Karma and Creativity* (Albany, State University of New York Press, 1986), 90,
13. Ibid., 30.
14. *Bhagavadgîtâ* 18:23.
15. *Chândogya Upanishad* VIII,7,1.
16. *Chândogya Upanishad* VIII,12,3.
17. Nicolás, *Avatâr*, 182-183.
18. Heinrich Zimmer, *Philosophies of India* (New York: Meridian Books, 1964), 287.
19. Ibid., 316.
20. Ibid., 319.
21. Sri Aurobindo, *Essays on the Gîtâ* (Pondichery: Sri Aurobindo Ashram, 1966), Second Series, Part II, Essay XXII, 498.

22. *Chandogya Upanishad* 8. 11-12.

23. *Bhagavadgîtâ* 18:36-39.

24. S. Radhakrishnan, *The Bhagavadgîtâ* (London: George Allen & Unwin, 1960), 363-364.

26. *Bhagavadgîtâ* 18: 51-56.

26. *Brihad-Aranyaka Upanishad* 4, 3.

27. *Bhagavadgita* 6, 27.

28. *Taittirya Upanishad* 2, 7.

29. *Taittirya Upanishad* 3, 6.

# 2

# DIONYSUS

Who was Dionysus? No one really knows, nor wherefrom he came, nor when. He may have originated in Phrygia or Thrace, in "the East," and his worship (for he was a god) may have grown in Crete before it appeared in Greece. Although he is referred to as "the new-comer god,"[1] his worship is well known to Homer, and the myths about his birth contain suggestions that point to a pre-Olympian, chthonic origin.

The earthness of Dionysus is conveyed by the myth that has him born of Persephone. Zeus, in one of his innumerable escapades, has disguised himself as a serpent and has made her pregnant. The child she gives birth to is horned. His name is Zagreus. He is a playful toddler who climbs on his father's throne, makes fun of him, and mimics him by holding the lightning in his tiny hand. Hera, however, enraged as usual by her husband's infidelity, orders the Titans to slay the new-born child. Easier said than done: Dionysus-Zagreus fights them valiantly turning himself into all kinds of shapes—that of old Kronos, that of a youth, a lion, a horse, a serpent, a bull. In this last form he is finally slain, dismembered, boiled with herbs, and eaten by the Titans. One version has it that Athena, his sister, saved his heart, and that Zeus enshrined it in a temple built in his honor. Other versions deny the theophagy and have it that Zeus commanded Apollo to reconstruct the body and bury it. Dionysus' tomb was believed to be next to Apollo's temple in Delphi. Still another version has it that Persephone, like another Isis, pieced together the limbs and made him youthful once again. There is still another version of the story: Zeus swallowed the heart of his slain infant, but when, in another of his escapades, he made Semele pregnant, the child she gave birth to was Dionysus.

Semele was one of King Kadmus' four daughters. They weren't about to believe that their sister had been made pregnant by a god. And who can blame them? So Semele took refuge in Zeus' temple. What did she have to fear? Was she not loved by the ruler of the gods? Had he not promised her, swearing his oath on the River Styx, that he would grant her whatever she asked? What she desired most was to look into the eyes of her exalted lover. Hera, fuming with anger at her husband's latest tryst, had disguised herself as Semele's nurse and had encouraged her to ask Zeus to show himself to her, knowing that no mortal can see god and live. The vision proved fatal. From Olympus flew the thunderbolt that crashed upon the shrine destroying Semele in the process. Zeus, however, saved the lately conceived infant, sewed him up within his thigh, and carried him to term. Upon his birth, Dionysus was cradled and cared for by nymphs who treated him as a girl, and who later became his ardent followers, the maenads. Besides the nymphs, the Muses inspired him, the satyrs taught him the dance and the pleasures of sexuality, and old Silenus taught him the virtues of ecstasy.

Grown to young manhood, Dionysus came to Thebes with his followers, mostly women, to install his cult. But Pentheus, his cousin, Agave's son, was king then, and neither he nor his mother and remaining aunts believed that Dionysus was "the son of god." Zeus' thunderbolt had been interpreted as a punishment of Semele for blaming her pregnancy on the god.

Dionysus was not intent merely on establishing his worship, he also wanted revenge on his kinsfolk for their disbelief and their disrespect for his mother. And so the madness ensued. The whole town flocked to Mt. Kithaeron at night to rock and roll in the woods amidst wild animals. Pentheus eventually was lured to the hills, and was there slain by his own mother who, blinded by the ecstasy and the orgy, imagined she had slain a wild boar. Dionysus drove the point home mercilessly: "Had ye learned wisdom when ye would not, ye would now be happy."[2]

The happiness that Dionysus brings is contained in another idyllic story. Sailing in the Aegean Sea, he found Ariadne, the young and beautiful daughter of King Minos, abandoned by Theseus in the island of Naxos. Dionysus consoled her, and they were soon married in a ceremony attended by the gods. Their marriage was perfect, ever happy and without quarrel, and they had many children. Upon Ariadne's death—she was, after all, mortal—Dionysus memorialized her by placing her crown among the stars, where it can be seen as the *Corona Borealis*.[3]

.oOo.

Dionysus is the god of passion, of euphoria, of ecstasy. In so far as wine induces drunkenness and therefore forgetfulness of self, he is Bacchus, the god of wine. He represents life, triumphant in death through rebirth—life in all its manifestations, not merely those sanctioned by custom, law, and reason. His myths and his worship bristle with contradictions. As Guthrie puts it, his worship

> presents us with the spectacle of annual festivals in the towns or fields in spring—and with biennial festivals on the bare mountain tops in winter; with daylight celebrations and torchlit midnight rovings; it has its joyful and bountiful side and its grim and gruesome side, for the same god is hailed as the giver of all good gifts and feared as the eater of raw flesh and the man-eater; he has animal incarnations, aniconic forms closely connected with tree-worship, a definite connection with ships and the sea; he offers ecstasy and spiritual union and wild intoxication in which he himself is the leader, so that he can be called the mad, the roving god; at the same time what disconcerts his adversaries and singles him out from them is an uncanny stillness and calm, and stillness and calm too are among the gifts he bestows on his infatuated worshipers; sexual license as a feature of his orgia is now admitted, now denied; his frenzied women votaries, in the passionate abandonment of his service, take young beasts in their arms and with maternal tenderness give them the breast--the same women who with scarcely conceivable savagery tear the limbs from the young creatures and fasten their teeth on them. So the list might be extended.[4]

His power is pervasive. He possesses his followers, dwells in them as enthusiasm, quickens their steps in dance, is the center of the satyr plays and later presides over the theater festivals. Transformed by Christianity into the Holy Ghost, he reappears in the Montanists, and later still among the Anastenari, in our contemporary Evangelicals, and in the American snake-handling cults. He inspires *glossolalia* ("speaking in tongues") and the trances of the Whirling Dervishes. He lurks around in every feast and celebration, whenever the Id triumphs, wherever ecstasy erupts, from Zorba's dance to the rock-'n-roll concert.

It can be seen from all this that Dionysus represents a pursuit of happiness that involves, in Nietzsche's words, "an ecstatic affirmation of the total character of life."[5] Such a pursuit of happiness assumes the forms of trance, rapture, enthusiasm; any standing out of oneself that de-individualizes the person and allows one to merge with others, humans and beasts, and with nature, in an orgiastic cosmicity. This is the happiness of the night, where order is disrupted, when time stands still, and where limits and boundaries merge and float away leaving everything undefined. This is the context of exhilaration. As Jaspers puts it, "nocturnal passion can make me say 'A god did it' as well as 'I did it'."[6]

The happiness of Dionysus is also the happiness that comes by chance, by luck, at the whim of fortune. As societies have become increasingly more organized and planned, this happiness has been crowded out. There does not seem to be room for the unexpectedness of Dionysian happiness in a world ruled by time-tables, clocks, and the regularity of the six o'clock news.

.oOo.

What is Dionysian, ecstatic happiness? It is one of the sublimest things one can aspire to. "Our greatest blessings come to us by way of madness," wrote Plato,[7] not the madness of sickness, but "the madness given by divine gift . . . by a divinely wrought change in our customary social norms"[8] —the madness of Dionysus. This is the madness that makes men and women crown themselves with ivy, burst forth with blossoms, and with boughs of oak and pine join in the Bacchic revelry; don coats of dappled dawn-skin and wield the sportive wand; and often go dancing and reveling in the hills of Kithaeron.[9]

Ritual dances of one form or another are among the earliest expressions of ecstatic happiness. The "Sorcerer" of Lascaux, the "Three Women" from the Valltorta Gorge and "The Dancers" from Tin-n-Tazarift, are just a few of the many ancient samples of ecstatic happiness and dance. Ecstatic dances associated with the Mother Bear, with fairies, or stags, have been recorded since antiquity. The little "Dancing Girl" from Mohenjo-Dâro is a precious example, continued in the Indian tradition by the many statues of Shiva Natarâjâ, Shiva "Lord of the Dance," who is dancer, stage, and audience to himself, abiding alone in his happiness. Shiva's dance represents his five activities as creator, sustainer, destroyer, illusionist, and savior.

In the Hebrew tradition dancing and singing were customary expressions of ecstasy. The *Psalms* give ample witness to this. But perhaps the most convincing example of the connection between dancing and happiness is the story of David dancing before the Ark of the Covenant.

> David danced before the Lord with all his might . . . girded with a linen ephod. . . . leaping and dancing before the Lord . . . .
> But Michal, the daughter of Saul. . .said to him, "How the King of Israel honored himself today, uncovering himself before the eyes of his servants' maids, as one of the vulgar fellows shamelessly uncovers himself!" And David said to Michal, "It was before the Lord [that I danced] . . . and I will make merry before the Lord."[10]

The near-elimination of ecstasy from the Western tradition is due largely to Christianity's infatuation with asceticism and its condemnation of everything physical as devilish.[11] For, as Nietzsche says in "The Dancing Song," "the devil is the spirit of gravity."[12] That the seriousness that has characterized Christianity was not necessarily original with it may be gauged from an early hymn of the apocryphal *Acts of John*, in which Jesus is depicted as dancing with his disciples after the Last Supper.[13]

The pursuit of happiness in ecstatic modes, in revelry and dance, is not common any more in Western cultures,[14] but this was not always the case, and there remain a few instances of ecstatic happiness in our contemporary societies, the Holi festival in India, Carnival in New Orleans and Brazil, New Year's Eve in New York City, Oktoberfest in Germany, and rock-'n-roll concerts all over the world. During the late Middle Ages, St.Vitus' dance was celebrated, especially in the Alsace, and the Feast of Fools took place in England. Roman times saw a proliferation of such festivals,[15] as is clear from the references to feast and revelry; this kind of happiness is joyous. Enthusiasm (literally, indwelling by the god) is one of the words used to describe it. A certain passivity is implied, not so much in renunciation of activity (which can be quite enervating) but in the sense that the experience is undergone. The enthusiastic reveler is acted on; he/she feels driven, lived, inhabited. This experience occurs often in the orgiastic dance, the main vehicle of Dionysian happiness:

> In the dance of life, male and female, work and play, creativity and fallowness, day and night, life and death belong together in a rhythmic unity. Identity is in movement, in the economy of fractions which create a community in diversity. Authentic thought is, as Nietzsche said, thought which dances. Kazantzakis' figure of Zorba the Greek might well be taken as a concrete illustration of the Dionysian way and of the centrality of dance . . . for life.[16]

Besides enthusiasm, however, which is like an inner boiling, there is also the mode of ecstasy, exhilaration, the superabundance of joy: "Ecstasy literally means the state of being outside oneself. Such a state is accompanied by joy, enthusiasm, a sense of being a part of a moving reality that is greater than the self. We say that someone is "beside himself with joy." This is a strange metaphor. Why should the experience of being beside oneself be so intensely pleasurable?[17]

As I said above, ecstatic happiness is often ritualized in festivals. Festivals represent one clear example of ways in which this riotous happiness may be experienced. According to Harvey Cox, "The festival, the special time when ordinary chores are set aside while man celebrates some event, affirms the sheer goodness of what is, or observes the memory of a god or hero, is a distinctly human activity. It arises from man's peculiar power to incorporate into his own life the joys of other people and the experience of previous generations. Porpoises and chimpanzees may play. Only man celebrates. Festivity is a human form of play through which man appropriates an extended area of life, including the past, into his own experience."[18] Festivals are characterized by revelry, by a celebrative affirmation of life in all its manifestations, and they are typically juxtaposed with periods of seriousness that we observe during the course of ordinary life.[19]. It also involves passion—the passion that leads to excess. This is one of the realms that render this form of happiness and its pursuit a rarity in our culture. But Paul Kurtz insists that it must be included in the pursuit of happiness.

> A vital ingredient of the full life is the ability to enjoy pleasures that are erotic, to find delight in the sensual, to be aroused by beauty, to be allured by the caress of touch, to savor the sensuous form, the fragrance and romance of sexuality and love. . . . Not to suffer the pangs of passion or be moved by their fervor and attraction is not to have lived fully; without passion, life would be lacking

something poignant. The erotic thus plays a significant role in the full life. . . .[20]

Western traditions have frowned upon the ecstatic enjoyment and affirmation of life involving sexuality. In the East, on the other hand, such a pursuit of happiness has been preserved in the traditions of Tantra. The openness to the whole range of human activity described above was a fundamental ingredient in the Tantric practices of Mahayâna Buddhism. The enlightened person is one who has transcended the dualities of experience; it is one for whom labels and appellations have fallen off, having been peeled away by the paring knife of awakened vision. Such a one lives beyond good and evil, the forbidden and the allowed, totem and taboo. Living, for him/her, is endowed with great joy.

> Hence the great Tântric formula (so different from that of the earlier Hindu yogic disciplines): *yoga* (the yoking of empirical consciousness to transcendental consciousness) and *bhoga* ("enjoyment," the experience of life's joy and suffering) are the same. Bhoga itself can be made a way of yoga.[21]

.oOo.

# Additional Reading

## Sources

Euripides, *The Bacchae*.
Richard Schechner, ed., *Dionysus in 69*. New York: Farrar, Straus & Giroux, 1970.

## Commentaries

Bharati, Agehananda. *The Tantric Tradition*. New York: Doubleday Anchor, 1965.
Blofeld, John. *The Tantric Mysticism of Tibet*. New York: E.P. Dutton & Co., 1970.
Coomaraswamy, Ananda. *The Dance of Shiva*. New York: The Noonday Press, 1957.
Cox, Harvey. *The Feast of Fools* New York: Harper Colophon, 1969.
Cutler ,Donald R., and Herbert W. Richardson, eds., *Transcendence*. Boston: Beacon Press, 1969.
Dodds, E. R. *The Greeks and the Irrational*. Berkeley: University of California Press, 1971.
Durant, Will. *The Story of Civilization*. New York: Simon & Schuster, 1935—.
Garrison, Omar. *Tantra, the Yoga of Sex*. New York: Causeway Books, 1964.
Guthrie, William K. *The Greeks and their Gods*. Boston: Beacon Press, 1967.
Hennecke, Edgar, and Wilhelm Schneemelcher, *New Testament Apocrypha*. Philadelphia: The Westminster Press, 1964.
Jaspers, Karl. *Philosophy*. Chicago: University of Chicago Press, 1969.

Johnson, Robert A. *Ecstasy*. New York: Harper & Row, 1987.
Keen, Sam. *To a Dancing God*. New York: Harper & Row, 1970.
Kurtz, Paul. *Exuberance*. Buffalo: Prometheus Books, 1977.
Nietzsche, Friedrich. *The Will to Power*. New York: Random House, 1967.
————. *Thus Spoke Zarathustra*. New York: The Viking Press, 1966.
Otto, Walter F. *Dionysus, Myth and Cult* Bloomington, IN: Indiana University Press, 1965.
Rawson, Philip. *Tantra*. New York: Avon Books, 1973.
Zimmer, Heinrich. *Philosophies of India*. New York: Meridian, 1956.

## Notes

1. Euripides, *Bacchae* 219 and 272.
2. *Bacchae* 1340.
3. Robert A. Johnson, *Ecstasy* (New York: Harper & Row, 1987), 9-10.
4. William K. Guthrie, *The Greeks and their Gods* (Boston: Beacon Press, 1967), 145-146.
5. Friedrich Nietzsche, *The Will to Power* (New York: Random House, 1967), 1050.
6. Karl Jaspers, *Philosophy* (Chicago: University of Chicago Press, 1969), vol.3, 91.
7. Plato, *Phaedrus* 244A.
8. *Phaedrus* 265A.
9. Euripides, *Bacchae* 100 *ff*.
10. *2 Samuel* 6:12-21.
11. Johnson, *Ecstasy* (New York: Harper & Row, 1987), 22-24.
12. *Thus Spoke Zarathustra* II.10, 107.
13. *Acts of John* 95-97; Hennecke & Schneemelcher, *New Testament Apocrypha* (Philadelphia: The Westminster Press, 1964), 227-232.
14. Johnson, *Ecstasy*, vi.
15. Will Durant, *The Story of Civilization* (New York: Simon & Schuster, 1935—), Vol.3, 65-66).
16. Sam Keen, "Manifesto for a Dionysian theology," in Donald R. Cutler and Herbert W. Richardson, eds., *Transcendence* ( Boston: Beacon Press, 1969), 39.
17. Sam Keen, *To a Dancing God* (New York: Harper & Row, 1970), 77.
18. Harvey Cox, *The Feast of Fools* (New York: Harper Colophon), 1969), 7.
19. Ibid., 22-23.
20. Paul Kurtz, *Exuberance* (Buffalo: Prometheus Books, 1977), 91 and 94.
21. Heinrich Zimmer, *Philosophies of India* (New York: Meridian, 1956), 580.

# 3

# LAO-TZU

## (*ca.* 604-517 B.C.E.)

Once upon a time there was a man whose name was Lao Tan. He was born in China, in the village of Ch'ü Jen, in what today is the province of Honan. His mother, it is said, conceived him while looking at a falling star. Later she gave him birth while leaning against a graceful plum tree.

The little boy spoke soon after his birth. He grew up to become Archivist at the royal court of the house of Chou. He lived a quiet life, almost like a recluse, though he was married and had a son. His knowledge increased with the passage of the years. His fame spread far and wide, and he was called Master Lao (Lao-tzu).

In the last year of his life he was visited by Confucius, then in his mid-thirties. They held many conversations, which brought their differences clearly to the fore. For the Way (*Tao*), for Confucius, led to kindly action in the world, while for Lao-tzu it led to inaction (*wu-wei*) and dissolution in the void. At length Confucius parted, baffled by the obscure wisdom of the older Master. As he went away, shaking his head in wonderment and disbelief, he commented, "I have understood everything—how the birds fly, how the fish swim, and how animals run. But how does a dragon soar upon the wind and the clouds? Behold, Lao-tzu is a dragon!"

The last years of his life saw Lao-tzu grew increasingly critical of the mores and politics of the royal court. "The people starve," he wrote later, "because the tax levies are too heavy on them; they are hard to rule, because the government meddles too much in their affairs."[1]

Finally, in desperation, he quit his post and decided to leave the kingdom. He took the road West, which went over the mountains. As he climbed the Han-ku Pass, Yin Hsi, the Guardian of the Pass, begged him to leave his followers a legacy of his wisdom. Lao-tzu tarried awhile, and after a few days he entrusted Yin Hsi with a book in two parts, The Way (*Tao*) and The Power (*Te*) written in five thousand characters.

Then he moved on through the Pass, and became a legend.[2]

.oOo.

History tells us that there was, indeed, a man named Lao Tan—but he lived, rather, in the 4th century B.C.E. Another tradition ascribes the book to Li Erh, a contemporary of Confucius. The book *Lao-tzu*, also known as the *Tao Te Ching* (or the *Te Tao Ching*), was probably written in the 3rd or 4th century, either by one author or by many. The author may have been Lao-tzu. But then, again, it may not have been he who wrote the famous little treatise. For, after all, he may not have existed at all. So, we are left with a legend and a book, the contents of which are profound but difficult to understand. To begin with, the sequence of chapters has almost certainly been altered, and the pictograms/ideograms are often open to such varied interpretations that the many translations in existence differ considerably from one another.

Nonetheless there is a fairly consistent doctrine expounded in the book. The *Tao Te Ching* is like a road map to the land of wisdom and happiness, except that one errs if one thinks the way can be traced in a map as much as if one imagines that wisdom can be described or that reality is comprehensible. For "the Way [*Tao*] that can be mapped is not the unswerving way .... The source of the universe is hidden in mystery."[3] Tao is the source: it is "like a great womb" that gives birth to innumerable things ("ten thousand," in the Chinese expression). Tao, then, is ultimate reality, and even naming it is pretentious: how can one name the unnameable?[4] By definition, therefore, anything one may say of it must remain incomplete. It may even be misleading. However, since something must be said, I will content myself with a brief exposition of the moral and mystical aspects of the Way as these have a bearing on the pursuit of happiness.

.oOo.

Philosophical Taoism developed at a time of great turmoil in China. Whatever its quietism and pacifism might have been, therefore, they must not have been seen as impractical, or they would have been rejected, and that would have been the end of it. On the other hand, it would be false to suppose that the moral doctrine proposed in the *Tao Te Ching* had a universal impact. It probably appealed more to the individualistic minority and the more contemplative elite.[5]

Much of the *Tao Te Ching* is devoted to the problem of moral action. The term used here is *Te*. *Te* means power (or virtue, in the original meaning of the Latin *virtus* [Greek *dynamis*], potential). In a sense, *Tao* is *archê*, principle, in that *Tao* continues to grow in the things it originates. *Tao* is their nature, but in the meaning of the Greek *physis*, as *natura naturans*; *Te* is their potential. It also means what has been acquired. Hence, it is the moral power derived or obtained from *Tao*: "The many forms of *Te* all flow from *Tao*."[6]

Lao-tzu's understanding of moral power centers around the doctrine of non-action (*wu-wei* [lit., "not-doing"]), or actionless activity.[7] "Act non-action [wu wei]," Lao-tzu counsels; "do without doing,"[8] for "he who acts, harms."[9]

These statements are paradoxical, and deliberately so. Clearly, Lao-tzu is aware of the fact that actions have consequences which are often unwholesome. If the purpose of morality were to avoid at all costs any evil, then the appropriate advice would be to refrain from action altogether. But according to the legend, Lao-tzu was himself some kind of public figure. It would not have seemed reasonable to him to suggest absolute and complete withdrawal. Hence the paradox: one must act as if one did not act. One must act in such a way that one avoids the usual consequences of action. Krishna gives a similar advice to Arjuna: you must act yet not become attached to the results of your actions.[10] Lao-tzu must have intuited the applicability at the moral level of the physical law that action entails commensurate reaction. Actions, then, become self-cancelling through the reaction they prompt. In other words, as Spinoza would put it centuries later, every being strives to persevere in its being. If its being is opposed, it resists. One's action upon any thing, therefore, may be seen as an opposition to the thing's being. The result is a reaction that cancels the original action.

But Lao-tzu does not counsel inaction. Rather, he suggests that one act in such a way as to avoid conflict. To achieve this, action must be receptive rather than direct, yielding rather than aggressive. "To yield is to remain entire,"[11] he says. *Wu-wei* is like water, "the tenderest thing in creation, which yet prevails over the hardest, [that is, rock]."[12] *Wu-wei* is a way of accomplishing everything without doing it.[13] Therefore *wu-wei* connotes a power (*Te*) which arises from not trying or acting directly, but which is real and effective nonetheless.

An analogy may help. A field is barren in winter and fruitful in spring and summer. In it all flowers and weeds are supported without discrimination, and the field nourishes them all, but its "action" remains unseen, so that all change and growth seems to take place "uncaused," or "by nature," without any action (*wu-wei*).[14]

As a program of action, *wu-wei* is not easy to live by. It therefore requires the development of certain fundamental attitudes through some kind of ascetical regime. Concretely, those who aspire to practice *wu-wei* must learn to control their desires, especially those which arise from, or are generated by, the specific social environment in which they live. Conversely, they must learn to fulfill (with moderation) those desires which are natural, according to their capacity. They must also learn not to be ruled by public opinion.

Above all, they must learn to become indifferent to all things. "The perfect sage," says Lao-tzu, "is indifferent."[15] By indifference he does not mean apathy. Rather, indifference is the kind of attitude that takes things, persons, and actions, entirely and solely for what they are. It gives each one its due. It has toward each and every possible course of action the kind of openness that the Mother-Void has towards all things. Waley quotes an aphorism by St. John of the Cross, "Without effort you will control people and be served by things, if you forget them and yourself."[16] One could also refer to St. Ignatius Loyola's "we must make ourselves indifferent."[17] The point is that, according to Lao-tzu, the moral way of *wu-wei* requires in the follower an attitude of openness and acceptance without which true yielding action is impossible. On the other hand, where such an attitude prevails, virtue and power (*Te*) reign supreme.

.oOo.

Indifference and non-action entail an inward openness to everything and a disregard for every definition that may be imposed (that is, for every limit). To achieve this, says Lao-tzu, is to return to "the Uncarved Block" (*p'u*)[18] —the block of wood or marble before it is sculpted into this or that form; that is, before it is defined as this or that, and therefore limited to being a statue of this or a statue of that.

An ancient Zen story has it that a child sees a mountain and sees a mountain; an adult sees a mountain and sees many things; a sage sees a mountain and sees a mountain. Wisdom consists not merely in a return to the unsophisticated perception of the child, but in being able to go beyond things as they are defined to the undifferentiated matrix from which they all sprang.

We are beyond the moral realm here. Yet there are obvious parallels. As in the moral realm, quietude is the way here, too. The goal is a return to Nothingness (no-thing-ness), the dawning of a consciousness of non-determination, of absolute unqualifiednes, absolute non-differentiation. Moral indifference gives way to the indifference of the Void.

Why is the Void important? Because it is truly the source of everything. It is the Mother of All. In its unqualified no-thingness it can turn out all kinds of different things. As an empty womb, it can be filled with a myriad different children.

A mother, too, gives birth to offspring that grow up and make a life of their own. Nothingness, equally, bodies forth the multiplicity of creation without interfering with each thing's individual development: "Tao produces them, makes them grow, nourishes them, shelters them, brings them up and protects them . . . . It produces them without taking possession of them . . . . And because it does not lay claim to them, therefore it does not lose them."[19]

Hence the path of the mystic must be toward the Void, for in laying hold of it, one can have access to all It has produced—that is, to the whole universe: "When a man has found the Mother, he will know the children accordingly."[20]   This, therefore, is the aim of the mystical pursuit.

This implies that the mystical attainment of the Void takes one into the farthest reaches of the ethical. The non-judgmental, indifferent way of the ethical path (*wu-wei*) finds its consummation in the mystical grasp of the undifferentiated Void. Indeed, while the mystical may be seen as crowning the ascent begun at the ethical level, it is truly the foundation of the latter. Moral indifference is thus grounded on ontological indifference. Indifference as an ethical imperative flows out of the mystic's grasp of the nature of reality. Placid contemplation of the Void is not the point. Rather, it is a life lived in accord with it. After all, the book purports to deal with the (ethical) Power (*Te*) of the (mystical) Way (*Tao*). Happiness is living out what Nature is.

The way there is one of unknowing,[21] for what comes through the senses is an impediment. Welch writes: "When colors, sounds, and tastes are reduced, the Taoist will be ready to see the secret essences; in seeing the Secret Essences, he returns to Non-Being; in returning to Non-Being, he reaches the final and highest stage of mystical experience."[22]   True wisdom is achieved "without knowledge."[23]

Happiness, then, consists, first of all, in the attainment of power (*Te*) through indifference (*wu-wei*). This power is utterly enjoyable and it fills the heart of the seeker. But while the beginning of happiness is at the level of the outward, of the control of others, indifference leads inwardly to one's own nature. Happiness consists in the quiet possession of one's own natural self as it is in its pristine wholeness (*p'u*). Having achieved this level, the seeker moves on. Through various practices (*tso-wang*) he/she goes beyond the self's nature toward the Void, the absolute *Tao*, the Nothingness of undifferentiated being. The attainment of such vision and state of being constitutes the Taoist's ultimate happiness. But his happiness is in great contrast to the fun-filled experiences people usually associate with happiness. The sage's happiness is tranquil, peaceful, simple, and straight-forward. It is a deep and enduring happiness nourished by the joy that flows from the everliving fountains of the Void.[24]

.oOo.

# Additional Reading

## Sources

Bikshu Wai-Tao, *Tao-Teh-King*, in *A Buddhist Bible*, ed. Dwight Goddard. Boston: Beacon Press, 1970.
Ch'u Ta-Kao, *Tao Tê Ching*. London: The Buddhist Lodge, 1937.
J. J. L. Duyvendak, *Tao Te Ching*. London: John Murray, 1954.

Robert G. Henricks, trans. & ed., *Lao-tzu Te-Tao Ching*. New York: Ballantine Books, 1989.


## Commentaries

Wing-Tsit Chan, *The Way of Lao Tzu*. Indianapolis: The Bobbs- Merrill Co., Inc., 1963.
Chang Chung-yuan, *Tao. A New Way of Thinking*. New York: Harper Colophon, 1975.
Benjamin Hoff, *The Tao of Pooh*. New York: E. P. Dutton, Inc., 1982
Benjamin Hoff, *The Te of Piglet*. New York: E.P. Dutton, Inc., 1992.
Paul J. Lin, *A Translation of Lao Tzu's Tao Te Ching and Wang Pi's COMMENTARY*. Ann Arbor, MI: University of Michigan Press, 1977.
Fung Yu-lan, *A Short History of Chinese Philosophy*. New York: The Free Press, 1966.
———. *The Spirit of Chinese Philosophy*. Boston: Beacon Press, 1962.
Arthur Waley, *The Way and its Power*. Boston: Houghton Mifflin, 1935.
———. *Three Ways of Thought in Ancient China*. New York: Doubleday Anchor, 1939.
Holmes Welch, *Taoism*. Boston, Beacon Press, 1966.


## Notes

1. *Tao Te Ching* 75.
2. Paul J. Lin, *A Translation of Lao-Tzu's Tao Te Ching and Wang Pi's COMMENTARY* (Ann Arbor, MI: University of Michigan Press, 1977), 147-149.
3. *Tao Te Ching* 1.
4. *Tao Te Ching* 25.
5. Chan, *The Way of Lao Tzu* (Indianapolis: The Bobbs- Merrill Co., Inc., 1963), 3.
6. *Tao Te Ching* 21; Chan, *The Way of Lao Tzu*, 11.
7. *Tao Te Ching* 2.
8. *Tao Te Ching* 63.
9. *Tao Te Ching* 64.
10. *Bhagavadgîtâ* 2, 71.
11. *Tao Te Ching* 22.
12. *Tao Te Ching* 43.
13. *Tao Te Ching* 47.
14. Henricks, ed., *Lao-tzu Te-Tao Ching* (New York: Ballantine Books, 1989), xxi.
15. *Tao Te Ching* 5.
16. Waley, *The Way and its Power* (Boston: Houghton Mifflin, 1935), 46
17. St. Ignatius Loyola, *Spiritual Exercises*, No. 23.
18. *Tao Te Ching* 28.
19. *Tao Te Ching* 51.
20. *Tao Te Ching* 52.
21. *Tao Te Ching* 19.
22. Welch, *Taoism* (Boston, Beacon Press, 1966), 73.
23. *Tao Te Ching* 10.
24. *Tao Te Ching* 20.

# 4

# GAUTAMA THE BUDDHA

## (*ca.* 563-483 B.C.E.)

In the southern foothills of the Himâlayas, along the Rohini river, lived the Shâkya clan, proud farmers and warriors (*kshatryas*) but otherwise unillustrious. Their king, Suddhodana, ruled from Kapilavastu, in the modern district of Gorakh-pur.

For twenty years King Suddhodana and Queen Mâyâ, his wife, had lived without children. But one night, the Queen had a dream: a white elephant was entering her womb from the right side of her chest. That night the Queen became pregnant. As the time of her delivery approached, she set out to return to her own father's house, as was the custom. On the way she stopped at Lumbini Park, and there, in the gardens, as she raised her arm to pluck a flower, her son, Siddhartha Gautama, was born. Tradition places this date on April 8.

Celebration followed, but it was short-lived. Seven days later Queen Mâyâ died, so the Prince's upbringing fell to the care of his maternal aunt, Prajâpati Gautami.

Not long after the Queen's death, Asita, an ascetic who lived in the hills nearby, saw a strange light about the palace and came down to investigate its origin. On seeing the newly born Prince he prophesied cryptically:

> Behold this child
> will either rule the world in power
> or save the world in wisdom.

Legend has it that Suddhodana preferred power to wisdom. So, as the Prince grew, he was exposed to all manner of learning that would lead to military achievement and worldly power, and he was protected from every possible pain that might set him on the quest for wisdom. His father even had a tall wall built around the palace enclosure to secure the peace and innocence of his son. But the world's truth would not be denied. One day, as the Prince walked with his father through the palace garden, he saw a bird pull out a worm from the ground and fly away with it to feed its young. The thought occurred to him: "Do all creatures prey on each other?" On another occasion, as he played on the palace grounds, he climbed a tree and, perched on one of its branches, he peered at the world outside the compound. And, lo! a funeral procession was marching toward the river carrying the shrouded remains of a loved one. And he thought: "Is death the end of all?"

Siddhartha's musings slowly turned to the ways of wisdom, so that his father grew concerned. To distract his son from his spiritual leanings, Suddhodana arranged Siddhartha's marriage to his cousin, Princess Yasodhara. He was then sixteen. But the Prince's mind would not be side-tracked. Even the birth of his son, Râhula, thirteen years later, did not cure him from his mental unrest; rather, it exacerbated the questioning. Eventually he decided to renounce palace life and seek the answer to his queries as a mendicant (*sanyâsi*). And so one night he stole out of the palace, never to return. He was twenty-nine years of age.

At first he consulted the hermit Bhagava, but was not appeased. Then he became the pupil of two renowned Brahmin teachers; first, of Arâda Kalama, a follower of the Sâmhkya system, whose psychology was later useful to the Prince; and later of Udraka Râmaputra. But Siddhartha was not into psychology, so he left and joined five pupils of Udraka who had moved to the jungle of Uruvilva, near Gâyâ, to practice a strict asceticism of denial. Here he stayed for six years, doing extraordinary penance, seeking to subdue his matter so that it would not disturb his spirit, unawares that he was thereby increasing the very suffering he was trying to assuage. Eventually he became so emaciated and weak that one day, as he finished his bath in the river Nairanjana (modern Phalgu), he was unable to walk out of the water, and had to drag himself out, slowly, by pulling on the low-lying branch of a tree. Later that day, as he walked to the village for the customary begging, he fell down and fainted, but was succored by Sujata, the eldest daughter of a herdsman living near by, who offered him rice and curds. To the consternation and scandal of his companions, Siddhartha accepted the food from the woman, thereby parting from his friends.

Siddhartha was left alone, but he decided to make a final effort to achieve understanding. Seated under a Bo tree (a fig tree, *Ficus religiosa*) he meditated in earnest through the night, and by the advent of the day, December 8, 528 B.C.E., he achieved enlightenment (*bodhi*): he became the Buddha, the enlightened one. He was thirty-five years old. This enlightenment did not take place in the context of a belief in God; therefore it was essentially non-theistic.[1]

Shortly thereafter he began his preaching, first at Varanasi (Benares), then in

Râjâgriha. Some of his former companions joined him, and thus the Order (*sangh*) or community was born. Eventually his own father and his son joined him, and his aunt, Prajâpati Gautami, formed a company of women. The Buddha, the Dharma (*dhamma*), and the Sangh became known as the "Three Jewels" of Buddhism.[2]

For forty-five years his preaching continued. Thousands became his disciples. His fame grew, and so did antagonism to his person and his views, for he rejected the Vedas. There were several attempts on his life, and tradition has it that his death came by poisoning. He had stopped for a meal at the house of Chundra, a blacksmith, and whether by design or accident, something in the food made him very ill. He moved on, sick though he was, until he came to Kushinagarâ, where he died, and where he was cremated. Among his last words were the following:

> Be ye lamps unto yourselves.
> Rely upon yourselves.
> Hold fast to the Doctrine [*dharma*] as a lamp.
> Rely upon the Doctrine.
> Do not depend upon anything else but yourselves.[3]

.oOo.

What did the Buddha teach? To begin with, the Buddha's teachings were heterodox to the Hindus. He did not preach in pictures or mythologies; he did not propound a metaphysical system. He did not accept the authority of the Vedas. His teachings were heterodox also in that he saw *karma* not as a cosmic web of cause and effect but as immediate psychological causation. Souls are not immortal, he held. Consciousness is a stream of moments in which each instant of thought causes the next. Self is the sum of the sequence.

The world, too, is discontinuous. Its seeming continuity is co-produced by our thinking it continuous and our thinking ourselves continuous, all of which is the result of ignorance. If we die in this ignorance—if our last conscious act ignorantly assumes an "I" and a "world"—it has an effect, mixture of mind and matter; that is, that last act of ignorant consciousness co-produces a new foetus. There is, thus, re-birth, but "we" are not reborn.[4]

Enlightenment ends rebirth, for it disconnects the relationship of co-production. This is the ultimate, but each one must find the truth in his/her own way,

> Truth is within ourselves; it takes no rise
> From outward things, whate'er you may believe.
> There is an inmost center in us all,
> Where truth abides in fullness; and around,
> Wall upon wall, the gross flesh hems it in,
> This perfect clear perfection which is truth.
> A baffling and perverting carnal mesh

> Binds it and makes all error: and to *know*
> Rather consists in opening out a way
> Whence the imprisoned splendor may escape,
> Than in effecting entry for a light
> Supposed to be without.[5]

Hence, in the last analysis, the truth of the Buddha remains undefinable, unteach-able, and the Buddha himself is aptly named *Shâkyamuni*—the Silent Sage of the Shâkyas, an otherwise incomprehensible appellation, since he preached for forty-five years!

Tradition ascribes to the Buddha himself the preaching of the Four Noble Truths and the Eightfold Path.[6] This preaching took place for the first time at Isipatana, in the deer-park of Varanasi:

> What are these Four Noble Truths? They are the Noble Truth of Suf-fering, the Noble Truth of the Origin of Suffering, the Noble Truth of the Extinction of Suffering, and the Noble Truth of the Path that leads to the Extinction of Suffering.[7]

Let us take each Truth in turn.

The first Noble Truth concerns the existence of suffering and its pervasive character. Birth, growth, death, misfortunes, worries, alarms, fears, and pain; the frustration of desire; the impossibility of fulfillment–all this spells suffering, and not only for the individual: suffering is the universal condition of human existence.

Suffering, however, has a cause. It has an origin, encompassed in the Second Noble Truth. This origin is desire. Through desire one binds oneself to the world (*samsâra*) and thereby to endless cycles of death and rebirth determined by the ineluctable law of *karma*. The origin of suffering is "that craving which gives rise to fresh rebirth, and, bound up with pleasure and lust, now here, now there, finds ever fresh delight."[8]  To crave, to desire for anything, is mediately to desire and crave for existence. But existence is the cycle of death and rebirth. Therefore craving ties the craver to the cycle, and thereby to sorrow, lamentation, pain, grief, and despair.

This craving is rooted in ignorance (*avidyâ*), a positivistic ignorance that tricks us into believing that our immediate experiences, impressions, ideas, feelings, represent to us the true reality of the world. We think that what glitters is gold, that seeming is being, that construct is reality, surface is substance, convention is truth, war is peace, and so on. Caused by the ignorance of former lives these erroneous views plunge us into further errors, according to the psychological understanding of *karma*. Ignorance begets desire. Craving sweetness, like flies, we are mired in the molasses of *samsâra*; like children, mistaking the merry-go-round for the real thing, "we" move interminably in circles, unable to get off.

However, suffering can be eliminated. The Third Noble Truth proclaims this. Suffering can be stopped by the extinction of desire. By realizing that this world and everything in it are but passing shadows, that every joy is ephemeral, and that existence itself is impermanent, craving for it may disappear, and, with it, suffering may be eliminated. This is possible because the truth of the world is undifferentiated; reality is the same in this and that, though desire ignores it. It is as if desire craved for *this* wave or *that* wave, without realizing that the sea is the same in all waves. The fact that the *un*differentiated waters are the sea, makes it possible to transcend the surface difference of the waves. In the words of the Scriptures,

> There is an Unborn, Unoriginated, Uncreated, Unformed. If there were no Unborn, no Unoriginated, no Uncreated, no Unformed, escape from the world of the born, the originated, the created, the formed, would not be possible. But since there is an Unborn, Unoriginated, Uncreated, Unformed, therefore is escape possible from the world of the born, the originated, the created, the formed.[9]

If suffering occurs because of our attachment to form, escape from suffering can take place only when we withdraw from form—whereto?   To formlessness. According to a later sage, Maitreya (*ca.* 270-350 C.E.), this means that

> Neither is it asserted
> that everything is unreal
> nor that everything is real;
> because there is existence,
> and also non-existence,
> and again existence—
> this is the Middle Way.[10]

Suffering ends when we glimpse the no-thingness (*sunyata*) behind all formed is-ness. Craving for form is thus shed, desire is stilled, and the soul is tranquil and at peace.

How is such a feat to be accomplished?  How is desire to be extinguished? There is a way, the Buddha taught, to achieve this release from suffering. This is the message of the Fourth Noble Truth. The way encompasses eight categories of practice and is therefore called the Noble Eightfold Path. The Path does not consist in giving oneself up to sensual enjoyment, nor does it enjoin mortification and penance. Between the extremes of sense and non-sense, gratification and denial, *bhoga* and *yoga*, lies the Middle Way (*Madhyamika*) of right action.

This Middle Way is also philosophical, for it steers a middle course between the metaphysical extremes of reality (*atthita*) and unreality (*natthita*). Similarly, it rejects as heretical both the materialistic- nihilistic view that denies *karma* and deliverance, and its opposite, the belief in eternal, indestructible reality.[11] Instead, it upholds the view of conditioned co-production.

It is also epistemological, for it holds to the middle between a skepticism that denies the possibility of transcendental knowledge, and a naive dogmatism that upholds the truth of all metaphysical assertions.[12]

However, it is at the moral, practical level, that the Middle Way becomes most significant and enduring. Specifically, it consists of Right Understanding, Right Aspiration, Right Speech, Right Action, Right Living, Right Effort, Right Attention, and Right Concentration. How these are to be understood constitutes the essence of the *Dharma*, the main tenets that hold together the followers of the Buddha. In a metaphor that becomes history, life is seen as a river to be crossed; the *Dharma* is a ferryboat (*yâna*). According to some, only the few (*hîn*) achieve a safe crossing. According to others, the ferryboat is large enough (*mahâ*) to afford safe passage to the many. Thus, after many centuries, the two main branches of Buddhism became established, the Hînayâna or Theravada, and the Mahâyâna. The former stresses individual salvation, for which the best route is monastic discipline. It survives primarily in Sri Lanka, Burma, and Siam. The latter preaches universal salvation. It spread beyond the frontiers of India to Tibet, to China, and eventually to Japan, where it gave rise to Zen.

But the Buddha's teaching, despite the clarity, directness, and conciseness of the Four Noble Truths and the Eightfold Path, remains paradoxical and elusive. For it points to the need to let go of every description, understanding, doctrine, spiritual aid; nay, of enlightenment itself, in order to attain salvation. Thus, suffering ceases when it is understood that suffering itself is merely phenomenal, a condition of the realm of appearance, and therefore really non-existent. Even the Ferryboat, the *Dharma*, is a vehicle for beginners, and must eventually be transcended, as is clear from the following text:

> "What would be your opinion of this man—would he be a clever man if, out of gratitude for the raft that has carried him across the stream to safety, he, having reached the other shore, should cling to it, take it on his back, and walk about with the weight of it?"
>
> "No, certainly the man who would do that would not be a clever man."
>
> "Would not the clever man be the one who left the raft to the current of the stream, and walked ahead without turning back to look at it? Is it not simply a tool to be cast away and forsaken once it has served the purpose for which it was made?"
>
> . . . . . . . . . . . . . . . .
>
> "In the same way the vehicle of the *Dharma* is to be cast away and forsaken, once the other shore of *nirvâna* has been attained."[13]

In point of fact, there isn't even another shore, nor this one, nor a Ferryboat, really, nor a setting forth. For truly,

> no one has ever set forth in the Great Ferryboat; no one will ever set forth in it, and no one is setting forth in it now. And why is this? Because neither the one setting forth, nor the goal for which he sets forth is to be found; therefore, who should be setting forth, and whither?[14]

.oOo.

*Nirvâna* is the central idea of the Buddha's preaching. But on the nature of *nirvâna* the Buddha has been pre-eminently "the Silent Sage" (*Shâkyamuni*)—his utterances are cryptic, often mere silence to the rising questions of his followers. This is especially so with regards to the matter of the extinction of the self (*anatta*) or its continuation after death. The only thing that emerges with any reasonable certainty is that *nirvâna* must be reached rather than preached.

Among the common folk, and some times even among the more learned utterances, *nirvâna* seems to mean a cooling, a refreshment, a state of peace, spiritual joy, tranquillity—a "Pure Land."[15] But the predominant meaning, especially when discussion seeks exactness, is one of cessation of desire and craving, implying at times, though obscurely, the extinction of individual existence.

Discussion has flourished on this issue, but only three possibilities seem to be available to the discussants. The first is that the dead saint is annihilated. When cessation of desire is achieved this side of paradise, death simply completes it. In this life we cease to crave; in the other *we* cease. Happiness, in this sense, would be to cease to be. A second possibility sees *nirvâna* as a cessation of craving here on earth, and as a heaven in the hereafter, where the enlightened ones reap eternally the results of their labors and renunciations. The third possibility is to see *nirvâna* as, indeed, a release from desire and its consequences, as deliverance from the cycle, without saying anything positive about what this release means after death. As Welbon puts it, *nirvâna* is "deliverance from a certain condition and not unto a specific other condition."[16]

It seems to me that the third one is the only position that can be seriously defended. The essence of *nirvâna* is *nirvâna* (*ni[r]* = un-, *vâna* = utterable). The reason is that complete deliverance is not possible as long as the "I" is upheld; on the other hand, we cannot really know what it means to leave the "I" behind. This impossibility of understanding what a self-less state might be is one of the roots of the later Mahâyâna notion of the Bodhisattva.

The tradition of the Bodhisattva enshrines the belief that some extraordinary individuals, having attained enlightenment and therein understood the nature of reality, withhold themselves from the ultimate insight (*samyak-sambodhi*) and from the consequent release from death and rebirth into *nirvâna*. They do this willingly, out of a magnificent kindness of heart or compassion (*karunâ*) for all created things, whose salvation they place ahead of their own. These are the Bodhisattvas. They sit at the brink of eternal *nirvâna*, a sacrifice for the salvation of the world. It is this benevolence that engenders the appearance on earth of great teachers and saints whose example and doctrine hastens the salvation of all.

.oOo.

In an important passage of the *Lankavatâra Sûtra*, the Buddha is asked to explain the nature of *nirvâna*. As a good teacher, he begins with a detailed exposition of what *nirvâna* is not. The philosophical positions discarded are those of the Upanishads as well as of the systems of Samkhya, and of Jainism.[17]

The most common error about the nature of *nirvâna* is to think that it is a happiness to be found and enjoyed here and now, in this time-bound existence. But this error itself gives rise to suffering, as explained in the Second Noble Truth.[18] *Nirvâna* is an inner realization, beautifully described in this passage of the *Lankavatâra Sûtra*:

> Realization . . . is an inner experience that has no connection with the lower mind system and its discriminations of words, ideas, and philosophical speculations. It shines out with its own clear light to reveal the error and foolishness of mind-constructed teachings, to render impotent evil influences from outside, and to guide one unerringly to the realm of the good immanent . . . and to the full enjoyment of the fruits that arise therefrom.[19]

But what can be said positively about *nirvâna*? To begin with, that it is extinction, cessation:

> This, truly, is the highest, holiest peace: appeasement of greed, hatred, delusion. . . . this, I say, is free from coming and going, from duration and decay; there is no beginning and no establishment, no result and no cause; this, indeed, is the end of all suffering.[20]

Secondly, that it is something marvelous, a sense of which is communicated in this passage from the *Lankavatâra Sûtra*:

> *Nirvâna* is where the thinking mind with all its discriminations, aversions, attachments, egoisms, is forever put away; where logical measures, as they are seen to be inert, are no longer seized upon; where even the notion of truth is treated with indifference because of its causing bewilderment; where, getting rid of the four propositions, there is insight into the abode of reality. *Nirvâna* is where the twofold passions have subsided and the twofold hindrances have been cleared away, and the twofold egolessness is patiently accepted; it is where, by the attainment of the turning about in the deepest seat of consciousness, self-realization of Noble Wisdom is fully entered into. . . . *Nirvâna* is where the Bodhisattva stages are passed one after another; it is where the sustaining power of the Buddhas upholds the Bodhisattvas in the bliss of contemplation [*samadhi*]; where compassion for others transcends all thoughts of self; where the Tathagata stage is finally realized.
>
> *Nirvâna* is the realm of the true nature of the Dharma; it is where the manifestation of Noble Wisdom that is Buddhahood expresses itself in perfect love for all; it is where the manifestation of perfect love that is Tathagatahood expresses itself in Noble Wisdom for the enlightenment of all—there, indeed, is *nirvâna*![21]

Again, *nirvâna* involves transcendence in that it requires going beyond the accepted understandings of self, world, reality, and even *nirvâna* itself. Moreover, eventually, this transcending itself must be transcended:

> Thus, Sariputra, all things having the nature of emptiness have no beginning and no ending. They are neither faultless nor not faultless; they are neither perfect nor imperfect. In emptiness there is no form, no sensation, no perception, no discrimination, no consciousness. There is no eye, no ear, no nose, no tongue, no sensitiveness to contact, no mind. There is no sound, no sight, no smell, no taste, no touch, no mental process, no object, no knowledge, no ignorance. There is no destruction of objects, no cessation of knowledge, no cessation of ignorance. There is no Noble Fourfold Truth, no pain, no cause of pain. There is no decay, no death, and no destruction of the notion of decay and death. There is no knowledge of *nirvâna*, there is no obtaining of *nirvâna*, there is no not obtaining of *nirvâna*.
>
> And why is there no obtaining of *nirvâna*? Because *nirvâna* is the realm of no-thingness. If the ego of personality were an enduring entity it could not obtain *nirvâna*. It is only because personality is made up of elements that pass away that personality may attain *nirvâna*. So long as man is seeking the highest, perfect Wisdom, he is still abiding in the realm of consciousness. In highest contemplation [*samadhi*], having transcended consciousness, he has passed beyond discrimination and knowledge, beyond the reach of change or fear; he is already enjoying *nirvâna*.[22]

Finally, in a very true sense, but in a mystical, paradoxical way as well, the essence of *nirvâna* consists in the realization that nothing can be said about *nirvâna*: "There is no *nirvâna* for the Buddhas,"[23] that is, the enlightened ones. That is why, perhaps, the Buddha is represented as forever sporting an enigmatic smile. For how else can this paradox be confronted?

To the earnest seeker, the Buddha offers the Noble Eightfold Path as the way to happiness. But ultimately, even this path must be abandoned. Therein alone lies sublime, un-utterable (*nir-vâna*) happiness.

> Mahâmati asked the Blessed One: "Tell us, Blessed One, about the One Vehicle which you said characterizes the attainment of inner self-realization and Noble Wisdom."
>
> . . . . [The Blessed One replied:] "Really, Mahâmati, there are no vehicles."[24]

.oOo.

# Additional Readings

## Sources

Edward Conze, ed., *Buddhist Texts through the Ages*. New York: Harper Torchbooks, 1964.
Dwight Goddard, ed., *A Buddhist Bible*. Boston: Beacon Press, 1970.
*The Teaching of Buddha*. Tokyo: Bukkyo Dendo Kyokai, 1977.
Nârada Thera, trans. & ed., *The Dhammapada*. London: John Murray, 1959

## Commentaries

Edward Conze, *Buddhist Meditation*. New York: Harper Torchbooks, 1956.
Alfred Foucher, *The Life of the Buddha*. Middletown, CT: Wesleyan University Press, 1963.
Mirko Fryba, *The Art of Happiness*. Boston: Shambhala, 1989.
Richard E. Gard, ed., *Buddhism*. New York: Braziller, 1962.
Rune E. Johansson, *The Psychology of Nirvâna*. New York: Doubleday Anchor, 1970.
David J. Kalupahana, *Nâgârjuna: The Philosophy of the Middle Way*. Albany: State University of New York Press, 1986.
Robert H. Lawson Slater, *Paradox and Nirvâna*. Chicago: University of Chicago Press, 1951.
Guy Richard Welbon, *The Buddhist Nirvâna and its Western Interpreters*. Chicago: University of Chicago Press, 1968.
Heinrich Zimmer, *Philosophies of India*. New York: Meridian, 1951.

## Notes

1. Ninian Smart, *The Religious Experience of Mankind* (New York: Scribner, 1976), 97.

2. Ibid., 98 and 115.

3. *Mahâparinirvâna Sûtra.*

4. Smart, *The Religious Experience*, 99-100.

5. Goddard, ed., *A Buddhist Bible* (Boston: Beacon Press, 1970), 8.

6. Smart, *The Religious Experience*, 98-99, 101-102.

7. *Majjhima-Nikâya* 141.

8. *Digha-Nikâya* 22.

9. *Udana* VIII.3.

10. Gard, ed., *Buddhism* ( New York: Braziller, 1962), 129.

11. Heinrich Dumoulin, *A History of Zen Buddhism* (Boston: Beacon Press, 1963), 15; Kalupahana, , *Nâgârjuna: The Philosophy of the Middle Way* (Albany: State University of New York Press, 1986), 1.

12. Heinrich Zimmer, Philosophies of India (New York: Meridian, 1951), 469-470.

13. *Majjhima-Nikâya* 3.2.22.135.

14. *Ashtasâhasrîkâ Prajñâpâramitâ* 1.

15.Smart, *The Religious Experience*, 120, 122, 224.

16.Welbon, *The Buddhist Nirvâna and its Western Interpreters* (Chicago: University of Chicago Press, 1968),  277.

17.*Lankavatâra Sûtra* 13.

18.*Digha-Nikâya* 22.

19.*Lankavatâra Sûtra* 7.

20.*Udana* 80.

21. *Lankavatâra Sûtra* 13.

22. *Prajñâpâramitâ-hridaya*.

23. *Lankavatâra Sûtra* 13.

24. *Lankavatâra Sûtra* 7.

# 5

## PLATO

### (428/7-348/7 B.C.E.)

Pericles was dead but a year or two, and the glory that was Athens' during his tenure had begun to wane, when, in the month Thargelion (May-June), 428 or 427, a son was born to Ariston and Perictione, noble citizens of Athens. They named him Aristocles.

Ariston and Perictione belonged to Athenian aristocracy. He traced his family to the ancient Athenian kings, and she was a direct descendant of Solon (*ca.* 639-559 B.C.E.), the great Attic legislator. Their union had already been blessed with the birth of two sons, Glaucon and Adeimantus, and was graced eventually by a daughter, Potone. Perictione († *ca.* 366) would survive her husband, marry her uncle Pyrilampes, and give birth to a boy, Antiphon, who would thus be the stepbrother of Aristocles.

Young Aristocles was a talented child. He loved music and sports, and as he grew into his teen years he added women to his loves. He wrestled at the Isthmian games, where his exploits earned him the nickname *Platon*—"broad-shouldered" —by which he is still known.

He may have known Socrates (469-399) from childhood, though it is not certain when he came within his sphere of influence. This probably occurred during his late teens, but the effect was not immediate: Plato's early ambitions were political, not philosophical.

In 404 (Plato was 23 years old) the oligarchic revolution of "the Thirty" seized power in Athens. Plato felt a call to join, but he was too young (according to Cleisthenes's law). Moreover, the Thirty tried to implicate Socrates in unlawful procedures by ordering him to make an illegal arrest. Even though disobedience to such a command entailed the penalty of death, Socrates refused. He was indicted, but in 403 the exiled democrats, Anytus chief among them, seized power from the Thirty and restored a measure of democracy.

Old, rankling jealousies soon prompted a new indictment of Socrates. The charges, this time, brought by Anytus, were that he corrupted youth and did not honor the gods of the city. In a trial that Plato has described in the *Apology*, Socrates was condemned to death (399). His last days and his death are movingly preserved in Plato's *Phaedo* and *Crito*.

The experience of Socrates's trial and execution unsettled Plato personally. It also shook his faith in democracy and in the human capacity to rule with justice. For how could a government call itself just when it had put to death unjustly the most just person of the age? Plato may have also feared for his life, for by this time he was a well-known "follower" of Socrates. So he left Athens for Megara, where he stayed at the home of Eucleides, and where he probably wrote the so-called Socratic dialogues.

He visited Athens a few times, and even fought for it against Corinth in 395. But he also traveled a great deal, to Magna Graecia and to Egypt.

In 388/7 he visited Sicily. Dionysus I (413-367) was then the ruler of Syracuse, and he received Plato graciously. In Syracuse Plato met young Dion, son-in-law of Dionysus, and Plato was impressed by the young man's eager desire to learn. But Dionysus's interest turned, and so did his favor. Plato had to leave in a hurry, was sidetracked to Aegina (then at war with Athens), and was promptly sold into slavery there. Anniceris of Cyrene ransomed him, and so Plato returned to Athens in 387, when he was 40 years of age. His friends there raised a substantial sum of money to repay Anniceris, who refused to be re-imbursed. The money, then, was used to purchase a grove dedicated to the god Akademos, and there Plato established his university.

The Academy was run like a religious fraternity (*thiasos*), very much on the model of Pythagoras's school at Crotona. No fees were charged, and men as well as women were welcome, the latter, perhaps, under the influence of Plato's hetaira, Archeanassa. During these years in the Academy Plato published his more mature dialogues, including the *Republic* (*Politeia*).

For twenty years Plato led the quiet but exciting life of the mind. But in 367, when he was 60 years old, he received an invitation from Dion to return to Syracuse. Dionysus I had died, and in his stead, his young son, Dionysus II, brother-in-law of Dion, had ascended the throne. Plato accepted the invitation, afraid that, if he didn't, people would say he was merely a man of words, not action. But nothing really came of this visit. Dion was virtually banished, and Plato returned to Athens and the serenity of the Academy. Once more, in 360 (he was 67) he traveled to Syracuse in the hope of effecting a reconciliation between Dion and Dionysus, but he failed and barely escaped with his life. Later he helped Dion overthrow Dionysus, and when Dion was assassinated in 354, he lent his support to Hipparinos and the friends and parents of Dion in their attempts to avenge Dion's death (353-352).

After his return to Athens in 360 Plato settled quietly in the Academy. For twelve years he taught some and wrote more, and he was still writing the *Laws* when death overtook him in 348/7. He was 81 years of age.

.oOo.

Plato himself maintained that he had never written technical treatises on his own ideas.[1] He made this statement when he was in his late sixties. What, then, is one to make of the dialogues, the best preserved collection of works from antiquity? Whatever one may say of them, one must agree with Whitehead that "the safest general characterization of the European philosophical tradition is that it consists of a series of footnotes to Plato."[2] For better or for worse, we are his heirs. Plato did not develop his ideas into a system. He was a thinker, not a philosopher (as thinkers became known until recently). He was an artist, also, crafting the language of his dialogues with exquisite care while discussing art.

At the core of Plato's thinking is intuition.[3] Intuition is the source of all true knowledge, and it is the highest possible form of knowing. Plato terms it *noësis* and *episteme*.[4] Intuition is the only form of knowing that gives us truth, the only form of knowing that gives us certainty. It is the pinnacle of the knowing process.

At its opposite pole stands imagining (*eikasia*). This is representational or imaginative knowing, the knowing that makes use of allegory and metaphor. Slightly higher than imagining is common sense belief or opinion (*pistis*). The certainty content of opinion is higher than that of imagining, but it is far below that of intuition, for it lacks irrefutable proof. Between intuition and opinion Plato places thinking (*dianoia*), especially mathematical and philosophical thinking. By *dianoia* Plato means a knowing that is more certain than mere opinion, but which cannot be called absolutely certain because it lacks the impregnability of intuition. This thinking, as illustrated by mathematical thinking, is more certain than mere opinion because it is more abstract; that is, it deals with the more permanent and universal characteristics of reality distilled by thinking and depicted in diagrams and formulas. It is, in other words, less sensorial; but, on the other hand, it lacks the perfect certainty of intuition because it hangs from assumptions which may not be absolutely certain. Discursive thinking, in other words, is hypothetical (it takes place below [*hypo-*] the premiss [-*thesis*]).

Thus we have, according to Plato, a four-tier hierarchy of knowing, ascending from imagining and opinion to discursive thinking and, finally, intuition. The two lower rungs constitute generally the realm of belief and empirical inquiry, while the two higher ones make up the realm of knowledge and truth.

This conception of knowing stages is tied by Plato to a fourfold, hierarchical view of reality. The deciding principle here is that of stability. At the bottom level we have shadows, images, dreams, reflections in mirrors, and the like; that is, objects of perception characterized by great instability and by a dependence on other objects for their own reality. Immediately above are the somewhat more stable objects that create the shadows and images of themselves, and about which we dream. This is the realm of living creatures and of manufactured objects. The third level contains objects that *we* tend not to count as real, but which were so for Plato. This is the realm of mathematical calculations, geometrical diagrams, and scientific formulas. It is, indeed, a world abstracted by the mind from the lower realm of things; but it *is* a real world, nonetheless, though its reality is of an intelligible, not a visible, nature. Thus, for example, the formula $E=mc^2$ gave us the reality of atomic power even before an atomic bomb was built, and the formulations of geometry about the circle are real even though no perfect circle exists. Not merely that, but even when the formulas and diagrams are arrived at inductively from the observation of actual things, their life lasts immeasurably longer than that of the very objects upon which they rest. Newton's legendary apple, for example, is gone, but the law of universal gravitation endures.

Still, the realm of discursive thinking does not support itself. It hangs from certain assumptions, certain statements which, though unprovable, are presumed to be true. Thus, for example, the whole of Euclidean geometry rests on a set of unprovable postulates, and the whole of science is built upon hypotheses. Therefore, argued Plato, this realm does not possess the kind of absolute stability, the kind of absolute truth one expects to find at *some* level of reality. It cannot be, therefore, the most real of the real. This kind of ultimate, stable reality is to be found by rising from this lower (*hypo*-) realm to the pegs (-*thesis*) from which it hangs. These pegs, immutable, unchanging, timeless, universal, perfect, real in themselves as well as the prototype of every lower real, are the Forms (*eidos, idea*). They are the summit of the real. They are what *is*.

Thus we have an ascending hierarchy of stability and reality, from dreams and shadows to things, from things to formulas, from formulas to Forms. The two lower realms make up what Plato called the visible world; the higher two compose the intelligible world. The lower two are accessible to physical eyes; the higher ones only to "the eyes of the soul" (*tò tês psychês ómma*).[5] Above all is the Form of the Good. Plato compares it and its function to the sun: in its light we apprehend everything we apprehend.

The lower realm of the physically visible encompasses, in a sense, reality as Herakleitus saw it: mutable, fluid, transient.[6] The upper realm of the intelligible comes close to the Parmenidian world: static, one, and eternally permanent. Thus, in Plato's intuition of reality are unified the two main world-views of his predecessors.

Plato also envisages a close relation between the stages of knowing and the levels of reality. Imagining (*eikasia*) is that function or power of the mind through which we know images and dream dreams; belief is the state of mind accompanying the perception of things; discursive thinking (*dianoia*) is how we deal with mathematics, geometry, and logic; finally, intuition (*noësis*) is the only way to apprehend the Forms, and is the only knowing that can give us certain, true knowledge (*episteme*).

Moreover, Plato conceives knowing as a developmental process. One begins by perfecting one's imaginative capacities through music, poetry, literature, and the arts. As one matures, the physical world in all its multiplicity is encountered and studied: perception must be developed. Then comes the refinement of thinking by a systematic exposure to mathematics, geometry, astronomy, and musical theory. Finally one hopes that the psyche, readied through years of exercise and dialectical discourse, will rise to the intuition of the Forms—as Plato puts it, "they must lift up the eye of the soul to gaze on that which sheds light on all things . . . the good itself."[7] Based on these insights Plato structured a course of education designed to lead the child, the adolescent, and the mature person, through stages of progressive enlightenment adapted to their own mental development, and he saw teaching as the art (*techne*) of adapting subject matter to the stage of development of the mind, and of making sure that the soul's eye "is turned the way it ought to be."[8] The Allegory of the Cave[9] was devised as a way to illustrate how we may become enlightened.

Plato's view of happiness is tied to his definition of justice. He confronts the question of justice in the *Republic*. After some preliminary skirmishes, he (Socrates) suggests that it may be easier to discover the meaning of justice by looking for it in the state at large rather than in the individual, for the state is the individual writ large.[10]

Plato assumes the existence of four "virtues" or capacities for action, namely, wisdom, courage, temperance, and justice.[11] These characteristics must be realized in any ideal state in the persons of its citizens. Wisdom is realized when the state's rulers or guardians are wise and prudent; courage is realized when its defenders—the military—are brave; temperance is realized when the citizenry is self-controlled; that is, when they are masters of themselves so that they always do what is the prudent thing to do rather than what is prompted by their intemperate desires.[12] Having defined three of the characteristic virtues of the ideal state, only justice remains to be discovered.

Plato begins with the common conception of distributive justice: to each his/her own (*unicuique proprium*). Each should get as each deserves or needs. To this idea Plato adds a pre-requisite: each should get what each deserves or needs as long as each does *what is proper to each* (*tá autou prattein*).[13] This pre-requisite comes out of the general teleological principle that everything has a function or orientation for which nature has suited it.[14] This function ought to be performed at all times,[15] and education prepares one to know, understand, and accept (i.e., choose) one's function and to perform it. In a true sense, one must be educated to choose one's fate.

Now, when in a state, each citizen (and each stratum of the citizenry) does what is proper to it (i.e., acts according to its function), each and every citizen, as well as the whole state, receive what is proper to them, and the whole state is harmonious. This is justice.

But at the individual level, this is also happiness: it is peace of mind and freedom from fear, since each and everyone is master of him/herself; it is wealth, since desires are tempered by wisdom; it is a pleasant life, since inner and outer balance makes for good feelings; it is pleasurable, too, for all pleasures are apportioned wisely, and those of the mind are not excluded; it cements friendships, which are a primary factor in happiness; and it is the highest good obtainable. Thus, "the best and most just are also the happiest, and they are those who are most kingly and masters over themselves."[16]

> The just man does not permit the several elements within him to interfere with one another, or any of them to do the work of others,—he sets in order his own inner life, and is his own master and his own law, and at peace with himself; and when he has bound together the three principles within him, which may be compared to the higher, lower, and middle notes of the scale, and the intermediate intervals—when he has bound all these together, and is no longer many, but has become one entirely temperate and perfectly adjusted nature, then he proceeds to act, if he has to act, whether in a matter of property, or in the treatment of the body, or in some affair of politics or private business; always thinking and calling that which preserves and cooperates with this harmonious condition, just and good action, and the knowledge which presides over it, wisdom, and that which at any time impairs this condition, he will call unjust action, and the opinion which presides over it ignorance.[17]

The inner psychic balance that is justice makes a person whole, integral. No imbalance exists, no opposition or division (*dypsychia*) within the psyche. This experience of wholeness the Greeks called *eudaimonia*, "good spirits," or "psychic harmony." It is happiness itself.[18] If only the just person can be counted happy, it is because justice is happiness.

.oOo.

## Additional Reading

### Sources

Plato, *The Dialogues of Plato*, trans. Benjamin Jowett and *The Seventh Letter*, trans. J. Harward. *Great Books of the Western World*, ed. Mortimer J. Adler. Chicago: Encyclopaedia Britannica, 1952.

Plato, *The Republic*, trans. Francis M. Cornford. New York: Oxford University Press, 1945.

### Commentaries

E. R. Dodds, *The Greeks and the Irrational*. Berkeley: University of California Press, 1971.

Paul Friedländer, *Plato*. 3 vols. New York: Pantheon, 1958.

William C. Greene, *Moira: Fate, Good and Evil in Greek Thought*. New York: Harper Torchbooks, 1944.

W. K.C. Guthrie, *The Greek Philosophers*. New York: Harper Torchbooks, 1950.

Werner W. Jaeger, *Paideia, The Ideals of Greek Culture*. 3 vols. New York: Oxford University Press, 1939-1944.

Richard L. Nettleship, *Lectures on the Republic of Plato*. London: Macmillan, 1937.

A. E. Taylor, *Plato, the Man and his Work*. New York: Meridian, 1963.

Gregory Vlastos, ed., *Plato*. 2 vols. New York: Doubleday Anchor, 1971.

Alfred North Whitehead, *Process and Reality*. New York: Harper Torchbooks, 1960.

### Notes

1. *Epistula* VII. 341C.

2. Whitehead, *Process and Reality* (New York: Harper Torchbooks, 1960), 63.

3. Plato, *Epistula* VII. 341C-D; Friedländer, *Plato* (New York: Pantheon, 1958), I, 19-20.

4. *Republic* VII. 533E.

5. *Republic* VII. 533D.

6. Herakleitos, *Fragment* 20W; Plato, *Cratylus* 440C.

7. *Republic* VII. 540.

8. *Republic* VII .518.

9. *Republic* VII. 514A-521B.

10. *Republic* II. 368.

11. *Republic* IV. 427.

12. *Republic* IV. 430-431.

13. *Republic* IV .441C-442A; Vlastos, *Plato* (New York: Doubleday Anchor), II, 76-77.
14. *Republic* I. 352-353.
15. *Republic* IV. 432.
16. *Republic* IX. 580.
17. *Republic* IV. 443-444.
18. *Republic* I. 354.

# 6

# ARISTOTLE

## (384-322 B.C.E.)

For Aquinas, he was *the* Philosopher; Erasmus called him "the God of our teachers";[1] and he is said to be the only pagan in Jewish heaven. He is Aristotle, and he was born in 384 in the Greek town of Stagira (modern Stavró), on the north-east coast of Chalcidice.

His father, Nicomachus, belonged to the guild of the Asklepiads, and he practiced medicine in the court of Philip's father, Amyntas II of Macedonia. Aristotle grew up in Pella, the court city, and he was probably initiated by his father into the study of medicine, since, according to Galen, Asklepiads traditionally trained their sons in dissection. His mother, Phaestis, was a native of Chalcis. Both parents died when Aristotle was still a boy, so he became a ward of a relative named Proxenus.

At eighteen he entered Plato's Academy in Athens, where he remained for nineteen years (till he was thirty-seven years old) as student, at first, and then lecturer. He followed Plato generally, but not uncritically, and always with respect. His *amicus Plato, magis amica veritas* ("Plato is my friend, but a closer friend is truth"[2]) is an indication of this.

In 348/7 Plato died and was succeeded in the leadership of the Academy by his nephew, Speusippus, who favored the mathematization of Plato's philosophy. Dissatisfied with this turn of events, Aristotle accepted an invitation from a former fellow-student, Hermeias, who was then the ruler of Atarneus and Assos in Mysia. There he spent about three years, married Pythias (niece and adopted daughter of Hermeias) in 345, and promptly fathered a daughter, also named Pythias.

Hermeias was assassinated in 344 by the Persians, so Aristotle moved to Mitylene, the major city in the island of Lesbos. Shortly after, in 343/2, Philip of Macedonia, for whose father Aristotle's father had been the physician, invited him to undertake the education of his son, Alexander, then thirteen years of age. So Aristotle moved to Pella, the city of his childhood, and began the task of cultivating the mind and mores of the future conqueror of the ancient world. For Alexander he composed treatises on monarchy and on colonizing (now lost), and began the collection and commentary of the constitutions of the great states of his time, of which only that of Athens survives. He also served Philip as emissary to various cities, and presided over the reconstruction of his own birth place, Stagira, devastated during Philip's war with Olynthus.

His formal stay at Pella ended when Alexander was appointed regent in 340, but Aristotle retained a warm friendship with him. Records of a correspondence between the two are extant, though considered spurious by most scholars. In one of the letters (in the keep of a monastery in Athens), Alexander addresses his former teacher touchingly as "the father of my soul."

Aristotle, then, moved to Stagira, and, after Philip's death in 335, he returned to Athens. He was forty-nine years old. Shortly after his arrival, his wife, Pythias, died. Aristotle did not marry again, though thereafter he lived with the hetaira Herpyllis, a native, like himself, of Stagira. By her he had a daughter and a son, whom they named Nicomachus, who would later edit his father's lectures on ethics (which therefore are titled with his name).

In Athens, in a grove to the north-east of the city dedicated to Apollo Lykeios and the Muses, Aristotle rented some buildings and founded his university, the Lyceum. There, every morning, he walked with his pupils through the covered porticos (*peripatoi*) or among the trees; in the afternoon, his lectures were open to the public. The walking about eventually gave rise to the nickname by which his scholars became known, *peripatetikoi*, the "round-about walkers."

At the Lyceum he collected the first large library, with hundreds of manuscripts and maps. Also a large number of specimens of animals and plants to make up the first natural science museum. Alexander provided both financial support as well as specimens. Aristotle's extant works, dating from this period at the Lyceum, are most probably notes for his lectures. The finished works, published mainly during his years at the Academy, are lost, but were reputed to have been good enough to have deserved the praises of Cicero and Quintilian.

In 323 Alexander died. Athens seethed with anti-Macedonian feelings, abetted by Demosthenes, who had returned from exile. Aristotle felt he was under suspicion. Eventually he was accused of impiety for a hymn and epitaph he had written twenty years before at the time of the assassination of his friend and father-in-law, Hermeias. So, determined, as he put it, not to let the Athenians "sin twice against philosophy" (a reference to Socrates's trial and death in 399), he left the Lyceum in Theophrastus's hands and moved to Chalcis, where he had land inherited from his mother. He died there in 322. He was sixty-two years old.

What kind of a man was he? No one has ever amassed the wealth of knowledge and detail that Aristotle did. There is no branch of knowledge that does not bear the imprint of his thought. He originated most areas of research, and the ones he did not, he re-oriented radically. But he was more than a superbly functioning thinking machine.

There is an exquisitely carved, small, French statuette of a bearded man, naked, on all fours. Astride his back rides a girlish, happy, naked woman. It is a statue of Aristotle and Herpyllis, and clearly it conveys the belief that he was not just the logical robot his extant works make him out to be, but a fun-loving and caring man who could enjoy sexual play as much as a perfect syllogism.

There is a painting, too, by Raffaello, titled "The School of Athens" (1509-1512). At its center is Plato, his right hand and index finger raised upwards, undoubtedly making a point about the Forms. By his side stands Aristotle, his right hand raised even with his waist, palm down, pointing neither upwards nor downwards but poised, in balance between the intelligible and the sensory, the abstract and the concrete, the universal and the particular.

There is, finally, his last will and testament, providing for his children and for Herpyllis; freeing some of his slaves and protecting others from being sold; and directing that the remains of his wife, Pythias, be placed in the same tomb as his own.

This man was balanced, sensitive, affectionate, prone to witticism, and capable of enjoying a good meal and a sexual escapade. He loved stories, the more so as he grew older. And he relished the use of his powerful mind. If ever there was one, he was the quintessential Renaissance man eighteen hundred years before the Renaissance. In fact, he was what Renaissance men sought to emulate.

In his discussion of friendship Aristotle remarks that perfect friendship is rare because good friends are rare[3]. This remark applies paramountly to him: he was one of the rare ones.

.oOo.

Why does a seed germinate into a tree? Because it has the potential to do so. Why does a child grow up to be an adult? Because it has the potential. Why does the human mind acquire knowledge? Because it is capable of doing so. To learn, then, is the actualization of the potential to know, just as to grow is the actualization of the potential to grow.

This way of speaking, so common to us today, was invented by Aristotle. It arose out of his effort to understand how things change, how they come to be and cease to be. Perceptively, he concluded that things change because they *can*. Not that if they can they will, but that if they do, it is because they are able to. Further, *what* things become defines them. Therefore these two principles (*aitía*), capacity to change and accomplishment or perfection, characterize all change. Aristotle called them *potency* (*dynamis*) and *act* (*energéia*).

Now, change in the broadest and most general terms is the actualization of what exists only potentially.[4] This applies to all change and to all things, whether living or inanimate. When speaking of physical objects, however, Aristotle employed the terms *form* (*morphe*) and *matter* (*hyle*), to correspond to act and potency. For example, in a bronze statue, bronze is the matter that has the potential to become a statue; and form is the actual shape or figure of the finished statue.[5] In the case of human generation, Aristotle would say that matter is the bodily conceptus while form is the psyche or soul. Here is to be found the Scholastic identification of the body with matter and of the soul with form.

The use of the term "matter" for potency creates some problems for us because modern physics and contemporary language see matter as a "thing" complete in and of itself. But for Aristotle, matter as potential was not a thing (*ti*); simply, it was one of the constituents of things (*ens quo*). By itself, matter was "neither this (*ti*), nor a quantum, nor anything else by which a thing can be defined."[6] It was, in a true sense, "no-thing." In saying that things are "composed of" act and potency, form and matter, Aristotle did not mean that things were a mixture of two "things," but, rather, of two "principles" (*aitía*). Matter does not exist by itself; it exists only as a thing's potential. It is that in things by which things come to be, and once they are, come to be whatever they come to be or are made to be.

*Why* do things come to be? *Why* are things made? *What/who* makes them be? Aristotle answers these questions by referring to two other principles, efficiency and finality. To make things come to be, an impetus or force is necessary—a maker. The maker acts because of a motivation, a desire to achieve something envisaged or planned. Thus, to form and matter, efficiency and goal-seeking are added, raising the number of principles to four. These are the so-called "four causes." But the word "cause" requires explanation.

We tend to restrict the meaning of cause to mere efficiency. But Aristotle shows how, clearly, efficiency without potential can no more effect anything than vision without efficiency. The truth is that the four principles contribute to the coming to be of anything that comes to be, but they do so differently, each providing a different but essential element in the coming to be of the thing. A sculptor, thus, conceives in her/his mind the idea of a statue. The image of the finished statue enthralls her/him; it appears as something desirable (good). It becomes the *goal* (*telos*) to be achieved. Next, the sculptor looks for a piece of marble of the size and color, etc., necessary for the carving of the statue. She/he envisages in the block of marble its *potential* to become the statue. The sculptor sets to work, and by means of various instrumentalities produces the statue—that is, *actualizes* in the marble the potential she/he had envisaged originally. The sculptor is the efficient cause; vision/image is the final cause; marble is the material cause; the shape of the finished statue is the formal cause. The thing thus wrought is actual, actualized, realized. It is an *entelechy* (*en-telos-echein* = having its end within; full-filled). In one of Aristotle's examples:

a house: the producer or agent of the house is the building art and the work of the builder; its "wherefor" [or "what-for"] is the use to which the house is put; its material [*hyle*] is earth and stone; its form [*eidos*] is its plan or definition.[7]

In brief:

> There are four causes underlying everything: first, the final cause, that for the sake of which a thing exists; secondly, the formal cause, the definition of its essence (and these two may be regarded pretty much as one and the same); thirdly, the material; and fourthly, the moving principle or efficient cause.[8]

As is clear from the foregoing, Aristotle views the whole of nature as well as human action as goal-seeking. Whatever we do or make, we do or make for a goal, and nature, which cannot be credited with forethought, seeks the goals imbedded in it by the Creator of the world. Teleology is thus the perennial refrain of the world.

Teleology, however, is not haphazard. Things do not have infinite, indiscriminate potential, nor do they, consequently, aim at just any goal; their potentials are quite definite, being directed, as it were, to an end or goal quite specific to themselves.

Such potentials are either inborn or acquired, but in any case they empower (render capable) the being to achieve what the potential is potential for. Habits, for example, are acquired second nature; they give us the potential to act in certain ways. Now, it is along the line of habits that we must understand Aristotle's definition of virtue. Virtue, he says, "is a state [*hexis, habitus*] concerned with choice, lying in a mean . . . determined by reason."[9] Virtue, that is, is an acquired disposition or potential that has become a habit in us. It is, as Yves R. Simon says, an "existential readiness"[10] to make certain kinds of choices, treading, as far as possible, a middle way between extremes, as determined by reason.

Virtues are of two kinds, intellectual and moral. Aristotle arrives at this distinction by noting that we are both reasoning and desiring beings. Reasoning is exercised according to the habits of thinking we have developed; desire, according to our habits of behavior. In both instances reasoning is exercised, but differently. In other words, reasoning can be exercised in a more theoretical or in a more practical fashion, for the sake of contemplation or for the sake of action. After all, determining the mean between extremes is an act of reasoning, albeit of a practical nature.

At a more intellectual level, reasoning can concern itself with the quest for truth (with the necessary) or with matters of opinion (the contingent), such as political theory, economics, etc., and with matters of art (*techne*). Depending on the area of exercise, the intellectual virtues enable us to conduct our thinking properly; they are the virtues (powers) of scientific demonstration, intuition, art, deliberation, and pure theorizing (wisdom).

The moral virtues have to do with the channeling of desire in action. These are the virtues of courage, temperance (including liberality, munificence, self-respect, gentleness, truthfulness, ambition, good taste, wittiness, friendliness, modesty, and righteous indignation), and justice. As is clear, Aristotle's treatment of the virtues is more detailed than Plato's, though it follows the general lines of the traditional "cardinal" virtues.

This conception of teleology and virtue places a premium on rationality. To desire a goal, to see it as good and wish to achieve it, the goal must be known. Knowing, or the capacity to know, distinguishes human goal-seeking from other forms of teleology. This capacity to know, therefore, is the distinctive *form* of the human, its specific difference. If human nature is "composed" of body and soul (i.e., matter and form), the soul (*psyche*) is the human form. What is highest in it is what is distinctively human. This is reason. Thus Aristotle arrives at his definition of the human: a rational or thinking animal.[11]

If the "rational element" defines the human, then its exercise will be what is most characteristically human. This exercise is governed by the highest of the intellectual virtues, wisdom. Contemplative theorizing, therefore, is the highest activity that humans can aspire to. Engaging in contemplation is the fulfillment of the highest human potential, the highest virtue. It is doing what is most distinctly human; it is the highest human function. It is happiness.

.oOo.

Aristotle begins the *Nichomachean Ethics* with an application of teleology to human activity. In everything we do we aim at a good. This does not mean that what we aim at or desire is actually good, but simply that what we want appears to us as a good. We cannot choose evil *per se*, but only what appears good to us. "Good" and "end" or "goal" are interchangeable.[12] But among ends, some are higher than others. So the acquisition of lower ends may be seen as a means toward the higher ends. Similarly, some ends are temporary, or immediate; but they are truly means toward those ends we consider final (in the sense that their acquisition implies cessation of pursuit). Again, some ends are desired and pursued only as means to further ends; as stepping stones, so to speak, while others are desired for their own sake because, when they are achieved, they suffice in themselves. Some activities, in brief, are heterotelic, some are autotelic.[13]

Aristotle then identifies the ultimate good or end with happiness. In other words, when people are asked what they want most in life they answer, happiness. When asked why they do what they do, they answer that, ultimately, it is for the sake of being happy. Happiness, then, is their primary end or goal.[14] But there is disagreement as to what happiness consists in. So, in order to clarify this question further, Aristotle undertakes a brief survey of opinions of happiness current in his time. His conclusion is that none of them really qualify as the ultimate good, basically, because none of them are self-sufficient, things we want for their own sake:

Now such a thing happiness, above all else, is held to be; for this we choose always for itself and never for the sake of something else, but honor, pleasure, reason, and every virtue we choose indeed for themselves . . . but we choose them also for the sake of happiness, judging that by means of them we shall be happy. Happiness, on the other hand, no one chooses for the sake of these, nor, in general, for anything other than itself. . . Happiness, then, is something final and self-sufficient, and is the end of action.[15]

Still, this does not tell us much about what this end consists in, and calling it happiness adds nothing to our knowledge, so Aristotle introduces the notion of "function." This notion is derived from Plato, and it was used by Plato, too, to arrive at his definition of happiness. In Aristotle, it is developed in the context of his analysis of the intellectual and moral virtues, that is, capacities. Function is the power-potential to act in specific, distinctive ways. What he wants to determine is the highest human potential (*virtue*, function), the most excellent exercise of which will lead to a definition of happiness.

The function of man is an activity of soul which follows or implies a rational principle. . . . Happiness [then] consists in the *exercise* of this function or virtue. Not merely that, but it must consist in an exercise or activity that is autotelic, that is, its own end.[16]

Happiness, then, "is an activity of the soul in accordance with perfect virtue."[17] But what kind of virtue or potential? It must be in accordance with the highest virtue, which is the intellectual one. But since virtue itself involves moderation, the contemplative activities that constitute happiness must not be exclusionary; rather, they must include other activities and the pleasures derived from them. In conclusion, then:

If happiness is activity in accordance with virtue, it is reasonable that it be in accordance with the highest virtue; and this will be that of the best thing in us. Whether it be reason or something else that is this element which is thought to be our natural ruler and guide and to take thought of things noble and divine, whether it be itself also divine or only the most divine element in us, the activity of this in accordance with its proper virtue will be perfect happiness. That this activity is contemplative we have already said . . . for man, therefore, the life according to reason is best and pleasantest, since reason more than anything else *is* man. This life therefore is also the happiest.[18]

.oOo.

# Additional Readings

## Sources

Aristotle, *The Works of Aristotle*. 2 vols. *The Great Books of the Western World*, ed. Mortimer J. Adler. Chicago: Encyclopaedia Britannica, 1952.
*The Complete Works of Aristotle*, ed. Jonathan Barnes. 2 vols.; Princeton, NJ. Princeton University Press, 1985.

## Commentaries

Copleston, Frederick. *A History of Philosophy*. 9 vols. New York: Doubleday-Image, 1977.
Guthrie, W. K. C. *Aristotle: An Encounter*. Cambridge: Cambridge University Press, 1981.
Höffding, Harald. *A History of Modern Philosophy*. 2 vols. New York: Dover Publications, Inc.,1955.
Jaeger, Werner W. *Aristotle*. New York: Methuen, 1934.
McGill, Vivian. *The Idea of Happiness*. New York: Praeger, 1947.
Pieper, Josef. *Happiness and Contemplation*. New York: Pantheon,1958.
Ross, W.D. *Aristotle*. New York: Meridian Books, Inc., 1960.
Simon, Yves R. *The Definition of Moral Virtue*. New York: Fordham University Press, 1986.
Taylor, A. E. *Aristotle*. New York: Dover Publications, 1955.

## Notes

1.Erasmus, *Praise of Folly* 63.
2.This is a lapidary version of a statement in *Nicomachaean Ethics* I.6 [10196$^a$ 17].
3.*Nicomachean Ethics* VIII.3 [1156$^b$ 24-25].
6.*Physics* III.1 [201$^a$ 10-19].
7.*Metaphysics* VII.3 [1029$^a$ 3-5].
8.*Metaphysics* VII.3 [1029$^a$ 20-21].
9.*Metaphysics* III.2 [996$^b$ 4-7].
10.*De Generatione Animalium* I.1 [715$^a$ 3-6].
11.*Nicomachean Ethics* II.6 [1107$^a$ 1].
12.Yves R. Simon, *The Definition of Moral Virtue* (New York: Fordham University Press, 1986), 105.
13.*Nicomachean Ethics* I.7 [1098$^a$ 1-4].
14.*Nicomachean Ethics* I.1 [1094$^a$ 1-17].
15.*Nicomachean. Ethics* I.2 [1094$^a$ 17- 1094$^b$ 11].
16.*Nicomachean Ethics* I.4 [1095$^a$ 13 - 29].
17.*Nicomachean Ethics* I.7 [1097$^a$ 15 - 1097$^b$ 21].
18.*Nicomachean Ethics* X.6 [1176$^a$ 34 -1176$^b$ 8].

# 7

# THE QÔHÉLETH

## (*ca.* 350-250 B.C.E.)

Many humans go through life and even leave a sizable imprint upon the sands of time, though little is known about them. Such a one was the Qôhéleth, the Preacher, or Convener, who lived in ancient Palestine between the fourth and third centuries B.C.E., and who wrote a short treatise that is still filed in the Bible under his name—not his proper name, for we do not know it, but the name given him for his function and his accomplishment.

He was some kind of professional sage, a seeker after wisdom, who probably roamed, at least for a time, the countryside in the vicinity of Tyre. But he seems to have been living in Jerusalem when he composed his little treatise. And he seems to have had disciples faithful enough to have undertaken the publication of their master's words.[1] He comes across to us as something of an aristocrat. His at-titudes are refined and he seems to have had enough means to acquire servants and to indulge in expensive sensual pleasures, including women. But his experiences with these were memorable only for the disappointment they spawned in him. As a result, he probably died a confirmed bachelor.

He was an honest man who told it like it was. No romanticizing of reality for him, no palliating of truth. He saw the pain, oppression, and injustice of social life, and he deplored it—not because of an exalted sense of justice, but because it was unfortunately the real thing. He searched for wisdom, but with the knowledge that it could not be obtained. His love for truth was tempered with the cynicism of the skeptic. He learned to hate life for its inconstancy,[2] yet to love it for its sensuousness (8:15). For Qôhéleth, says Scott, "to relish being alive is man's chief good. Life ought to be enjoyed."[3]

His book was controversial, if not during his lifetime certainly after it. It did not fit the usual religious mold of other Biblical narratives. In fact, it was not accepted into the canon until late, some time during the first century of the Common Era, when it was sponsored by influential leaders of the community. The general argument for its acceptance seems to have been that it belonged in the canon "because its beginning is religious and its end is religious"[4]—improper reasons, since the beginning and the end were not Qôhéleth's writing. But it was included, and that is the reason why we know of him what we know of him.

Such was the man, whoever he was.

.oOo.

What did he teach? What philosophy did he espouse? Even though the book is short, many points are raised and treated with exemplary succinctness. I wish to single out two, the generally skeptical tenor of his outlook and of his conclusions, and his quasi-existential affirmation of life, an affirmation tinged with hedonism.

For the Qôhéleth, all human pursuits are vain and useless, for whatever positive results one may achieve are counterbalanced by negative points. Positive and negative cancel each other. Thus, for example, the search for wisdom does not dispel all ignorance; nor does knowledge obliterate evil; and, at any rate, death overtakes both the wise and the foolish, the seeker and the non-seeker. Human pursuits, therefore, are vain and useless.

The Qôhéleth arrives at this conclusion not *a priori*, but through careful reflection on experience, his own and that of others. It would be contrary to his spirit to take conclusions for granted. No; he mentions in detail the various experiments he has undertaken, so that the conclusions he arrives at come as no surprise. This point is important. Disagreement with the conclusions would pit one against the data—no mean feat even in our own day. His conclusion?

Plain hot steam!
Everything is emptiness!
What does a man gain by all the things at which he toils under the sun?
A generation goes, a generation comes, but the earth remains the same.
The sun rises and sets, and it hastens again to the place where it is to rise.
To the south and to the north the wind blows, turning and turning upon its tracks.
All streams run to the sea, but the sea is not full; wither the streams flow they continue to flow.
Weariness overcomes the teller, he becomes speechless; yet the eye is not satisfied with seeing, nor the ear filled with hearing.
What has been once will be again, and what has been done will be done again, there is nothing new under the sun![5]

How is one to act in such a world? Should one even consider action rather than suicide? What life-plan should one follow within a fated world in which everything ends in decay and death?

The Qôhéleth chooses life. Like Gilgamesh, and like his anonymous Egyptian counterpart two thousand years before (and like Camus two thousand years later), he counsels enjoyment of life: "Eat, drink, and find happiness in your toil."[6] The program is one of affirmation of the sensual experience of living as an answer to the brevity of the life-span and the incompleteness of all attainments. As Scott puts it,

> The good of life is in the living of it. The profit of work is in the doing of it, not in any profit or residue which a man can exhibit as his achievement or pass on to his descendants. The fruit of wisdom is not the accumulation of all knowledge and the understanding of all mysteries. It lies rather in recognizing the limitations of human knowledge and power. Man is not the measure of all things. He is the master neither of life nor of death. He can find serenity only in coming to terms with the unalterable conditions of his existence, and in enjoying its real but limited satisfactions.[7]

.oOo.

In his search for happiness, the Qôhéleth decides that he should inquire into various modes of life, and find for himself whether or not it is possible to attain happiness in any of them. He begins with wisdom. Perhaps the wise man is happy, for knowing much he may have attained contentment. But he soon discovers that it is impossible to know everything, and that increases in knowledge lead inevitably to increases of worry.

Next comes pleasure. The Qôhéleth explores it all, fun, gourmandise, farming, cattle breeding, real estate, women—but none of it gives him the contentment he seeks. Women, especially, he finds disappointing.[8] Even money, and riches, offer no ground for a lasting happiness, for reversals of fortune may occur at any moment, and even the rich die. All pleasures are fleeting; all are unprofitable. Moreover, the Qôhéleth is shocked by the social injustice he witnesses around him, the overwhelming oppression of his fellow humans, a spectacle that leads to the perennial question, Why do the just suffer? Why do the evil prosper?

Almost in despair, the Qôhéleth reaches his first conclusion, he despises life. It is unreasonable for life to offer so many opportunities which turn out to be no more permanent than an empty dream:

> So I came to hate life, because it depressed me that all human activities under the sun are only like hot steam and a clutching at the wind.[9]

This is, however, the only life we have. It is the only stage we will ever know.

Imperfect though it be, in it we must act out our lives. It would be foolish, and more than foolish, not to pursue one's happiness in it. What matters is the living and the doing; in them one must make one's happiness consist.

More specifically, it is in pleasure that one must search for happiness. Contentment is the thing. The happy person enjoys living in all its sensuous multiplicity, but knowing full well that no enjoyment can be perfect or permanent:

> So I reached the conclusion that what is satisfying and suitable is to eat and drink and enjoy oneself in all one's struggle under the sun, during the few years God grants us here. That is what one gets out of it. Furthermore, every man to whom God grants riches and possessions, and enables him to benefit from them, and to possess his share and be happy in his work—he has a bonus from God. Such a one will not brood over the shortness of life, for God keeps his mind occupied with many thoughts. So I commend enjoyment, for we have no other good in this life than to eat and drink and be happy. This will accompany us in our struggle during the few years which God grants us beneath the sun.
>
> There is nothing better for us than to eat and drink and find satisfaction in doing our work. Even this, I came to see, is in God's hands. For who can eat and rejoice apart from God? Indeed, to those whom he favors God assigns wisdom, knowledge, and happiness; whereas to those who offend him, he gives the task of gathering and collecting what they must hand over to those whom God favors. This, too, is futility and a grasping at the wind.[10]

.oOo.

# Additional Reading

## Sources

B. Y. Scott, trans. and ed., *Proverbs and Ecclesiastes*. The Anchor Bible, vol.18; New York: Doubleday & Co., Inc., 1965.

Morris Jastrow, *A Gentle Cynic*. Philadelphia, J. B. Lippincott Co., 1919.

Robert Gordis, *Koheleth, the Man and his World*. 3rd ed.; New York: Schocken Books, 1971.

## Commentaries

Julian Jaynes, *The Origin of Consciousness in the Breakdown of the Bicameral Mind*. Boston: Houghton Miflin Co., 1976.

Bika Reed, *Rebel in the Soul*. New York: Inner Traditions International, Ltd., 1978.

T. W. Thaker "A dispute over Suicide," in *Documents from Old Testament Times*, ed. D. Winton Thomas. New York: Harper Torchbooks, 1958.

Addison G. Wright, "The Riddle of the Sphinx: The Structure of the Book of Qoheleth." *Catholic Biblical Quarterly* 30:3 (July, 1968): 313-334.

## Notes

1. Cf. *Ecclesiastes* 12:9-12.
2. *Ecclesiastes* 2:17.
3. Scott, *Proverbs and Ecclesiastes* (New York: Doubleday, 1965), 196.
4. Talmud, *Shabbath* 30b.
5. *Ecclesiastes* 1: 2 b-9.
6. *Ecclesiastes* 2: 24.
7. Scott, *Proverbs and Ecclesiastes*, 206.
8. *Ecclesiastes* 7: 26-28.
9. *Ecclesiastes* 2:17-23.
10. *Ecclesiastes* 5:18-20; 8:15; 2: 24-26.

# 8

# EPICURUS

## (341--270 B.C.E.)

The glory that had been Athens was beginning to wane. Social injustice was widespread, as often happens when oligarchies rule. Facing growing unrest, the Athenian government decided to relocate about two thousand of its citizens to the island of Samos, in the Aegean Sea, to farm land acquired for them at government expense. Among them was a certain Neocles. Thus it came to pass that Epicurus, the second of Neocles's four sons, was born in Samos, in 341 B.C.E. His mother's name was Chairestrata. His older brother, also named Neocles, attained some fame later as a philosopher. His younger brothers were Chairedemos and Aristoboulos.

Cicero[1] remarks that Neocles was unhappy with the paltry proceeds from his tilling, so he became a gym teacher. At any rate, young Epicurus did not lack instruction, and soon he was studying Platonic philosophy under Pamphilus. But in 323, when he was eighteen years old, he had to journey to Athens for his *ephebeia*, the military service incumbent upon all Athenian citizens. Shortly after his arrival, the news spread of the death of Alexander the Great. A wave of anti-Macedonian feeling arose in many states, among them Samos. All Athenians were thrown out, so that by the time Epicurus was done with his military duties, he had to travel to Colophon, in Asia, to be with his family.

This move was not as bad as it seemed. Teos, the city of Anacreon, was close to Colophon. It was the home of Nausiphanes, an atomist follower of Democritus, and a respected philosopher. Epicurus was not particular enthused. Having been schooled in Platonism, he had an almost instinctive aversion for atomism. Still, philosophy was philosophy, and he applied himself earnestly to the study of atomism.

This event proved to be one of the most significant in the history of ideas. Epicurus, who was in his late twenties at the time, soon came to an unalterable disagreement with Nausiphanes. The quarrel seems to have centered on the deterministic views held by the atomist, to which Epicurus, mindful of Socrates, could give no assent. There may also have been some moral objection to the *paiderasteia* of Nausiphanes.[2] But instead of walking away and rejecting atomism altogether, Epicurus set about to produce a synthesis of the best elements of atomism and the moral philosophy espoused by Socrates. Out of this conflict and synthesis Epicureanism was born.

Karl Marx was one of the first modern thinkers to understand this. He developed this point in his doctoral dissertation, the title of which was, "The Difference between the Democritean and the Epicurean Philosophies of Nature" (1841). In it Marx criticized those who had equated both views, and catalogued at length their differences.

One of the things that Marx noted was that Epicureanism did not depend on Plato and Aristotle, but went back, rather, to the naturalistic philosophies of Leukippos and Democritus, combining them with the moral point of view espoused by Socrates. His system is not a further elaboration of either Platonism or Aristotelianism, but, rather, an entirely new synthesis of subjective and objective elements. Given the objectivism of Aristotelian philosophy, the only path to follow was that of the spirit, of the subjective, and Epicurus found this in Socrates. However, no philosophy can be complete without the objective, so Epicurus went back to Democritus for the material counterpart he needed. But he did not take atomistic materialism as he found it, for it was deterministic, and this contradicted the libertarian subjectivism of Socrates. So, in a stroke of genius, Epicurus stepped beyond his predecessors and began doing his own thing.

The year was probably 312. His brothers were impressed, swore their allegiance, and remained with him all his life. And thus, with this nucleus, Epicurus began his career as a philosopher. Perhaps he was a prophet, a seer, a saint, rather than a philosopher; a Socrates at another time, except that he wrote "books"—three hundred, according to Diogenes Laërtius, of which only a few letters and many fragments survive—and that he died, eventually, of natural causes.

From Colophon, Epicurus moved to Mytilene, in Lesbos, in 310. There he obtained permission to lecture, but was opposed strenuously by the established school of Aristotle, and eventually, his license to teach was withdrawn. However, one of his pupils, Hermarchus, followed him, and forty years later succeeded him in the leadership of the school.

Epicurus moved to Lampsacus, where the reigning Platonic school was in disarray, therefore raising little opposition to his teaching. Here he met with success and raised many disciples, among them Metrodorus. Eventually, in 306, he moved to Athens, where he established his school near Dipylon with a generous gift from the Lampsacenes. The school consisted of a House and a Garden, which became famous as "the Garden of Epicurus." It appears that part of the Garden was reserved for the growing of vegetables and the dwelling in tents of his many disciples. Over the entrance was the inviting legend, "Guest, thou shalt be happy here, for here happiness is esteemed the highest good."[3]

The school admitted men and women and made no distinctions because of social status. Epicurus's favorite pupil was his own slave Mys ("Mouse"). "The courtesan Leontium," writes Durant, "became his mistress as well as his pupil, and found him as jealous a mate as if he had secured her by due process of law. Under his influence she had one child and wrote several books,"[4] which were published by the community. In fact, the House served as some sort of publishing enterprise.

Epicurus lived and taught in Athens for thirty-six years. He died in 270 from an attack of the stone. In his will, made with extraordinary care, he left the House and the Garden to Hermarchus to be used as the property of the school.

Epicurus seems to have been a kind, temperate man, whose motto was *lathe biosas*—"live unobtrusively." He was keenly interested in ideas and considerate with his friends, though his enemies painted him as a hypocrite, alternating between debauch and recovery. His pupils revered him to the point that, even after his death, they admonished each other, saying, "Live as though the eye of Epicurus were upon thee."[5]

.oOo.

Between 1838 and 1844, a team of archaeologists unearthed a long wall in the ancient town of Oenoanda, in Lycia, Asia Minor. It dated from the second century C.E. On it, in many blocks of stone, was carved a summary of the teachings of Epicurus. This colossal scriptural task was financed by a certain Diogenes, now appropriately known as Diogenes of Oenoanda.[6] This was devotion with a vengeance. What was this teaching that commanded even greater reverence than Plato's?

"The nature of the universe consists of bodies and void,"[7] Epicurus maintained. The void (*kenon*) is the intangible emptiness necessary for matter to fill. Matter itself—bodies (*somata*), the objects of perception—is compounded of indivisible (*átoma*) and unalterable (*ametábléta*) particles that cannot be destroyed. They are the permanent, indestructible components of everything that is.[8] The reason for their permanence and indivisibility is, simply, that something solid must remain, for otherwise matter *as we perceive it* could not exist: everything would be constantly dissolving into its component parts.[9] Thus, in an unmistakable way, Epicurus affirms the priority of sensory experience, the importance of common sense perception, and the atomism of Leukippos and Democritus. But by taking sense perception as a standard, Epicurus can answer questions that had troubled his predecessors, such as the size of the atoms. He admits variability, but not such as would make the atoms visible, for in fact, we never see them.[10] On the other hand, variability is needed in order to explain the various kinds of perceptions, as will be explained later.

Atoms are perennially in motion, falling of their own weight, in a straight line, "like drops of rain,"[11] and at enormous speed. But some of the atoms "swerve" (*parenklisis*) a little from the straight downward paths, colliding with other falling atoms, and creating movement in all directions. In this way atoms merge with atoms to produce the compounded "bodies," the things of our sensory experience. Illogical and unscientific as this "swerve" of the atoms may seem, it is of momentous importance, for it introduces an element of indeterminacy in a system that, up to Democritus, had been thoroughly deterministic. It is as if two thousand years ago Epicurus had been an Einstenian against the background of the rigid, Newtonian atomism of Democritus.

From the point of view of physics, the introduction of the "swerve" appears to be gratuitous, an unjustifiable answer to the questions regarding the rise of compounds whose existence was impossible to explain if the atoms fell for ever in a straight line. But Epicurus's claim makes perfect sense within the totality of his system. *Experience* gives us the datum of choice; that is, indeterminacy. But choice is a matter of the mind's atoms behaving "freely"; that is, of their not being un-alterably pre-determined. Therefore some kind of "freedom" must exist in the movement of the atoms. By placing this freedom of movement—the "swerve"—at the very heart of the system, Epicurus accounts for the totality of the system's anomalies while remaining true to his original empiricism.

While many among the ancients criticized Epicurus severely for the introduc-tion of uncertainty at the atomic level, perhaps the judgment of Diogenes of Oenoanda comes closest to the truth: "do you not know . . . that there is also a free motion in the atoms, which Democritus did not discover, but Epicurus brought to light, a 'swerving' motion, as he proves from phenomena?"[12] Diogenes understood that this stroke of genius liberated Epicurus from the traditions of his predecessors. At the same time he acknowledged experience as the ground. The challenge was to place atomic indeterminacy in the context of a system that for the first time was more humanistic than scientific, and that, perhaps for the first time in history, truly made human experience "the measure of all things."[13]

.oOo.

Epicurus himself understood philosophy as "a practical activity intended by means of speech and reasoning to secure a happy life."[14] By reasoning, however, he meant inference, for the basis of all reasoning is experience. Therefore he mistrusts formal logic and any artificial technique (*kakotechnia*) of argumentation. Similarly, any schooling that might be geared to this end is shunned, a point that was misunderstood and exaggerated in ancient times.

The reasons for this mistrust were two, according to Bailey,[15] that the mind is material, and therefore the laws of its functioning are the very laws of the functioning of matter in general, and that the only meaningful logic is the one that keeps the mind in close relation to the material world. Therefore not logic but physics, on the one hand, and "canonics" (*kanonika*) or methodology, on the other.

And it makes sense. To be happy one must be practical; that is, one must know how to live. Intellectually, it may help to know how the mind works and how its laws are the laws of the material universe; but the point is to live.

According to Diogenes Laërtius,[16] the *Canonicon* described "the method of approach to the system," but this method was less logic and more a criterion of truth. For Epicurus, truth is not just the truth of propositions but the truth of things, for "it is the same thing to call a thing true as to call it existing. True means that which is as it is said to be."[17] The position is, of course, that our senses are trustworthy in what they perceive; they give us faithfully the reality of things. Perception is infallible. Truth consists in experiencing only what is perceived, which is reality. As long as we do only that, we know and speak the truth.

It follows that sensation is the primary criterion of truth (in the sense that what is sensed is true), and that it itself is incontrovertible and unprovable (*alogon*, non-logical) as are all first principles.

Sensation itself is understood as the result of atoms from the object impinging directly on the atoms of the senses. We have here a sort of ancient quantum theory. In objects that are seen, the object's atoms coalesce into a kind of irradiation (*phantasia*) that strikes upon the eye in successive waves. Only those perceptions that are clear (*enargés*) and distinct are true. Cognition (combination, relation, synthesis, etc.) follows upon perception in order to complete knowledge. This inner cognition, distillation from sensation, is a kind of "tacit" schema (*prolepsis*)—what James called "a sort of wraith"[18]—that in some way anticipates the actual confrontation with a sense datum. It is like a mental attunement to the object. By means of it the mind receives the new datum into itself and integrates it, thus completing the process of knowing. Error arises when in the process we express opinion (*doxa*) based on inadequate comparisons and identifications. Error is a matter of judgment, not perception.

Finally, all sensations produce in us a certain feeling (*pathos*). That is, every sensation makes us feel either related to the object or alien to it, and this feeling is indubitable: we "know" what gives us pleasure and what gives us pain. This is not a criterion of the existence of the object, but of its nature, whether it is good or bad for us. As such, it is the foundation of ethics. It is for ethics what sensation is for empirical knowing and what attunement is for cognition[19] These notions, sensation, attunement, and feeling, constitute the three criteria of truth contained in the *Canonica*.[20] However, the *Letter to Herodotus* § 38 and the *Principal Doctrines* XXIV[21] add a fourth criterion, "intuitive apprehension" (*epibolé tes dianoias*), by which Epicurus seems to have meant the apprehension of very subtle skeins of atoms emitted by the gods and perceived, not by the senses, but directly by the mind. But the mind, too, is composed of atoms, so we do not have here some sort of immaterial perception. Rather, and on the model of ordinary sense perception, we have a kind of refined apprehension of refined substances (the gods), equally clear and distinct, and therefore equally certain.[22]

.oOo.

For Epicurus, the soul is material. It has to be, for there are only two substances that enter into combination, atoms and the void. The soul cannot be void; therefore it is "body."[23] It is composed of four kinds of atoms, of fire, air, breath, and a nameless, most subtle element, by which we love, hate, judge, remember, and understand, whether in a practical or a theoretical way.[24] When the body perishes in death, the material soul's atoms are dispersed. Therefore the soul, as *this* soul, perishes, too, after death. Thus death should pose no threat to our happiness, for after death we are not sentient any more, for *we* are no more: "Death is nothing to us; for that which is dissolved is without sensation, and that which lacks sensation is nothing to us."[25]

Since the soul is material, the emotions we experience are literally that, *e-motions*, movements of the atoms. The whole process of cognition, choice, and action, is explained as motion stimulated by outward objects in the soul, which in turn stimulates the body to act. The whole process is a mere transmission of movement from the outside to the inside and out again. But the sequence is not predetermined, because the atoms of the will may "swerve" slightly, altering the direction of the motion. It is this "swerve" that accounts for the freedom of the will characteristic of human choice. The fact that this "swerve" originates within the will and is not the result of the sense data impinging on the soul, but is spontaneous and undetermined, makes us free from necessity. This is the meaning of self-determination. In so far as this freedom originates in the soul, we may be conscious of it. We are, therefore, both self-conscious and self-determined in our actions.

What does experience show is the primary choice of human beings? Pleasure. Even before they are taught (*adidaktos*) they choose pleasure and avoid pain.[26] That the goal of life is pleasure, therefore, is not the conclusion of a syllogism but an inference from life. But what we desire and seek is good, and what we seek paramountly is paramountly good, for we are unable to desire anything except *sub specie boni*. Therefore pleasure is the ultimate good: "it is enough to have sensation and to be a creature of flesh and blood, to see that pleasure is a good."[27] By pleasure Epicurus means simply a *feeling* of compatibility (*oikeion*) between us and the object, which accompanies the perception of the object; by pain, similarly, a *feeling* of strangeness (*allotrion*).[28] It is thus that feelings are a criterion of perception, as explained above.

Two points must be noted here. First, in stating that pleasure is the goal of life, Epicurus is being faithful to his empirical premises. Second, Epicurus never constructed an ethic of duty; he never concluded that, because pleasure *is* factually what we all desire, we *ought* to pursue it. What he set out to do was to conceive a way of life centered around the enjoyment of pleasure and the avoidance of pain.[29]

If pleasure is the feeling accompanying sensation, then the stronger the feeling and the more numerous the occurrences of it, the greater the pleasure. Quantity and intensity are the only acceptable distinctions among pleasures, and Epicurus admits that the most intense pleasures have to do with the visual, with sexuality, and with eating. In fact, he is reputed to have said that "the beginning and root of all good is the pleasure of the stomach,"[30] a statement that has accounted for a great deal of the disrepute in which hedonism has been held through the centuries. However, for Epicurus, the quantity of pleasure was not to be estimated in terms of particular, discrete instances of satisfaction, but by overall pleasure throughout a lifetime. The point was to live in such a way that over the length of one's life one would experience a greater amount of pleasure over pain. As he wrote to Menoeceus,

> since pleasure is the first good and natural to us, for this very reason we do not choose every pleasure, but sometimes we pass over many pleasures when greater discomfort accrues to us as the result of them; and similarly we think many pains better than pleasures, since a greater pleasure comes to us when we have endured pains for a long time. Every pleasure, then, because of its natural kinship to us is good, but not every pleasure is to be chosen, just as every pain also is evil, yet not all must be avoided.[31]

The point, as Bailey notes,[32] is one of balancing pleasure and pain over a long life in the pursuit of pleasures that are simple and easily reached. In such a balance is happiness (*eudaimonia*) to be found.

Epicurus is aware that this balance is often disturbed by accidents of one sort or another over which we have no control. To guard against the evil effects of such occurrences and to preserve happiness, we must develop a permanent equanimity or peace of mind (*ataraxía*)[33] that will secure for us whatever happiness may be in store for us. *Ataraxía*, therefore, is an essential condition of happiness. It alone makes us masters of ourselves; and self-mastery (*autarkeia*), as Epicurus says, "is the greatest of all riches."[34]

In summary, then, the secret of happiness is to achieve an inner peace of mind that is secure from external reverses of fortune and even accidents and cataclysms. It is by paying attention to our reactions that we can discover their origins, and once this is done, we can be free from their effects on us. Pleasure must be understood in a broad sense, and Epicurus makes clear that it extends to the enjoyment of contemplative and intellectual activity.

> When, therefore, we maintain that pleasure is the end, we do not mean the pleasures of profligates and those that consist in sensuality, as is supposed by some who are either ignorant or disagree with us or do not understand, but freedom from pain in the body and from trouble in the mind. For it is not continuous drinkings and revelings, nor the satisfaction of lusts, nor the enjoyment of fish and other luxuries of the wealthy table, which produce a pleasant life, but sober reasoning, searching out the motives for all choice and avoidance, and banishing mere opinions, to which are due the greatest disturbance of the spirit.[35]

Such a life steers clear of gloominess and solemnity. As Epicurus is reputed to have said, "We must laugh and philosophize at the same time."[36]

.oOo.

## Additional Readings

### Sources

*Epicurus: The Extant Remains*, ed. Cyril Bailey. Oxford: Clarendon Press, 1926.
Hermannus Usener, *Epicurea*. Leipzig: B.G. Teubner, 1887.
Diogenes Laërtius, *Lives of Eminent Philosophers*. New York: G.P. Putnam, 1925.
*Diogenes of Oenoanda: The Fragments*, ed. C. W. Chilton. London: Oxford University Press, 1971.

### Commentaries

Cyril Bailey, *The Greek Atomists and Epicurus*. Oxford: Clarendon Press, 1928.
Frederick Copleston, *A History of Philosophy*. Garden City: Doubleday, 1962.
Norman W. DeWitt, *Epicurus and his Philosophy*. Minneapolis: University of Minnesota Press, 1954.
————. "Organization and Structure of Epicurean Groups." *Classical Philology* 31 (1936): 205-211.
Will Durant, *The Life of Greece*. New York: Simon & Schuster, 1939.
Benjamin Farrington, *The Faith of Epicurus*. New York: Basic Books, 1967.
A.J. Festugière, *Epicurus and his Gods*. Cambridge: Harvard University Press, 1956.
Richard W. Hibler, *Happiness through Tranquility: The School of Epicurus*. Maryland: University Press of America, 1984.
David McLellan, *Marx before Marxism*. New York: Harper Torchbooks, 1970.
George A. Panichas, *Epicurus*. New York: Twayne Publishers, Inc., 1967.
J. M. Rist, *Epicurus: An Introduction*. Cambridge: Cambridge University Press, 1972.
G. K. Strodach, *The Philosophy of Epicurus*. Evanston, IL: Northwestern University Press, 1963.

### Notes

1. Cicero, *De Natura Deorum* I, 26, 72.
2. Panichas, *Epicurus* (New York" Twayne Publishers, Inc.), 21.

3. Durant, *The Life of Greece* (New York: Simon & Schuster, 1939), 647.

4. Ibid., 645.

5. Ibid.

6. Farrington, *The Faith of Epicurus* (New York: Basic Books, 1967), xii.

7. Sextus Empiricus, *Adversus dogmata* III.333 = Usener, *Epicurea*, No.75.

8. *Ad Herodotum* § 41 = Usener, *Epicurea*, 6-7)

9. Bailey, *Greek atomists* (Oxford: Clarendon Press, 1928), 282.

10. *Ad Herodotum* § 55 = Usener, *Epicurea*, 15.

11. Lucretius, *De Natura Deorum* II.222.

12. *Fragments* 32, in Chilton, *Fragments* (London: Oxford University Press), 15; Bailey, *Greek atomists*, 317

13. Protagoras, *Fragments* 1.

14. Sextus Empiricus, *Adversus dogmata* XI, 169 = Usener, *Epicurea*, No.219.

15. Bailey, *Greek atomists*, 235.

16. Diogenes Laërtius, *Lives* (New York: G. P. Putnam, 1925), X, 30.

17. Sextus Empiricus, *Adversus dogmata* II,9 = Usener, *Epicurea*, No.244).

18. William James, *Principles of Psychology* (Chicago: Encyclopaedia Britannica, 1952), Ch. IX.

19. Bailey, *Greek atomists*, 250 and 486.

20. Diogenes Laërtius, *Lives* X,31 = Usener, *Epicurea*, 371.

21. Usener, *Epicurea*, 5 and 75.

22. Bailey, *Greek atomists*, 251 and Appendix III.

23. *Ad Herodotum* § 63 = Usener, *Epicurea*, 19.

24. Plutarch, *Adv. Colot.* 20 = Usener, *Epicurea*, No.314.

25. *Principal Doctrines* II = Usener, *Epicurea*, No.139.II.

26. Sextus Empiricus, *Adv. dogmat.* V, 96 = Usener, *Epicurea*, No.398.

27. Plutarch, *Adv. Colot.*, 27.1122$^d$ = Usener, *Epicurea*, 279 note.

28. Diogenes Laërtius, *Lives* X, 34 = Usener, *Epicurea*, 373.

29. Bailey, *Greek atomists*, 486.

30. *Athenaeus deipnosoph.* XII = Usener, *Epicurea*, No.409; Paul, *Philip*ians 3:19.

31. *Ad Menoeceum* § 130.

32. Bailey, *Greek atomists*, 490 and 496.

33. Panichas, *Epicurus*, 20.

34. *Frag.* 70

35. *Ad Menoeceum* § 131-132.

36. *Vatican Sayings* 41.

# 9

## ZENO AND EPICTETUS

(*ca.*336-264 B.C.E.) (*ca.*50-138 C.E.)

Zeno, some times called the Phoenician (to denote perhaps a Semitic origin), was born in Citium, Cyprus, around 336/335 B.C.E. By his late teens he was a misshapen, wealthy merchant, who, however, happened to lose his fortune in shipwreck, and thus found philosophy in poverty.

He arrived in Athens in 314, age 22, four years ahead of Epicurus. By this time, the Cynics, under Crates, had become the Franciscan monks of antiquity,[1] though their love of poverty had not led them to preclude the love of women. Crates married Hipparchia, and they consummated their marriage in public, since they had no permanent abode; but they lived honorably and affectionately until their deaths.

Zeno was originally attracted to the Cynics, and he studied under Crates, and later with Xenocrates, at the Academy, and with the famed Stilpo at Megara. But he remained fixated on the image of Socrates he had first discovered in Xenophon's *Memorabilia* and Plato's *Apology*.

In 301, at the age of 35, Zeno finally began to expound his own philosophy. His favorite haunt was the Stoa Poikile, a painted porch with an ample colonnade, to which young and old, rich and poor, flocked in numbers. For nearly forty years he taught there, and from the location came the name of his doctrine, Stoicism.

Zeno died in his seventies, in 264/3, apparently by his own hands, having interpreted a fall he had had as a call from the gods to depart this life.

Stoicism was developed further by Zeno's successors, and a number of the ideas still associated with Stoicism were expounded by them. Both as a philosophy and as a way of life, it spread far and wide, taking from, and contributing to, the many religions and philosophies it came in contact with. It had a profound influence on Christianity, as can be seen from the letters of Paul and from later theological speculation. But it was in Rome that Stoicism finally coalesced, to the point that we associate it with the expression it gained in the lives and writings of Epictetus and Marcus Aurelius, to whom may be added Cicero and Seneca.

.oOo.

It is customary to divide the development of Stoicism into three periods, the Early Stoa, comprising primarily the development of the doctrine by Zeno and Chrysippus; the Middle Stoa, which extended itself through the Hellenistic period; and the Later Stoa, which consisted mainly of the contributions of the Stoics during the Roman period. For the purpose of this exposition, however, I will emphasize those tenets that remained pretty much unaltered through the centuries.

The Stoics divided their endeavors into three parts: logic, physics, and ethics. Logic was for them more than a tool of inquiry, as it had been for Aristotle, although even in this field they made important contributions. But the greater part of logic was, for them, a theory of cognition that today we would classify as empiricism.

All knowledge, they taught, begins with sensory impressions; that is, the impressions made on our senses by things in the outside world. Abstract concepts do not exist—they do not "walk about." Neither are we born with ideas. Our souls are like smooth clay tablets on which impressions (*typoseis*) are made like those of a seal on wax. Even inner states are "perceived." Thus all knowledge originates in the senses.

As the individual grows it develops a reasoning power, pretty much as Freud thought the Ego developed from the Id. This power is brought to bear on the data of experience and leads eventually to comparisons and syntheses which constitute knowledge. The assent of reason to the data of sensation constitutes the judgment of truth. This judgment, to be reliable, must be necessitated by the sensory datum itself and its corresponding arresting image (*phantasía kataleptiké*). The criterion of truth, therefore, is some kind of clarity that commands assent. If assent is not forthcoming it is because of "hindrances" (a term Buddhists would have recognized); that is, subjective states and emotions that interfere with the evidence which would otherwise necessitate assent.

The simplicity of this epistemology is rendered possible by a monistic and materialistic understanding of reality. The "stuff" of the universe is one, even though it encompasses two modes, as it were, an active and a passive one. The passive one is recognizable as the gross *materia prima* of Aristotle; the active one is reason, which is divine. But *both* form the one whole of reality, which therefore is both Nature and God (*deus sive natura*).

Since God is nature and God is reason, the whole universe is permeated with consciousness, though this manifests itself differently at different levels. In God, too, are the rational seeds (*logoi spermatikoi*, adopted by Augustine as *rationes seminales*), the designs of everything that exists in the universe. This is a kind of materialized conception of the Platonic forms as prototypes of reality. God, then, is conceived as a Fiery and Creative Breath' (*pyr technikon kai pneumatikon*) blowing through the universe, eventually to consume all and regenerate all in a process of eternal recurrence. While the world is, God stands to it as the soul to the body. The world, therefore, is God's body, an idea dear to St. Paul.

Not only is the universe permeated by the divine *logos*, it is ruled by God, too, in a most rational way. This is the Stoic notion of providence (*pronoia*; literally, "fore-knowledge"). Within this over-reaching providence of God there is no room for human freedom; there is only fate (*eimarméne*). Freedom means only to assent consciously to what will be anyway,[2] seeing everything that happens as the expression of the reason that is God active and present in the world. Since God is rational (God *is* reason) the ends to which the world is directed cannot but be good. Evil, therefore, does not exist as such, once the universe, and life itself, are seen from God's (that is, reason's) point of view. Even evil acts are "good" in themselves, or in so far as they exist. Really, they are just what they are. Their malice derives from the intention of the doer, and is therefore adventitious. In a sense, the essence of moral evil is unreasonableness; it consists in the will being out of harmony with right reason.[3] As can be seen, the system is shot through and through by a strong sense of reason.

Reason, too, is the essence of Stoic ethics. In fact, philosophy and ethics are almost indistinguishable. A later Stoic, Seneca (*ca.* 3 B.C.E.-65 C.E.), defined philosophy as "the right ordering of life, or the science of living honestly, or the art of leading one's life properly."[4] The meaning is clear: philosophy's most important role is the guidance of life. It is eminently practical.

The goal of life is happiness (*eudaimonia*), which for the Stoics was the life of virtue, understood as a life in accord with Nature; that is, God; that is, reason. Their maxim, "live according to Nature" (*Zen kata physin*), may sound very contemporary, but the rationality implied by it is miles apart from the romanticism of contemporary nature lovers. In the words of Diogenes Laërtius,

> life in accordance with nature is rightly understood to mean life in accordance with reason. Hence Zeno's definition of the end is to live in conformity with nature, which means to live a life of virtue, since it is to virtue that nature leads. On the other hand, a virtuous life is a life which conforms to our experience of the course of nature, our human natures being but parts of universal nature. Thus the end is a life which follows nature, whereby is meant not only our own nature, but the nature of the universe, a life wherein we do nothing that is forbidden by the universal—that is, by right reason, which pervades all things.[5]

.oOo.

Being caught up in the determinism of nature forced the Stoics to define freedom as mastery, or self-mastery (*enkrateia*) vis-à-vis the predetermined course of living. The truly free person is the one who understands determinism and places him/herself alongside it. To be free is to discover the rational ends of the universe and to will them as one moves along one's path, along which one would have to move anyway. Seneca wrote: "Fate leads the willing and compels the unwilling,"[6] a doctrine that endeared itself to Spinoza and to Nietzsche two thousand years later.

And since the end will be the same for both the willing and the unwilling, willing can only be something one does purely for itself, for it will not alter the results the least bit. Being virtuous, therefore, which is the same as being happy, is the only thing willed entirely for its own sake. And what a happiness! Seneca, again, defines it as "being able, with a cheerful mind, to tolerate adversity; being able to undergo whatever may befall as if you had willed it to happen; for you should have willed it anyway, if you knew that everything takes place according to God's design."[7]

Stoicism found a ready ear among the Romans hankering for the old republican virtues. Slowly it took root, and it thrived even during the intemperate, extravagant, and dissolute reigns of Caligula and Nero. In fact, one of its most beautiful expressions is to be found in the *Meditations* of the Emperor Marcus Aurelius (121-180). But perhaps the best known are the *Discourses* of Epictetus, the slave-turned-philosopher whose down-to-earth style did much to popularize what at bottom is a very demanding way of life.

Epictetus, the "Acquired One" (his real name is not known), was born in Hierapolis, in Phrygia, between 50 and 60 C.E., the son of a slave woman. When still a boy, he was bought as a slave by Epaphroditus, one of Nero's bodyguards, and thus he may have come to live in Rome. While still a slave he attended the lectures of Musonius Rufus, who was one of the reigning Stoic luminaries in Rome at the time, and who obviously did not discriminate between slaves and masters. In fact, he was somewhat of a feminist, claiming that women as well as men had received from the gods the gift of reason[8]. The lessons of Musonius took root. It is narrated that once, when Epaphroditus was mad at Epictetus, he sat on a leg of the slave boy to punish him. Epictetus warned him, "You are going to break my leg." The pressure increased, and the leg snapped loudly, at which point Epictetus quipped calmly, "I told you!" The leg healed, but from then on the "philosopher" walked with a limp.

It is not known when Epictetus was freed, but by the year 89 he was teaching philosophy in Rome, apparently none too successfully. This stint as a teacher did not last long, for the Emperor Domitian expelled all philosophers from Italy around 90 or 93, so Epictetus moved to Nicopolis, in northwestern Greece, where he resumed his teaching.

His fame grew, and pupils came from all over the Empire. It is thus that, probably in 123-126, a certain Flavius Arrian, who later became consul under Hadrian, took notes in shorthand of Epictetus's "lectures," and published eight books of *Discourses*, of which only four are extant. These seem to contain the *ipsissima verba* of the master. He also compiled a compendium, which he titled *Encheiridion.*

Having remained single most of his life, Epictetus married in old age for the purpose of bringing up a little child whom the parents, friends of his, could not support. He also travelled a little, and probably visited Athens.

Epictetus died *ca.*138, having written nothing, and leaving no material inheritance, only the simple tenets of his Stoic philosophy. Summarizing Epictetus's views, Arrian wrote:

> Success in life does not result from the accumulation of wealth, or of power. Success in life can only be measured in terms of happiness and contentment achieved as a result of acting in accordance with right principles. Right principles are those which create goodness for all men, which itself is a creation of God.[9]

The touchstone of Stoic happiness, then, is reasonableness. But this reasonableness could be imperiled by desire, as we saw above. Therefore Epictetus concluded as St. Ignatius Loyola did fifteen hundred years later: "*Es menester hacernos indiferentes*": "We must make ourselves indifferent"[10] to all things that do not depend on us. If things are indifferent to us, we should be indifferent to them.[11]

Indifference (*apatheia*), then, was the principle and foundation of all virtue, and the key to happiness. Obviously, by indifference Epictetus did not mean apathy, in our modern sense, a careless and uncaring attitude of resignation and defeat. Neither did he mean an unfeeling life, a life devoid of affect. Rather, it was a state of serenity and peace of mind to be striven for, a mastery of oneself to be pursued for its own sake, and in whose possession—and, if one may add, enjoyment—true happiness could alone be found. When such a state was achieved, as a later writer put it, good actions would spring from it as gently as a shadow fell from a body.[12]

.oOo.

Epictetus insists that it is important to make a clear distinction between things and events external to us, and those which are internal to us. On this distinction is based his inquiry into the meaning of happiness and the way to attain it.

> The rational animal, man, sees that he has some of the things which are about him free from hindrance and under his control, but that others are subject to hindrance and under the control of others. Free from hindrance are those things which lie in the sphere of the moral purpose, and subject to hindrance are those which lie outside the sphere of the moral purpose. And so, if he regards his own good and advantage as residing in these things alone, in those, namely, which are free from hindrance and under his control, he will be free, serene, happy . . . .[13]

Now, the only thing within our control is how we react to the world and its happenings.[14] The *Encheiridion* summarizes this point: "You can be invincible if you never enter a contest in which victory is not under your control. . . . Now there is but one way that leads to this, and that is to despise the things that are not under our control."[15]

Even when adverse things befall us, we can count ourselves fortunate if we have learned to preserve our equanimity and peace of mind.[16] And he concludes: "He who is dissatisfied with what he has and what has been given him by fortune is a layman in the art of living, but the man who bears all this in a noble spirit and makes a reasonable use of all that comes from it deserves to be considered a good man."[17]

Epictetus presents three arguments or reasons to persuade us that the attainment of happiness is in our reach. The first, already stated, says that our will alone is within our power, and therefore it is the only thing we can control. Such control protects us from the uncertainties of the world around us, which could imperil our happiness. Secondly, he reminds us that everything is under God's rational control. God, however, is to be understood in the pantheistic fashion peculiar to Stoicism. Hence, the "influence" of the divine felt by the earth must be understood as sympathetic vibrations of the whole cosmos. The third reason for holding that happiness is within our reach is based on the distinction between things that we can control and things we cannot control, as was explained above. Things not under our control we should leave in the hands of God; that is, the Cosmos.

Epictetus argues further that the will, "the faculty of moral purpose" (*proairetikê*), is the sole controller of our actions, and is therefore the center of value. It alone is the source of value, whether good or evil.

How are we to use the things around us? Epictetus answers with an apt simile: "He must imitate those who play at dice. The counters are indifferent, the dice are indifferent; how am I to know what is going to fall? But to make a careful and skillful use of what has fallen, that is now my task. In like manner, therefore, the principal task in life is this: distinguish matters and weigh them one against another, and say to yourself, "'Externals are not under my control; moral choice is under my control. Where am I to look for the good and the evil? Within me, in that which is my own.'"[18] If the good gambler is the one who knows how to play the game, the moral person is the one whose inner poise is not disturbed by any external occurrence.[19]

How do we acquire this equanimity? By means of education. "To be getting an education means this: To be learning what is your own, and what is not your own."[20] Further, it means understanding oneself and one's prejudices.[21] Put differently, education is needed to learn how to apply the principles one has committed oneself to, to particular cases.

It is not the things themselves that disturb men, but their judgments about these things. For example, death is nothing dreadful, or else Socrates too would have thought so, but the judgment that death is dreadful, *this* is the dreadful thing. When, therefore, we are hindered, or disturbed, or grieved, let us never blame anyone but ourselves, that means, our own judgments. It is the part of an uneducated person to blame others where he himself fares ill; to blame himself is the part of one whose education has begun; to blame neither another nor his own self is the part of one whose education is already complete.[22]

Education and practice, then, enable us to turn every experience in life into a happiness that is August and enviable.[23] Secondly, in order to attain happiness one must rid oneself of desire, which is desire for external things, and cultivate the one thing that is desired for itself alone, inner peace and serenity; that is, happiness.

There is but one way to serenity (keep this thought ready for use at dawn, and by day, and at night), and that is to yield up all claim to the things that lie outside the sphere of the moral purpose, to regard nothing as your own possession; to surrender everything to the Deity, to Fortune; to yield everything to the supervision of those persons whom even Zeus has made supervisors; and to devote yourself to one thing only, that which is your own, that which is free from hindrance, and to read referring your reading to this end, and so to write and so to listen.[24]

Epictetus remarks that happiness is a kind of serenity and peace precisely because in not desiring what we cannot be sure of obtaining, and in procuring only what is within our power to possess, we achieve a kind of fullness: we can be more easily, and more completely filled, when our emptiness is dovetailed to what can fill it, and no more[25]. In achieving this happiness, we fulfill the end for which we were created.

.oOo.

# Additional Readings

## Sources

Epictetus, *Moral Discourses*. New York: Washington Square Press, 1964.
———. *A Dialogue in Common Sense*, ed. John Bonforte. New York: Philosophical Library, 1974. (This is an edition of the *Discourses* arranged in a different order).
———. *The Enchiridion*, tr. Thomas W. Higginson. Indianapolis: Bobbs-Merrill Co., Inc., 1955.
———. *Discourses, Manual, and Fragments*, tr. W.A. Oldfather. 2 vols.; Loeb Classical Library. Cambridge: Harvard University Press, 1978.
H. von Arnim. *Stoicorum Veterum Fragmenta*. 4 vols.; Leipzig, 1924.

## Commentaries

A.H. Armstrong, *An Introduction to Ancient Philosophy*. Boston: Beacon Press, 1966.
Edwyn Bevan, *Stoics and Sceptics*. Oxford: The Clarendon Press, 1913.
Peter Brown, *The Body and Society*. New York: Columbia University Press, 1988.
Frederick Copleston, *A History of Philosophy*. New York: Image Books, 1962.
Will Durant, *The Life of Greece*. New York: Simon & Schuster, 1939.
———. *Caesar and Christ*. New York: Simon & Schuster, 1944.
Cora E. Lutz, "Musonius Rufus, 'The Roman Socrates.'" *Yale Classical Studies* 10 (1947):
    38-43.
Gilbert Murray, *The Stoic Philosophy*. New York: Putnam, 1915.
———. *Five Stages of Greek Religion*. New York: Doubleday, 1955.

## Notes

1. Durant, *Greece* (New York: Simon & Schuster, 1939), 651.

2. Frederick Copleston, *A History of Philosophy* (New York: Image Books, 1962), 133.

3. Copleston, *A History of Philosophy*, Vol. ½, 135.

4. Seneca, *Frag.* 17.

5. Diogenes Laërtius, *Lives* VII. 86 *ff.*

6. Seneca, *Epistula* 107, 11.

7. Seneca, *Nat. Quaest.* III, *Praef.*, 10-17.

8. Cora E. Lutz, "Musonius Rufus, 'The Roman Socrates.'" *Yale Classical Studies* 10 (1947), 39.

9. John Bonforte, ed., *A Dialogue in Common Sense* (New York: Philosophical Library, 1974), 11.

10. St. Ignatius Loyola, *Spiritual Exercises*, No. 23.

11. Epictetus, *Discourses* I, 30.

12. Peter Brown, *The Body and Society* (New York: Columbia University Press, 1988), 131.

13. Epictetus, *Discourses* IV.7.

14. *Discourses* I.12.

15. Epictetus, *Encheiridion* XIX.

16. Epictetus, *Frag.* 28$^b$.

17. Epictetus, *Frag.* 2.

18. *Discourses* II.5.

19. *Discourses* I.18.

20. *Discourses* IV.5.7.

21. *Discourses* I.2.5-11 and 33.

22. Epictetus, *Encheiridion* V.

23. *Discourses* III.20.15.

24. *Discourses* IV.4.

25. *Discourses* III.24.17.

# 10

## SAINT AUGUSTINE

### (354-430)

It has been said that his was the greatest mind to think in the Western world, but his passionate temperament made him an extremist. The sweetness of his love of God was countered dramatically by the harshness of his view of humanity as a "damned mass (*massa damnata*)."[1] His health was always precarious, but he lived to a ripe old age. He plunged headlong into sin for a while, but he could write after his conversion, "Thou hast made us, Lord, for Thee, and our hearts are restless until they rest in Thee."[2]

This man of contrasts was Aurelius Augustine. He was born at Tagaste (modern Souk-Ahras), North Africa, on November 13, of the year 354. He was the youngest of three children born to Patricius and Monica. Both parents were probably of Roman stock but with Numidian ancestry. Patricius, a pagan at the time of his son's birth, was an official in the Roman administration. He was hot tempered and a philanderer, but not a wife beater like many of his countrymen,[3] who punished their virtuous wives for their own unvirtuous loves. Monica was a Christian, a strong-willed woman whose faith, in her son's estimate, was virile, though how faith could differ by gender he never explained. Against everybody's advice she enrolled her young son as a catechumen in the local church.

The young boy was not particularly fond of learning, but was forced to study at Madaura, a town about twenty-five miles south of Tagaste. He hated Greek, which he never mastered, but he became proficient in grammar and literature.[4] These early studies finished, he returned to Tagaste where he idled his life away for a year while his father sought funds to finance further studies of rhetoric in Carthage, prerequisite to becoming a lawyer. Eventually Romanianus, a wealthy citizen of Tagaste, came up with the money, but not before idleness had led to wildness,[5] and a pattern of life had been set that would last for quite a few years.

Augustine was all of sixteen years of age when he finally moved to Carthage. His father died shortly after (371), an event he recorded without emotion.[6] Not that he was bereft of feeling, but his love was spent on women and friends in the course of riotous and promiscuous living. At last he calmed down enough to settle into concubinage, the fruit of which was a son, naïvely named Adeodatus (382-389).[7]

The life of a lawyer did not attract him, so when his studies at Carthage were finished in 373, he moved back to Tagaste and taught grammar there for a while, but was deeply shaken by the sudden death of a dear friend,[8] and left after a year to teach rhetoric in Carthage.

In 377 he entered and won a poetry contest, and wrote his first book, *On the Beautiful and the Fit*, which later he considered not worth preserving. In 383 he became Professor of Rhetoric, and could look ahead, at twenty-nine, to a secure and successful teaching life. However, as many teachers have since then, he found that teaching would be wonderful were it not for students. His were inattentive and undisciplined and he despaired of teaching them anything. Lured by rosy reports from Rome he moved there that same year, but he found, to his distress, that students in Rome were not really better listeners, though they proved to be shrewd money makers: they cheated him of his fees.[9]

Dissatisfied and disillusioned he moved to Milan in 384, where he taught rhetoric and listened to Ambrose (339-397), bishop there since 371. Ambrose was a classicist, a musician (Ambrosian chant still rivals Gregorian chant), and a brilliant and courageous preacher who had opposed Arianism even when espoused by the emperor, Valentinian II. Initially at least, Augustine attended his sermons for purely professional reasons, in an effort to learn from Ambrose's performance and polish his own oratorical style.[10]

One year later, in 385 (he was 31 years of age), under the advice and pressure of his mother and friends, and on the pretext of getting married, he broke the liaison he had sustained for some twelve years with the mother of his son, kept the boy with him, and sent the mother to Carthage, where she went reluctantly, swearing eternal loyalty to him. Then, in a most unrealistic move, he became engaged to a young lady who was still a minor, and who could not become his wife for two years. The wait proved too hard: he picked up another mistress in a flash.[11]

While in Carthage, Augustine had become a Manichaean "auditor" (beginner), and even a zealous proselytizer. Obviously, he was on a quest, but the Manichaeans he knew were not paragons of morality, and his own insightful mind could not be satisfied by the superficiality of their explanations. Even Faustus, a touted leader and philosopher, acknowledged his ignorance,[12] thereby leaving Augustine adrift in a sea of questions.

His association with Manichaeism continued through his stay in Rome, but in

Milan he began to be drawn to Neo-Platonism.[13] Plato's influence on him was profound, and it is through his writings that Platonism became inextricably tied to Christianity.

In the late spring of 386, Augustine received a visit from a certain Pontitianus, a fellow African and a powerful man in the Emperor's court. Pontitianus discovered by chance that Augustine was reading the letters of St. Paul, whereupon the conversation took a Christian turn. Pontitianus talked glowingly about St. Anthony the eremite, in such a way that Augustine's mind was greatly moved. Very upset and troubled inwardly, Augustine went out to the courtyard, followed by his friend and pupil Alypius who was concerned about his safety. In the midst of much commotion and even physical pain, Augustine heard from a neighboring house a voice from either a boy or a girl (he couldn't tell), chanting repeatedly, "Take up and read; take up and read." Instantly he picked up St. Paul's letters and read: "Not in rioting and drunkenness, not in chambering and wantonness, not in strife and envying: but put ye on the Lord Jesus Christ, and make no provision for the flesh."[14] The effect was immediate and extraordinary. As he put it himself, "instantly at the end of this sentence, by a light as it were of serenity infused into my heart, all the darkness of doubt vanished away."[15]

Augustine decided to give up teaching, but he waited the three weeks remaining in the term before the long vacation of the Vintage. Then, in the fall of 386 (he was 32 years of age), he retired to the farm of a friend at Cassiciacum to prepare for baptism. With him were his mother, his son Adeodatus, his brother Navigius, his friend Alypius, his pupils Trygetius and Licentius (sons of his old benefactor, Romanianus), and two relatives, Lastidianus and Rusticus. There was also an army of scribes charged with keeping an accurate record of their discussions. These he later published. Interestingly, one of them was titled, *On the Happy Life*.

Augustine and his entourage returned to Milan in the spring of 387. He and Adeodatus were baptized by Ambrose on Holy Saturday. His mother, Monica, stood proudly by.

At this time, Augustine made the decision to retire permanently from teaching and to settle with his friends into a prayerful community. He made arrangements to return to Africa, but was delayed in Rome for about a year, which he used to his advantage by preparing his first manuscripts as a Christian. Christianity added, too, a higher dimension to his relationship to his mother. The two conversed intimately and mystically. It was like a presage, for Monica died in Ostia in 387.

Eventually Augustine sailed back to Africa and settled in Tagaste in 388, where he founded a small monastic community, the first of its kind. It has endured the centuries, and still exists as the Augustinian Order.

However, this quiet life was shattered by the death of his son, Adeodatus, in 389, and then by his being chosen by the people of Hippo (Bône, in modern Algeria), to be one of their priests. He was ordained in 391. But Augustine did not renounce the monastic life; he simply moved the monastery to Hippo, and even when he was made a bishop in 396, he continued to live with the austerity and simplicity of a monk.

New responsibilities were thrust upon him. The bishop's task was to instruct, and so he started his life-long commitment to preaching. He also began the composition of one of his best known works, the *Confessions*, which was published in 400.

Affected profoundly by the Barbarian sack of Rome in 410 and by the sentiment, widely felt, that Rome had fallen because of its abandonment of the ancient gods in favor of Christianity, he began *The City of God*, a refutation of such views and the enunciation of a philosophy of history, which he published serially for thirteen years beginning in 413. Many treatises, polemic, theological, and devotional, occupied much of his time (and that of his secretaries). In 426, at age seventy-two, he wrote his *Retractions*, a book of revision and self-criticism, in which he reviewed two hundred and thirty-two separate titles, excluding letters and sermons.

In 430, when Gaiseric attacked Hippo with his Vandals, Augustine encouraged the military to resist. The city was sieged, and life became increasingly harsh. During the summer, Augustine fell ill, and he died on August 28. He was seventy-six years of age.

.oOo.

We do not find in Augustine's writings a system of philosophy. Neither does he present a developed theology in the modern sense of the term.[16] In fact, philosophy and theology are always mixed, for what Augustine was after was a particular truth at a particular moment. That he lived long and wrote plenty account for the complexity and comprehensiveness of his views; for the illusion of system rather than the reality. There is, however, a remarkable consistency in most issues, and the corrections he made in his *Retractationes* (426-427) strike one sometimes as petty. He strove to achieve exactness where there can be none, and he knew that. He said, in fact: "If you understand, it is not God . . . . To attain God somewhat through one's mind is great happiness; to comprehend, however, is totally impossible."[17]

All his life Augustine searched for wisdom, but it was not the search alone that concerned him. Rather, it was the apprehension of truth, and ultimately, of the Divine Truth. In his search he felt drawn, acted upon, attracted by the wonderful beauty of the divine mystery, and he thought that every human being was similarly pulled toward the eternal, though some people misinterpreted the promptings of the Spirit, or got sidetracked, or mistook temporary truths for the eternal One. In some sense, as Copleston remarks, he universalized his own experience,[18] feeling that his quest was essentially synonymous with the human quest for truth.

In a kind of quasi-Platonic scheme, Augustine placed sensory perception at the lower level of cognition, for the senses give us primarily material or sensory knowledge. He did not condemn the senses or their apprehensions. It is not the senses that deceive us, he explained, when we see the oar bent in the water. It is our judgment that is at fault. The senses report accurately what they observe, but in our haste to judge *we* are often mistaken[19]. Higher than the senses is reason, a power peculiarly and distinctly human, which, although it engages the data of the senses, is still capable of abstracting and generalizing, of going beyond the immediacy of what the senses report.

This mind of ours is a powerful instrument. It has the capacity to know something with certainty and to distinguish truth from error. It is capable of being infallible. Twelve hundred years before Descartes, Augustine stated his proof for the certainty of his own existence, *Fallor, ergo sum*. The passage is brilliant and typical:

> I am not at all afraid of the arguments of the Skeptics, "What if you are deceived?" for if I am deceived, I am; for he who is not cannot be deceived; if I am deceived, by this same token I am. And since I am if I am deceived, how am I deceived in believing that I am since it is certain that I am if I am deceived? Therefore, since I, the one deceived, would be even if I were deceived, certainly I am not deceived in knowing that I am.[20]

But this kind of philosophical certainty was sterile for Augustine. The point was the use of the mind for the attainment of wisdom. Supreme knowledge was not the result of the ratiocinating work of the intellect, nor was the pursuit of knowledge itself the objective. He argued this point against Licentius in the *De Beata Vita* IV.27. Striving to have wisdom implies that one does not have it: we pursue what we have not. Therefore we cannot call a person wise who is merely in pursuit of wisdom. And if wisdom leads to happiness, then lack of wisdom, even if wisdom is being pursued, makes one unhappy. And he concludes: "There is no greater and more miserable lack than the lack of wisdom; conversely, one who lacks not wisdom, lacks nothing at all."

This may sound exaggerated, but Augustine explains. Jesus called himself Truth (*John* 14:6), or Wisdom, and Jesus is God. Now, "if God is wisdom . . . then a true philosopher ["lover of wisdom"] is a lover of God"[21]—literally: wisdom (*sophia*) = God (*Deus*), *ergo* love (*philia*) of wisdom (*sophiae*) = love (*philia*) of God (*Dei*). And he adds:

> Here is truth itself for you: embrace it if you can, and rejoice in the Lord, and he will grant you the desires of your heart [*Psalm* 36:2]. What more can you ask than to be happy? And who is happier than the one who enjoys unsullied, unchangeable, and excellent Truth?[22]

Further, Augustine seems to have held that the capacity for certainty is not merely a human power, but rather a function of God's illumination which allows the mind to see things clearly and distinctly. The human mind is like a mirror in a dark room, ready to reflect the objects presented to it when there is light. It is the light that occasions the reflection, the certainty, the recognition. By it we are factually ascertained. Augustine wrote: "Whatever we perceive through the mind, that is, by means of intellect and reason . . . we see immediately in that interior light of truth by virtue of which he himself who is called 'the interior man' is illumined."[23]

This view is a modification of Plato's theory of learning as recollection. Confronted with the question, How do we know that something is true? Plato answered that the soul, even as it is born, possesses all the knowledge it had acquired in previous existences, but has forgotten it all. Learning is remembering what we knew but have forgotten; hence the sense of recognition that we often experience in learning, as if something forgotten were suddenly remembered.

To ground this view and render it plausible, Plato relied on the common view of reincarnation or metempsychosis. For doctrinal reasons, Augustine could not follow him in this, so he substituted illumination for recollection, and turned God into an inner Master: "no one is taught through words, but by means of the things themselves which God reveals to the soul."[24] Clearly, the power to be certain is not entirely the mind's only. Ultimately, it is God's light that effects the certainty: "No creature, however rational and intellectual, is lighted of itself; rather it is lighted by participation in Eternal Truth."[25]

While this illumination affects the mind in its pursuit of truth through the senses, it is, *a fortiori*, present in the mind's knowledge of the truths of God. Here we approach the acme of knowledge in pure contemplative activity without admixture of the senses. It is in contemplation that one envisages the truths of God, not separate and by themselves, like Platonic Forms or archetypes, but as grounded in the Divine Essence with which they are identical. For Truth, Beauty, and Being are interchangeable (*convertuntur*) paramountly in the case of God.

The contemplation of the Divine, however, is not a mere intellectual activity, because the mystery of God is really the goal, and before that mystery, human knowledge must give way to faith. Knowledge precedes, indeed; understanding takes the mind to the very limits of its power, demonstrating in the process that it is legitimate and reasonable to believe. Faith, for Augustine, was obviously not irrational.

> Who does not see that thinking comes before belief? For people do not believe anything unless first they think it must be believed. However instantly, however quickly some thoughts fly before the will to believe, and the will follow ever so closely that it be felt to accompany it intimately, still it is necessary that everything that is believed be preceded by thought. For belief itself is nothing but thinking with assent.[26]

Not merely that, but faith adds to reason a certain extension, so that the questions to which the understanding seeks answers are only answered fully in faith. Thus, for Augustine, faith is the crown of reason, the extension of the understanding, and six hundred years before St. Anselm, he could truly ask and truly answer:

> Do you want to understand? Believe! For God said through the prophet, "Unless

you believe you will not understand""[*Is.* 7:9]. . . . So I say: if you do not understand, believe. Understanding is the gift of faith. Therefore do not seek to understand that you may believe, but rather believe that you may understand.[27]

Now, it is this faith that brings us to the truth of God, and it is that truth that makes us happy. "The happy life," he writes, "is joy in truth. This joy comes from you, who are Truth [*John* 14:6]. . . my God. And it is this happy life that is desired by all."[28] And he adds: "For there is a joy which is not given to the ungodly, but only to those who love You for your own sake, whose joy You yourself are. This is the happy life, to rejoice with You, from You, for You; this is it, and there is no other. For they who think there is another pursue some other, and not the true joy."[29]

.oOo.

At the beginning of his Christian life Augustine set down this doctrine, from which he never deviated. Happiness, he argued with his companions in the conversations recorded in *On the Happy Life*, means having what you want if what you want is appropriate. But fear of losing what one has interferes with happiness. There is also suffering. "People," he says, "have attempted to make for themselves a happiness of this unhappy life."[30] Therefore the truly happy person is the one who possesses only what cannot be lost through reverses of fortune; that is, the one who enjoys the possession of an enduring object. The only such object is God. The only thing left, then, is to find out who possesses God, for surely such a one will be the happy one. Augustine concludes that those alone possess God who have a pure spirit, or who do what God commands; in short, those who live well[31]. Only they possess God, both here and hereafter. Hence, he says, "we are commanded to live righteously for the reward of being worthy to live eternally happy."[32] But God is not only the sole enduring object: he is also the sole absolute, and therefore the one object whose possession eliminates all want. If to be happy is to lack nothing forever, to be happy is to possess God.

Again, to lack nothing is to be wise. Wisdom, thus, is the balance (*modus*) of the soul. Therefore to be happy is to have the balance that is wisdom.[33] This wisdom, however, as we have indicated, is paramountly the knowledge of God. But *knowing* God is *having* God, not merely intellectually but also, and paramountly, in love; for "no good is perfectly known that is not also perfectly loved."[34] And so it happens that "when the will cleaves to the immutable good [that is, God]. . . such is the happy life."[35]

Therefore happiness consists in the knowing of God that is the having of God,[36] a knowing achieved especially in faith and love, and achieved perfectly only after this life, in the "beatific vision"—that is, the vision that renders the wise eternally happy in heaven.

There we shall rest and see, see and love, love and praise. This is what shall be in the end without end. For what other end do we propose to ourselves than to attain to the kingdom of which there is no end?[37]

.oOo.

# Additional Reading

## Sources

*Opera Omnia*, in *Patrologiae Cursus Completus*, ed. Migne. Paris: Garnier, 1800-1875. Vols. 32-47.
*Corpus Scriptorum Ecclesiasticorum Latinorum.* Vienna, 1908.
St. Aurelius Augustine, *Concerning the Teacher and On the Immortality of the Soul*, transl. George. G. Leckie. New York: Appleton-Century-Crofts, Inc., 1938.
Francisco Moriones, O.R.S.A., *Enchiridion Theologicum Sancti Augustini.* Madrid: Biblioteca de Autores Cristianos, 1961.

## Commentaries

David Bentley-Taylor, *Augustine: Wayward Genius.* Grand Rapids: Baker Book House, 1980.
Vernon J. Bourke, *Augustine's Quest for Wisdom.* Milwaukee: Bruce Publishing Co., 1945.
Frederick Copleston, *A History of Philosophy.* New York: Doubleday, 1962. Volume 2.
Will Durant, *The Age of Faith.* New York: Simon & Schuster, 1950.

## Notes

1. *Enchiridion* 27 [ML 40, 245].

2. *Confessions* I.1.

3. David Bentley-Taylor, *Augustine: Wayward Genius.* (Grand Rapids: Baker Book House, 1980), 12.

4. *Confessions* I.19-23.

5. *Confessions* II.6.

6. *Confessions* II.7.

7. *Confessions* IV.2.

8. *Confessions* IV.7-11.

9. *Confessions* V.22.

10. *Confessions* V.24.

11. *Confessions* VI.25.

12. *Confessions.* V.12.

13. *Confessions* VII.13-26.

14. *Romans* 13:13-14.

15. *Confessions* VIII.29.

16. Frederick Copleston, *A History of Philosophy* (New York: Doubleday, 1962), Vol. 2, 63-65.

17. Augustine, *Sermo* 117,3.5; ML 38, 663.

18. Copleston, *A History,* 67

19. *Contra Academicos* 3,11,20.

20. *De Civitate Dei* XI, 26; also *De Trinitate* 15,12,21; Copleston, *A History,* 69.

21. *De Civitate Dei* VIII.1.

22. *De Libero Arbitrio* II.13,35.

23. *De Magistro* 40.

24. *De Magistro* 40.

25. Augustine, *In Psalmum* 119; *Sermo* 23,1.

26. *De Praedestinatione Sanctorum* 2,5; ML 44,962.

27. Augustine, *In Ioannis Evangelium, tractatus* 29,6; ML 35,1630.

28. *Confessions* X.23,33

29. *Confessions* X.22,32.

30. *De Civitate Dei* XIX.1.1.

31. *De Beata Vita* II.12 and III.18.

32. *De Divinis Quaestionibus, ad Simplicianum.* I.2.21.

33. *De Beata Vita* IV.33.

34. *De divinis quaestionibus.* 83, q. 35, 2.

35. *De libero arbitrio* 2,19,52.

36. *De Beata Vita* IV.34.

37. *De Civitate Dei* XXII.30.

# 11

## ABÛ HÂMID AL-GHAZÂLÎ

### (1058-1111)

Abû Hâmid Muhammad ibn Muhammad ibn Muhammad al-Ghazâlî at-Tûsî: that was his full name, without titles and honorifics. Aquinas, who mistransliterated the names of just about every Muslim writer he quoted, got this one almost right, and his spelling is still repeated by otherwise competent modern historians of philosophy, such as Russell and Copleston.

He has been hailed by some as the greatest Muslim after Mohammed; as "The Touchstone of Islam" (*Hajjat al-Islam*);[1] as "the greatest, [and] certainly the most sympathetic figure in the history of Islam";[2] or, in Renan's words, as "the most original mind among Arabian philosophers."[3] Tholuck compared him with Origen, and Montgomery Watt maintains that his greatness derives from the fact that "he was the leader in Islam's supreme encounter with Greek philosophy."[4] In many respects these estimates are correct; for Mohammed founded Islam, but al-Ghazâlî preserved it inviolate at a time when its purity might have been soiled and its essence diluted. For al-Farâbî (870-950) had been quite successful in his use of Aristotle and of Neoplatonism in constructing a kind of Islamic philosophy, and ibn Sînâ (980-1037), who created Muslim Scholasticism, had added a decidedly rationalistic track. Al-Ghazâlî, however, reverted to the pure faith of the Prophet and the mystic ardor of the *sûfîs* without abandoning the method of reason. Philosophy was retained but as a mere maid of theology. It never grew up and became independent as it did among Christian thinkers after Aquinas. Moreover, jurisprudence remained the queen of sciences in Islam, and among Muslims for the first two hundred years after his death, al-Ghazâlî's highest reputation was that of a genial jurist.

Al-Ghazâlî was born in Tûs, Persia, in 1058. His father died when he was quite young. He and his brother Ahmad (who later distinguished himself as a theologian) were raised by a guardian. His first studies took place in Tûs and later (1074) in Gurgan.

As a child he was precocious, so it was not surprising that in 1077 he went to Nishâpûr to study at the recently founded Nizâmiyya College. His teacher was al-Juwaynî, the reigning luminary of the day.[5] When al-Juwaynî died in 1085, al-Ghazâlî joined the court of vizier Nizâm al-mulk. Then, in 1091 he was appointed professor of law at Nizâmiyya College in Baghdad. He was thirty-three years old.

Al-Ghazâlî was a successful teacher. He himself sets the number of his students at three hundred. He was also a busy author.[6] During this time he probably composed the *Maqâsid al-falâsifa* ("Aims of Philosophy"), his main philosophical work. But after four years of teaching he was beset by harrowing doubts that eventuated in a colossal spiritual crisis. The crisis, it seems, was not between belief and unbelief; rather, it was a matter of the role that diverse rational and other claims had on the nature and extent of belief. Partly, he questioned whether it was possible to attain to any certainty at all,[7] and partly whether he could align satisfactorily the results of rational inquiry with the tenets of faith.[8] In the end, he was successful in achieving a synthesis. It was to put philosophy in its place that he composed the *Tahâfut al-Falâsifa* ("The Inconsistency of Philosophy"), which ibn Rushd later opposed with his own *Tahâfut al-Tahâfut* ("The Inconsistency of the *Inconsistency*"). Moreover, as he put it,

> it had already become clear to me that I had no hope of the bliss of the world to come save through a God-fearing life and the withdrawal of myself from vain desire. It was clear to me too that the key to all this was to sever the attachment of the heart to worldly things by leaving the mansion of deception and returning to that of eternity, and to advance towards God most high with all earnestness.[9]

But while all this was clear, he just could not muster the strength to act on it. He hesitated; he doubted; he prayed. In the meantime he was gripped by psychosomatic ailments: his speech slurred, his tongue dried so that he had to curtail his classes. One particular day, as he rose to lecture, he could not utter a word. Then his stomach began acting up: he could not retain or assimilate food. His sickness the doctors correctly diagnosed but could not cure: "The trouble arises from the heart," they said; "the only treatment is to dispel the anxiety gripping the heart."[10]

This crisis lasted six months, starting in July, 1095, when he was thirty-seven years old. He knew he had to leave Baghdad, but was afraid of being detained by the Vizier. Finally, on pretext of going to Mecca on a holy pilgrimage, he gave his teaching post to his brother Ahmad (1065-1126) and retired to Damascus. He did eventually visit Jerusalem, Abraham's tomb in Hebron, Medina, and Mecca (November and December 1096); but the longest time he spent in solitude in

Damascus, where a corner of the mosque still bears his name—"the Ghazâlî corner."[11] He returned to Baghdad in June, 1097 and moved on to Tûs where he established a sûfî community.

For many years he prayed and thought, concluding with his contemporary, Anselm of Canterbury (1033-1109), that one must believe in order truly to understand.[12] During this time he wrote his main theological work, *Al-Iqtisâd fî-l-i`tiqâd* ("The Just Balance in Belief"), and also the *Ih'yâ `ulûm al-Dîn* ("The Revival of the Religious Sciences"), a monumental work of some forty small volumes designed to show how the practice of Islam can be the basis for a genuine sûfî life.[13] This work was, in effect, a justification of faith above philosophy. His conclusion was that only mystical insight can give us the truth of God. To this truth, sûfîsm is the only path. His *Bidâyat al-hidâya* ("Beginning of Guidance") offers directions for the spiritual journey.

In 1105 Fakhr-al-mulk, son of Nizâm al-mulk and now vizier of Baghdad, appointed al-Ghazâlî as teacher at Nizâmiyya College in Nishâpûr. His friends and children prevailed upon him to accept the position. He was also moved by a sense of vocation confirmed by the holy men he consulted, and by a sense of mission. For there was a well-known tradition that at the beginning of each century God would send a man to revive religion.[14] The deliberations whether or not to return to teaching took place during the last month of 499 A.H. (July, 1106 C.E.). Al-Ghazâlî hoped he might be the chosen one to re-awaken the fervor of religion.[15] And so he taught again there between 1106 and 1109. But the lure of pure contemplation and spiritual companionship was too strong. He left Nishâpûr and went back to Tûs, the city of his birth. There he lived his last years surrounded by sûfî followers, and there, too, he penned his autobiography, *Al-Munqidh min al-dalâl* ("Deliverance from Error"). He died on December 18, 1111. He was fifty-three years old.

.oOo.

Besides being the record of an intellectual journey, al-Ghazâlî's *al-Munqidh* is a discourse on method written five hundred years before Descartes's.[16] There are differences, of course. For one, al-Ghazâlî was in his early fifties when he wrote *al-Munqidh*. For another, al-Ghazâlî may not have been concerned as much with the limits and conditions of thinking in general as with the (psychological) conditions necessary for claiming certainty in the knowledge of revealed truth.[17] In other words, al-Ghazâlî's quest may have been more Anselmian than Cartesian.

Al-Ghazâlî's starting point was the realization that we grow up with prejudices. To the human nature we receive at birth is added a second nature of belief, practice, and mores. To Christians, Jews, and Muslims who have been born into a Christian, Jewish, or Muslim society, their Christian, Jewish, and Muslim beliefs are as natural as their own humanness. Having noticed this, al-Ghazâlî "was moved to discover what this original nature really was and what the beliefs derived from the authority of parents and teachers really were."[18] In other words, as Augustine said we all must do, he became a question to himself.

But an effort to know and establish differences required first an examination of knowing itself; that is, to know what is real, he felt he must first establish the nature and conditions of knowledge itself.[19] True knowledge, he concluded, was certain and indubitable knowledge. And what made knowledge certain? He answered: "Knowledge in which the object is disclosed in such a fashion that no doubt remains along with it, that no possibility of error or illusion accompanies it, and that the mind cannot even entertain such a supposition."[20] The criterion of certainty, in other words, is compelling self-evidence; what Descartes will term "clear and distinct."

But in matters pertaining to God and the spirit, we need light in order to see clearly, for "light is the key to the greater part of knowledge. Whoever thinks that the understanding of things Divine rests upon strict proof has in his thought narrowed down the wideness of God's mercy."[21] This light, however, comes from God. As Augustine and Plotinus before him, al-Ghazâlî accepted Plato's vision of the Good as the source of all our knowing, though his immediate source was the Prophet:

> When the Messenger of God (peace be upon him) was asked about "enlarging" [*sharh*] and its meaning in the verse, "Whenever God wills to guide a man He enlarges his breast for *islâm* [i.e., for surrender to God: *Qu'rân* 6:126], he said: "It is a light which God most high casts into the heart." When asked, "What is the sign of it?", he said, "Withdrawal from the mansion of deception and return to the mansion of eternity."[22]

This light is vouchsafed by God to the mystics, "for to the mystics all movement and all rest, whether external or internal, brings illumination from the light of the lamp of prophetic revelation; and behind the light of prophetic revelation there is no other light on the face of the earth from which illumination may be received."[23]

In this way philosophy, science, and theology were tempered by mysticism, and the trend toward rationalization was halted. For the theologian seeks understanding and explanation, while the mystic realizes the limits of all conceptual schemes. For al-Ghazâlî it is not reason that makes the soul giddy, but in an unspeakable manner, God alone.

.oOo.

When it comes to happiness, Al-Ghazâlî begins with a statement similar to Plato's and Aristotle's and probably derived from their writings. In order to understand what happiness is one has to determine what is the highest human faculty, and what will be its fulfillment. Al-Ghazâlî concurs with the Greeks: reason is the highest human faculty, therefore happiness must be connected with it. Reason's exercise leads to knowledge, and the highest knowledge is the knowledge of the highest object, God. Al-Ghazâlî maintains that the knowledge of God arises out of self-knowledge, and by self-knowledge al-Ghazâlî means especially the knowledge of one's inner self, "according to the saying: 'He who knows himself knows God,' and as it is written in the *Qu'rân*, 'We will show them Our signs in the world and *in themselves*, that the truth may be manifest to them.'"[24]

The meaning of happiness emerges now: happiness lies in the actualization of the highest human faculty, reason, by the highest object of knowledge, God, and in the delight accompanying such a knowledge.[25] The summit of happiness is not merely knowledge of God; it is the joy accompanying the intellectual union with God in heaven. As with Christianity, this idea of happiness transforms the merely philosophical notion of happiness into a religious one.

But Islam is a personalistic religion. Happiness, therefore, cannot be defined or pursued in purely intellectual terms. Love is the other fundamental ingredient. Al-Ghazâlî defines love in traditional Greek fashion as the desire for the good (i.e., the desirable), the possession of which engenders joy. "This enjoyment of God is happiness. But if he had no delight in God before, he will not delight in Him then, and if his joy in God was but slight before it will be but slight then. In brief, our future happiness will be in strict proportion to the degree in which we have loved here."[26] Moreover, love admits degrees, and as in any relationship, the degrees of love are enhanced through close and continuous acquaintance and through purification of desire. Such ascetical efforts require spiritual direction.

Finally, the pursuit of happiness in knowledge and love does not exclude obedience to tradition (*sunna*) and the *imitatio Prophetae*. Ritual, custom, and tradition remain integral components of the spiritual life.

.oOo.

## Additional Reading

### Sources

W. H. T. Gairdner, transl., *Al-Ghazâlî's Mishkât al-Anwâr*. Lahore, 1952.

Abû Hâmid Al-Ghazâlî, *Kitâb al-Arba`în fî Usûl al-Dîn*. Cairo, 1925.

———. *Ih'yâ `Ulûm al-Dîn*. Cairo, 1939.

———. *The Alchemy of Happiness* [*Kûmiyâ-yi Sa`âdat*]. New York: E. P. Dutton & Co., 1910.

William McKane, *Al-Ghazâlî's Book of Fear and Hope*. Leiden: E .J. Brill, 1962.

W. Montgomery Watt, *The Faith and Practice of Al-Ghazâlî* [*al-Munqidh min al-Dalâl* ("Deliverance from Error") and *Bidâyat al-Hidâyah*]. London: George Allen & Unwin, Ltd., 1953.

L. Zolondek, *Book XX of Al-Ghazâlî's **Ihyâ' `Ulûm al-Dîn***. Leiden: E.J. Brill, 1963.

## Commentaries

Julian Baldick, *Mystical Islam*. New York: New York University Press, 1989.
Kenneth Cragg, *The House of Islam*. 2nd ed. Belmont, CA: Wadsworth Publishing Co., 1975.
Cyril Glassé, *The Concise Encyclopedia of Islam*. New York: Harper & Row, 1989.
Ignacio L. Götz, "The Quest for Certainty: Al-Ghazali and Descartes," *Journal of Philosophical Research* 28 (2003): 1-22.
Al-Hallâj. *Dîwân*, ed. Louis Massignon. Paris: Éditions des Cahiers du Sud, 1955.
P. Jabre, *La notion de la certitude selon Ghazali*. Paris, 1958.
William James, *Varieties of Religious Experience*. New York: The New American Library, 1964.
Duncan B. Macdonald, *Development of Muslim Theology, Jurisprudence and Constitutional Theory*. New York: Russell & Russell, 1903; reprint 1965.
Louis Massignon, *The Passion of al-Hallâj*. 4 vols. Princeton: Princeton University Press, 1982.
Marijan Molé, *Les Mystiques Musulmans*. Paris: Presses Universitaires de France, 1965.
Seyyed Hossein Nasr, *Ideals and Realities of Islam*. Boston: Beacon Press, 1972.
Mohammed Marmaduke Pickthall, *The Meaning of the Glorious Koran*. New York: Mentor, 1961.
Abû Nasr al-Sarrâj, *Kitâb al-Luma' fî'l-Tasawwuf*, ed. R.A. Nicholson. Leyden: E.J. Brill, 1914.
Fadlou Shehadi, *Ghazali's Unique Unknowable God*. Leiden: E.J. Brill, 1964.
M. Smith, *Al-Ghazali the Mystic*. London, 1944.
William Cantwell Smith, *Islam in Modern History*. New York: Mentor, 1957.
W. Montgomery Watt, *Islamic Philosophy and Theology*. Edinburgh: Edinburgh University Press, 1985.
————. "The Authenticity of Works attributed to al-Ghazâlî." *Journal of the Royal Asiatic Society* (1952): 25-45.
John Alden Williams, ed., *Islam*. New York: George Braziller, 1962.
R. C. Zaehner, *Hindu and Muslim Mysticism*. New York: Schocken Books, 1969.

## Notes

1. Molé, *Les mystiques Musulmans* Paris: Presses Universitaires de France, 1965), 91; Jabre, *La notion* (Paris, 1958), 378.

2. Macdonald, *Development of Muslim Theology* (New York: Russell & Russell, 1903), 215.

3. Quoted in Al-Ghazâlî, *The Alchemy of Happiness*, 7; Zolondek, *Book XX*, 16-17.

4. Montgomery Watt, *The Faith and Practice of al-Ghazâlî*, 14-15.

5. Jabre, *La notion*, 39 and note.

6. Montgomery Watt, "The Authenticity of Works attributed to al-Ghazâlî." *Journal of the Royal Asiatic Society* (1952): 25-45; Jabre, *La notion*, 9-11 and 40-41.

7. Montgomery Watt, *Islamic Philosophy* (Edinburgh: Edinburgh University Press, 1985), 87.

8. *Al-Munqidh* III. 96, 37.

9. *Al-Munqidh* III. 126, 56.
10. *Al-Munqidh* III. 129, 57-58.
11. *The Alchemy of Happiness*, 8.
12. *Al-Munqidh* II.76.
13. Montgomery Watt, *Islamic Philosophy*, 92; Molé, *Les Mystiques*, 28.
14. Jabre, *La notion*, 35, note.
15. *Al-Munqidh* IV. 152.
16. Montgomery Watt, *The Faith and Practice*, 12; Jabre, *La notion*, 125 note 2.
17. Jabre, *La notion*, 34.
18. *Al-Munqidh*, I. 70, 21.
19. *Al-Munqidh*, I. 70.
20. *Al-Munqidh*, I. 70.
21. *Al-Munqidh*, II. 76, 25.
22. *Al-Munqidh*, II. 76, 25-26.
23. *Al-Munqidh*, III. 131-132.
24. *The Alchemy of Happiness* I, 19-20.
25. *The Alchemy of Happiness* I, 27-28.
26. *The Alchemy of Happiness* VIII, 101-102.

# 12

# SAINT THOMAS AQUINAS

## (1224/25-1274)

The exact date of the birth of Thomas, the youngest son of the Count of Aquino, has been impossible to ascertain. But it was around 1224 that the greatest theologian of the Middle Ages was born in the family castle at Roccasecca, about mid-way between Rome and Naples.

His first years were spent in the family enclave, but at about the age of five, in 1230, he began his studies at the famous Benedictine monastery of Monte Casino, probably as an oblate. Being an oblate entailed little more than the promise, made by the father, that the son would become a cleric in due course, and would abide by the regulations of the community as long as he resided there. There was no formal taking of vows, no commitment for young Thomas formally to enter the religious life. At the monastery he learned to write (his handwriting remained distinctly illegible throughout his life); he studied Latin, the Sicilian dialect, and read assiduously the Scriptures and the Church Fathers.

Political intrigues between Pope Gregory IX and the Emperor, Frederick II, made the monastery a questionable haven for study. So in the Fall, 1239, Thomas left Monte Casino and entered the Imperial University at Naples, where he studied until 1244. His course of studies here probably included some natural philosophy based on the work of Aristotle, grammar, and logic.

Thomas' father died in December, 1243, and in 1244 he officially entered the religious life in Naples—*not* as a Benedictine but as a Dominican. The fact that he did not join the Benedictine Order, in whose monastery he had grown up as a young boy, may have incensed the members of his family. His mother was certainly upset, and his brothers proceeded to kidnap him and keep him in detention for several months. But eventually he was released, and in a short time traveled on foot to Paris to begin his theological studies.

In the year 1245, in Paris, when Brother Thomas began his studies, Albert the Great was the reigning Dominican luminary in the field of theology. He was Thomas' mentor during those years, and he chose him as his companion when, in 1248, he was summoned to Cologne to found a Studium Generale for the Order.

Thomas remained at Cologne for four years, but these were not counted toward the eight years in residence required by the University of Paris as a condition for the Master's degree. So in 1252 Brother Thomas was back in Paris, reading for his degree, which he finally received in 1256. At this time be began his magisterial teaching.

Three years passed, and in 1259 Brother Thomas was summoned to Italy, where he was to remain almost ten years in the service of the Pope and his Order. Anagni, Orvieto, Lucca, Rome, Viterbo: in all of them he spent time preaching, writing, teaching, and proffering advise to sundry dignitaries.

In 1268 he was back in Paris, resuming his old chair, and lecturing for four years. But in 1272 he was ordered to Naples to found a new Studium Generale as part of a general effort to revitalize the Imperial University. Here, again, he taught, he preached, he wrote, always with enormous energy and sincere commitment.

During Lent, 1273, Thomas began to undergo some moving spiritual experiences. These culminated in his decision, reached on December 6, 1273, to cease writing the third part of the *Summa Theologiae*. The reason, he confided to Brother Reginald, his companion and secretary, was that everything he had written so far seemed to him grossly inadequate in light of his recent insights.

At about this time his health deteriorated rapidly. He took some rest, but it did not help. Nevertheless he began the journey on foot to Lyons, where a general Council had been convened. But he did not go far. On March 7, 1274, he died at the Cistercian Monastery of Fossanova. He was just forty-nine years old.

Within the short span of his life Thomas Aquinas generated an enormous body of writings. Among his early works are the *Commentaries on the Scriptures* and on *The Sentences* of Peter Lombard, and several *Quaestiones Disputatae* and *Quaestiones Quodlibetales*, as was the custom at the time. He continued to write such *Quaestiones* virtually until the last year of his life, as part of his magisterial function. He also preached fairly extensively, as the record of his sermons indicates.

Between 1261 and 1272 he wrote commentaries on various treatises of Aristotle as part of the ongoing reconsideration of the importance and usefulness of the Stagirite. The *Summa Contra Gentiles* (1258-1263) and the *Summa Theologiae* (1267-1274) are his most important works.

.oOo.

It is impossible to summarize Aquinas' work in a few paragraphs, or even to point to the most important and salient aspects of his thought. But a context can be provided within which his idea of happiness may be better understood.

Aquinas did not develop a system of philosophy independent of his theology. Philosophy, however, plays a large and important role in his rational explanation of the faith. It is not that he did not write distinctly philosophical works—he did. Such are, for instance, *De Ente et Essentia* ("On Being and Essence"), *De Veritate* ("On Truth"), and the various *Commentaries* on Aristotle. But philosophy was for him subordinate to theology, *ancilla theologiae*. Furthermore, he saw philosophy as an instrument in the mind's search for the knowledge of God, while he saw faith as the very knowledge of God and a participation in the Divine Life.[1] For him, philosophy clearly proceeds on the strength of "natural" reason, while the knowledge of God that alone fully satisfies the human mind relies further on the gratuitous help God himself vouchsafes, the supernatural light of faith. Theological knowledge, therefore, rests on the authority of revelation, not reason; reason merely helps plumb the depths of the revealed mysteries. Anselm had already formulated this position in the *Proslogion*:

> I do not endeavor, O Lord, to penetrate thy sublimity, for in no wise do I compare my understanding with that; but I long to understand in some degree thy truth, which my heart believes and loves. For I do not seek to understand that I may believe, but I believe in order to understand. For this also I believe—that unless I believe, I should not understand.[2]

The distinction between philosophy and theology mentioned above is highlighted again in the discussion of humankind's end. Aquinas maintains that all human beings were created by God for a purpose, to attain one end, namely, their eternal beatitude. Now, this beatitude is supernatural, since it entails the vision of God, which is clearly above and beyond all purely human powers. It follows that though humankind is created for this end, namely, supernatural happiness, it cannot attain it by its own unaided powers. It requires God's enabling grace. All that humans can obtain on their own is imperfect happiness. This happiness they often term *the end* (meaning goal; Lat. *finis*), and philosophers discuss its nature. But true happiness is another matter. Its existence is known by faith, and its attainment rests ultimately with God.

Another important point to bear in mind is Aquinas' conception of the human mind. He is more concerned with understanding existing reality than with the knowledge of disembodied essences—he is more Aristotelian than Platonic. Nevertheless, he considers the primary and immediate object of the human mind to be the essence of things (*quidditas*; *quod quid est*),[3] apprehended in reflection. Truth consists in correspondence between the mind's ideas and their objects in the world, determined through evidence. From this point of view, he is an objectivist, and places heavy emphasis on the power of the human mind to be objective, that is, to apprehend the real as it is.

It goes without saying that for him, as for Aristotle, the total orientation of philosophy (and the same goes for his conception of happiness) is intellectual. The object of philosophical speculation is *ens quâ ens*, the bare reality of Being. This is especially so in metaphysics. But this speculation is cast in a theological context in which God is the Supreme Being, the *Ens Supremum*. Given the teleological orientation derived also from Aristotle, "the knowledge of God is the ultimate end of every human cognition and operation,"[4] as was mentioned above. Hence "nothing else is understood to be meant by the term happiness than the perfect good of an intellectual nature."[5]

The argument is exactly the same as that of Aristotle: happiness must be defined in terms of the most complete satisfaction (or actualization) of the best and highest potential of any being. But in humans, in so far as they are intellectual natures—this intellectual nature being their specific difference—perfect satisfaction must consist in an intellectual operation. Hence "the happiness of every intellectual nature consists in understanding."[6] For "the Philosopher expressly says," writes Aquinas—and for Aquinas, *the Philosopher* is always Aristotle—"that 'happiness is an operation according to perfect virtue";[7] and after enumerating many virtues in the tenth book,[8] he concludes that ultimate happiness consisting in the knowledge of the highest things intelligible is attained through the virtue of wisdom, which in the sixth chapter he has named the 'chief of the speculative sciences.'"[9] But while Aristotle rested satisfied with this basic definition of happiness, Aquinas goes on to suggest that intellectual activity can be truly and fully satisfying only when its object is the most thoroughly complete, absolute, and final. Such an object can only be God.[10]

.oOo.

Aquinas deals with the question of happiness in a short treatise in the *Summa Theologiae*. The treatise owes a lot to St. Augustine, but equally, if not more, to Aristotle. To begin with, Aquinas sees happiness as the cessation of pursuit because all desires have been satisfied by the possession of the supreme object of desire. So defined, all human beings desire happiness, that is, the full satisfaction of all their desires. Problems arise, however, when one seeks to specify what is the supreme object of desire, and in what its possession consists.[11] He discusses wealth, honors, fame and glory, power, bodily goods, spiritual goods, pleasure, and in short, created goods as objects possibly claiming preeminence in the quest of happiness. All of these are ruled out.[12] The only object that qualifies as the universal good is God, "Therefore human happiness consists in God alone."[13]

Furthermore, happiness is an activity, that is, the actual exercise of a human capacity. What kind of activity? Aquinas demonstrates that it cannot be an activity of the senses, nor of the will, but only of the intellect, which is the distinctive human capacity. The essence of happiness, then, consists in an act of the intellect, but the delight resulting from happiness belongs to the will. As Augustine says, happiness is "joy in the truth,"[14] because joy itself is the fulfillment of happiness.[15]

Moreover, says Aquinas, this activity of the intellect in which happiness consists is a speculative, not a practical activity. In other words, it is intellectual activity for its own sake. And while it is true that contemplation, that is, speculative intellectual activity for its own sake, cannot be sustained perfectly upon earth, it is the activity we look forward to in heaven. The object of this eternal contemplative activity is God. Happiness is the intellectual possession of God.

This intellectual possession of and union with God, called beatific vision, is the essence of the experience of happiness. Everything else—delight and joy, rectitude of the will, comprehension, the body and its physical perfections, all external goods and possessions, and even friends, are not essential to happiness, though they undoubtedly enhance the experience. The experience is also enhanced by the cultivation of virtue in this life, and by the development of one's disposition to contemplate the divine essence. Such tasks are the goal and purpose of this life.

Finally, it must not be thought that the vision of God, eternal happiness, can be earned or acquired solely through human effort, however strenuous. God, as the object of vision, infinitely transcends the human powers of intellection. Hence, in the last analysis, it is God who must empower the human mind to contemplate the divine essence and in that contemplation to be happy. "Man is made happy by God alone, if we are speaking of perfect happiness."[16]

.oOo.

# Additional Readings

## Sources

St. Thomas Aquinas, *Summa Theologiae*, translated by the English Dominican Fathers. London: Burns, Oates, Washbourne, and New York: Benziger, 1947-1948.
St. Thomas Aquinas, *Summa Contra Gentiles*, or *On the Truth of the Christian Faith*. Garden City: Hanover House, 1955-1957.

## Commentaries

Vernon J. Bourke, *Aquinas' Search for Wisdom*. Milwaukee: The Bruce Publ. Co., 1965.
Frederick Copleston, *A History of Philosophy*. Westminster, Md.: Newman Press, 1950.

Volume II.

————. *Aquinas*. Baltimore: Penguin, 1955.

Etienne Gilson, *The Christian Philosophy of Saint Thomas Aquinas*. New York: Random House, 1956.

A. D. Sertillanges, *Foundations of Thomistic Philosophy*.   Springfield, IL: Templegate, 1956.

Josef Pieper, *Guide to Thomas Aquinas*, New York: Pantheon Books, 1962.

## Notes

1. *Summa Theologiae* 2-2, 19, 7c and 2-2, 45, 1c.
2 .Anselm, *Proslogion*, I.
3. *Summa Theologiae* 1, 88, 1c.
4. *Contra Gentiles*. III, 25.
5. *Summa. Theologiae* 1, 26, 1c.
6. *Summa Theologiae* 1, 26, 2c.
7. *Nicomachean. Ethics* I, 10 [1101ᵃ 14].
8. *Nicomachean. Ethics* X, 7 and 8 [1177ᵃ 21; 1179ᵃ 30].
9. *Summa Theologiae* 1, 88, 1c. *Nicomachean Ethics* VI, 7 [1141ᵃ 20)].
10. *Summa Theologiae* 1, 26, 3c.
11. *Summa Theologiae* 1-2, 5, 8c.
12. *Summa Theologiae* 1-2, 2, 8c.
13. *Summa Theologiae* 1-2, 2, 8c.
14. *Confessions* X, 23.
15. *Summa Theologiae* 1-2, 3, 4c.
16. *Summa Theologiae* 1-2, 5, 6c.

# 13

## BENEDICT SPINOZA

### (1632 - 1677)

History is full of strange twists and turns. A man whose name was twice blessed ended up cursed, which goes to show that blessings do not always ward off evil. The man was Benedict Baruch Despinoza ( or de Spinoza, or d'Espinoza), "the noblest and most lovable of the great philosophers," as Russell called him.[1] He was born in Amsterdam on November 24, 1632, the second child and first son of a Portuguese Jew and local businessman named Michael Despinoza (1588-1654). The child's two names mean the same in Latin and in Hebrew, "Blessed Blessed" (or "Happy Happy"), though he would often be called Bento.

In Amsterdam, the Jews lived mostly in a Jewish ghetto about half a square mile in size, called Flooyenburg ("flea town" or "flooded land," take your pick). There were about two thousand of them, and they were mostly businessmen, so Portuguese became the business language of the enclave, though Ladino was also spoken. Portuguese was also the language of instruction in the schools, but the children learned at least to read Hebrew.

Michael had married Rachel in 1623, but she had died in 1627, so Michael married again a woman by the name of Hana Debora, who gave birth to Bento. Hana died in 1638, so Michael married a third time, a woman named Giomar de Soliz, known as Esther, a recent arrival from Lisbon. She became a stern stepmother to the three surviving children from the previous marriages, and she gave Bento a half-sister, Rebecca, who would outlive him. Esther died in 1654, the same year as her husband, when Bento was 22 years old.

The ghetto was a place of scholarship to which Christian scholars often came to consult the rabbis about Hebrew grammar and Jewish traditions.[2] Bento must have attended the elementary and secondary school of the community until he was about fifteen years of age, when he would have moved on to the senior division of the Talmud-Torah school to pursue studies leading to the rabbinate. But his name does not appear in any of the class lists of the senior class. Was he a dropout? Had he begun at such a young age to ask questions that upset his teachers? Or was his father putting pressure on him to follow in his footsteps and become a businessman? We do not know with certainty, but the fact is that the curriculum of the Talmud-Torah school was exclusively traditional involving only the study of the Bible texts, the Talmud, and the interpretations of great scholars like Rashi, Maimonides, and Cresca. In the community at large the Kabbala was popular, since this had been one of the major contributions of the Spanish Jews to the Jewish mystical tradition. Bento did not favor any of this. Lucas, his first biographer, says that "the teachings of his father, who was a man of good sense . . . taught him not to confuse superstition and genuine piety."[3] Lucas adds that Bento "decided, accordingly, to consult no one but himself in this matter."[4] Bento was 19 years old. So whatever learning he acquired during these years came from attendance at all kinds of discussion circles in the Jewish community and from borrowing books from the private libraries of people like Rabbi Morteira, the premier high rabbi and head teacher of the Talmud-Torah school.

In 1655 two young fellows, pretending to be Bento's friends, tried to get him to confess to views that were anathema to the Jewish religious authorities. They planned to report him to the Jewish council. This was not unprecedented: several others had been accused of impious and heretical ideas, and some had been excommunicated; one, Uriel Acosta, had actually shot himself in 1647 upset over his excommunication. As for the plan to trip Bento, nothing came of it, but the incident indicates that Bento's unorthodox ideas were known in the community.

During the following year, 1656, Bento met Affinius Van den Enden (1602-1674), a Catholic ex-Jesuit who had set up a school in which he taught Greek, Latin, the classics (like Ovid, Virgil, Cicero), the Stoics and Epicureans (rather than Plato and Aristotle), Descartes, Bacon, Hobbes, Locke, and "the New Philosophy." This curriculum colored Bento's outlook.[5]

Bento joined Van den Enden and actually taught in his school, probably Hebrew and the Hebrew Scriptures. Later he began the composition of a *Hebrew Grammar*, which he left unfinished. He seems to have lived in Van den Enden's house.

Precisely because of its commitment to the free practice of religion and for its protection of dissidents like Descartes, Holland experienced a certain amount of religious controversy. The Jewish community was not exempt from this and had to deal with its own heretics and freethinkers. In 1656, a generally bad year—the Dutch lost Brazil and "New Amsterdam" (New York)—and under pressure from the Calvinist religious authorities, the government imposed a loyalty oath to Scripture on its professors of philosophy and theology at the universities. The Jewish community became concerned about its young dissident, Bento Despinoza, and encouraged by one of its leaders, Saul Levi Morteira, Bento's former teacher and friend, the Council summoned Bento and excommunicated him on July 27, 1656. The Herem, or excommunication, is in Spanish. Morteira reported the excommunication to the civil authorities, and Bento was banished from Amsterdam for several months. Bento's comment on the whole sordid affair was, "At such price is freedom bought."[6] He was twenty-four years old.

Shortly before this event, and perhaps cognizant of what might happen if he did not act, Bento had himself declared officially an orphan, since both his parents were dead. He was therefore free of any debts incurred by them.[7]

Bento moved to Ouderkerk and boarded for a short time in the house of the artist Nicholas Tulp. From there he may have moved to Leiden, an appealing location because of the University there. Golius (1596-1667), Descartes's teacher and correspondent, was the Rector at the University. Bento was back in Amsterdam in early 1657, probably as a spectator at the performance of Terence's play, *The Woman of Andros*, staged by his friend Van den Enden. After the performance he was accosted near the theater by a young Jewish zealot who tried to stab him, but Bento escaped unharmed.

Shortly after this, in 1657, he moved in with the Mennonites at Rijnsburg, and during the three years or so he stayed there he wrote *Short Treatise on God, Man and his Well-Being*, a *Treatise on the Improvement of the Understanding*, and *Descartes' Principles of Philosophy Geometrically demonstrated*, with an appendix, *Metaphysical Thoughts*. These were published under his name, but did not impress many. He then moved to Voorburg, near The Hague, and wrote and published anonymously his *Theological-Political Treatise* (1670), which was violently received. In Germany, a pamphleteer claimed that the book was full of "the abominable doctrines and hideous errors which this shallow Jewish philosopher has—if I may say so—shit into the world."[8] The book, however, became a milestone in the history of Biblical criticism. Denunciations were issued against it, but still, a second edition appeared in 1674. He also began work on his *Ethics demonstrated according to the Geometrical Order* (1673), which was published only posthumously. While in Voorburg he was visited by Leibnitz in 1676. Finally he moved to The Hague, where he received an invitation to join the faculty of philosophy at the University of Heidelberg, which he graciously declined. In The Hague, too, he died, probably of tuberculosis, on February 21, 1677. He was 45 years old. He was buried in the cemetery of the Calvinist New Church in The Hague, where his grave is still shown to tourists, though it probably contains none of his remains. His last work, *Political Treatise*, was left unfinished.

During the last years of his life he survived on modest pensions provided by friends like the powerful Jan de Witt (1625-1672), Grand Pensioner of the Netherlands from 1650 until his murder in 1672, Simon de Vries (1633-1667), and others, and he worked as a grinder of lenses for microscopes, telescopes, and eyeglasses. He was not a recluse, by any means, but his health did not permit him to be more active. His letters show him as impatient at times with his critics and people who did not understand him, but also very sensitive to the feelings of those who disagreed.

.oOo.

The salient idea of Spinoza's philosophy is that there is only one substance, infinite and divine, and that this divine substance is Nature; not Nature as the variegated complex we encounter when we go for "nature walks," but as the abstract concept of physics, the summary of all that is. This Nature is divine, hence the equation *Deus sive Natura*, "God, that is, Nature." From this point of view God (that is, Nature) is *both* creator and creation; creator and creation are one and the same.[9]

The existence of God or Nature is proved by what is called "the ontological argument," famously developed by Anselm and, contemporaneously with Spinoza, by Descartes and Leibnitz. The argument basically states that "there is an essence which necessarily involves existence,"[10] or, in Anselm's words, that if we can think of an absolutely perfect being, existence would have to be an attribute of it, for otherwise it would not be absolutely perfect. But actually to possess this attribute of existence is to exist. Therefore God must exist. But while for Anselm the argument is used only to prove the existence of God, Spinoza places it at the very center of his philosophy, and draws from it the profoundest implications in a very strict and mathematical fashion. The clarity of his treatment gives an overwhelming force to his argument.

The essence of the divine substance involves existence. It cannot but exist. Moreover, it does not depend on any external cause in order to exist; it is totally self-sufficient. Also, it is the one and only thing that exists, because if there were another, neither would be absolute.[11] Therefore, every thing that in our traditional thinking is said to be created by God, and dependent on God, exists only as a modification of the divine Nature. Nature—that is, God—comprises in itself all reality. When one considers all these other modes of existing that are gathered into the one divine reality of Nature—that is, God—one speaks of *Natura naturata* ("Nature natured"), Nature as an established system; while when one speaks of Nature in itself, one speaks of *Natura naturans* ("Nature naturing"). In Spinoza's words, "By *natura naturans* we are to understand that which is in itself and is conceived through itself. . . . By *natura naturata* I understand everything which follows from the necessity of the nature of God."[12] But this distinction does not mean that "the world" is different from God, as we are used to thinking is the case. No. Everything is Nature, is God. And among the attributes of Nature are extension (physicality) and thinking; and this, in a particular way, is what we humans are: our bodies represent the mode of the attribute of extension and our minds are the mode of the attribute of thinking. The mind is the idea of the body; that is, there is a mode of Nature which expresses itself as body or as its idea, that is, mind.[13] Since extension and thought belong to the same substance, Nature, "there can be no ideas which are not ideas of extended things, or extended things of which there is no idea."[14] Self-consciousness is the idea of the mind; and thinking has always a physical basis: "*The mind does not know itself except in so far as it perceives the ideas of the affections of the body.*"[15]

In a world in which there is only one reality, Nature (that is, God), there can be no question of truth as the *correspondence* between idea and thing (object); truth consists in the *coherence* of all ideas,[16] and error is simply the incompleteness, mutilation, or confusion of ideas,[17] prompted often by the deluding imagination. So, if an idea fits, it is true; if it does not because it is confused or incomplete, it is false.

Mind and will do not exist by themselves, as separate entities or faculties of the human reality, since the human reality itself is nothing but an affection or mode of Nature. Mind and will are merely minding and willing.

I said earlier that for Spinoza God (that is, Nature) cannot but exist, and there is a certain determinism in this, as there was in the philosophies of Lucretius and of the Stoics, which Spinoza studied, and as was being preached in Amsterdam by the Calvinists, though for different reasons. Freedom, then means simply that God (that is, Nature) is self-originating or self-creating; God is free "in the sense that he acts merely according to the necessary laws of his own nature,"[18] not of any other cause. But in this determinism there is also a great liberation, the freedom of being what Nature has in itself to be, which is, of course, unknowable. Human freedom, too, is not a freedom *from*, as we often conceive it to be, but a freedom to be what we must necessarily be. In this necessity there arises the most extraordinary freedom, a freedom that Nietzsche called "*Our fatum,*"[19] ("our destiny"), and that Spinoza calls "blessedness."[20]

This is not different from what each of us does throughout a life-time, though we seldom stop to think about it. We are born into our own particular world with an endowment of genes which spell out physiognomies, propensities and inclinations we cannot obliterate or ignore. Living means unfolding these determinisms through a judicious exercise of our reason so as to maximize achievement. Thus we create ourselves, not out of nothing, but out of a pre-existing substance which constitutes our endowment. As Spinoza puts it, "*in so far as the mind understands all things as necessary, so far has it greater power over the affects, or suffers less from them.*"[21] Freedom is found in mastery. Our freedom, then, consists in becoming who we are meant to be; or, as Nietzsche put it, becoming who we are.[22] But, according to Spinoza, what we are is Nature (that is, God); therefore by becoming who we are we unfold what Nature (that is, God) *is*. To paraphrase Hopkins, we act in God's eye what in God's eye we are.[23] No idea could be more powerful than this at a time when we strive to deal with Nature intelligently and with respect; after all, Nature *is* God, and we *are* Nature, so that our preservation is totally dependent on the preservation of Nature.[24] And not just the preservation of us as individuals, but that of the entire human community: "He who counts himself more blessed because he alone enjoys well-being not shared by others, or because he is more blessed or fortunate than others, knows not what is true happiness and blessedness."[25] In loving God with our whole being we love as God loves himself, and in this our utmost well-being consists.

.oOo.

One corollary of this identification of God with nature (or of Nature with God) is that our ordinary notion of miracle is shown to be completely absurd. Most people believe that miracles are suspensions of the laws of nature by God in favor of a particular person or as a response to a person's prayers. People believe that God answers their prayers—that is, their requests that God suspend the normal functioning of the physical universe in order to favor their requests. To pray for someone not to die when that individual is terminally ill is to request God to interfere in the normal progression of a disease beyond what medicine and other interventions can achieve. It is to pray for a miracle. Similarly, to claim that a miracle has taken place when someone recovers from a serious illness for reasons the doctors cannot explain is to attribute to God an agency in such a cure. Generally, to claim that a miracle has occurred when we cannot explain why an unusual event has taken place is to assert that God, the author of Nature's laws, has prevented their usual exercise or execution. God is in control, so why not?

But this view of miracle assumes that there are two realities, God and Nature, and two powers, the power of Nature and the power of God, and that God has absolute power over Nature, which he exercises when he works a miracle. But this cannot be so if God *is* Nature. So, Spinoza asserts, "If anyone were to maintain that God performs some act contrary to the laws of Nature, he would at the same time have to maintain that God acts contrary to his own nature—of which nothing could be more absurd."[26] A great deal of Spinoza's *Theological-Political Treatise* is concerned with showing how such an aberrant belief could occur.

.oOo.

Most scholars see Spinoza's *Ethics* as his crowning achievement. We should therefore say something about his understanding of ethics, even though in a summary way. His views on ethics flow from his general philosophy, which we have explained briefly above. It is a matter of drawing conclusions from these views.

Perfection and imperfection are only modes of thinking.[27] So also are the terms "good" and "bad," because according to the mode of extension, things simply *are*: "Nature is always the same."[28] Nature itself is neither good nor bad. The idea of "original sin," therefore, of a vitiated Nature, is a mistake.

Mind and body are one and the same thing; they are diversified when Nature is perceived under the mode of extension (body) or of mind (thinking).[29]

Moreover, says Spinoza, each thing endeavors to persevere in its being;[30] its essence, as it were, is a striving toward self-maintenance.[31] This endeavor Spinoza calls *conatus*. In humans, being conscious of this endeavor is called *desire* (*cupiditas*). When humans are conscious of their actual self-preservation and self-perfection, they experience *pleasure*, but if, on the contrary, they are conscious of decay, they experience *pain* (*tristitia*). *Desire*, *pleasure*, and *pain* are the fundamental emotions. All others are derived from these.

Since we necessarily seek self-preservation, which translates into pleasure when we are aware of it, it can be said that we necessarily pursue pleasure.

We call *good* all kinds of pleasure, and *bad* all kinds of pain. Good and bad are modes of thought.[32] Good and bad say nothing about things. We call *good* the things we desire, and *bad* those we do not. When in our minds the idea of a thing becomes associated with pleasure (that is, with an increase of vitality and of the drive to self-preservation) we are said to *love* that thing, and we call it *good*. From this point of view we call good what we know with certainty will lead us to become the type of person we aspire to become.

Now, pleasure and pain are "passive" emotions (*passions*) in that we necessarily experience them as a result of their being connected with the essential striving (*conatus*) by which all things seek to persevere in their being. Pleasure and pain are passive reflections of such bodily modifications. But there are "active" emotions as well, which arise when the mind is active in trying to understand itself. These active emotions are connected with pleasure and desire *only*. They are fortitude and its constituents, courage, and generosity, and their various forms, temperance, sobriety, presence of mind, etc. Moral development consists in a progressive liberation from passive emotions by changing these into active ones, as far as this is possible. Since active emotions draw their active character from the understanding, moral development is essentially rational, and it parallels intellectual development.[33]

To be moral is to be free from the servitude to the passions, the passive emotions. Understanding achieves this. Even in the case of pain, to understand that it is connected with Nature (that is, with God) is to cease to be a slave to it, thereby lessening its effects.[34] This Spinoza calls "understanding *sub specie aeternitatis*,"[35] which means that we see ourselves connected with Nature (that is, God).

Moral progress is achieved through the clarification of confused ideas of freedom and control. This is not easy, but it is possible.[36] The question, how can there be moral behavior if we are determined, rests on a misunderstanding of freedom. We become moral precisely by understanding how we are implicated in the evolution of the essence of Nature, which is determined: "For insofar as we understand, we can desire nothing but that which must be, nor, in an absolute sense, can we find contentment in anything but truth . . . [being] in harmony with the order of the whole of nature."[37] Understanding how one's actions are determined confers on the wise an extraordinary freedom that makes them "blessed."

.oOo.

And what is happiness? Since we are nothing but affections or modes of the divine Nature—that is, God—happiness consists only in the knowledge and love of God alone. This love is not personalistic, the love of a person; it is, rather, a kind of self-knowledge, for God, in a sense, knows and loves himself through our knowing and loving.[38] Here it helps to understand that Nature manifests itself ineluctably according to its own inner necessity, that is, "according to that same necessity by which it follows from the essence of a triangle that its three angles are equal to two right angles."[39] Everything is perfectly determined, nothing is fortuitous or accidental. We may not know how Nature will unfold, but we know that this will be according to its inner necessity. Inspecting these things in the coolest light of reason, therefore, is the surest way to achieve personal as well as social happiness, and a perfect society is one which seeks rationally to help all its members in the pursuit of their self-fulfillment. According to Hampshire, "the happiness of the free man, which is the free exercise of his understanding, is essentially uncompetitive, and requires from others only peacefulness and respect for law and order."[40] Thomas Jefferson, who had three volumes of Spinoza's works in his private library, would have agreed wholeheartedly.

Happiness does not depend on freedom in the usual sense of the term, because this meaning is false even though popular, as we showed above. Freedom means acting out of the necessity of one's nature, and of nothing else.[41] Since there is nothing else, unfreedom would be acting out of a mixed-up or confused sense of ourselves and of our nature; that is, out of a misconception of our identity with Nature, that is, God.

Why does happiness consist in the knowledge and love of God? Because happiness depends on the quality of the object known and loved.[42] Augustine had already asserted this, but in Spinoza this knowledge and love of God in which happiness consists is explained differently, in that the knowledge and love of God do not reject the physicality of God—after all, God *is* Nature, and therefore is qualified by extension. In us, Nature's mode of extension is the body, and it is through this body that we become aware of Nature and can eventually come to know and love God. This love of God in which happiness consists is a recovery of the awareness of our identity with Nature—that is, with God—very much as in the Vedanta there is a mystical and ecstatic awareness of the soul's identity with the divine It, Brahman-Atman. As Spinoza puts it, "If once we get to know God, at least with a knowledge as clear as that which we have of our own body, then we must become united with him even more closely than we are with our body, and be, as it were, released from the body."[43] In other words, happiness consists in a mystical transcending of the apparent difference between our own bodies and the "body" that is Nature; happiness is a kind of paroxysmal re-absorption into Nature, a rediscovery of our oneness with Nature, that is, with God; it is the consciousness of a drop of water dissolving in an infinite ocean. Only in this sublime reunion, both spiritual and material, does perfect happiness consist.[44] I should add that, for Spinoza, this happiness is sublimely joyful, and that he felt that there could never be an excess of joy in the world. "Joy is always good!"[45]

.oOo.

# Additional Readings

## Sources

Spinoza, *Werke*, ed. Carl Gebhardt. 4 vols. Heidelberg: Akademie der Wissenschaften, 1925.
Jean-Maximilian Lucas, *The Oldest Biography of Spinoza*, ed. A. Wolf. New York: Dial Press, 1927.
*The Correspondence of Spinoza*, ed. A. Wolf. London, 1929.
*The Chief Works of Benedict de Spinoza*, translated and edited by R. H. M. Elwes. 2 vols. London, 1883, revised 1903, reprinted 1951.
*Spinoza. Complete Works*, ed. Michael L. Morgan. Indianapolis, IN: Hackett Publishing Co., 2002.

## Commentaries

Copleston, Frederick, S. J. *A History of Philosophy*. New York: Doubleday, 1963.
Dungan, David Laird. *A History of the Synoptic Problem*. New York: Doubleday, 1999.
Durant, Will. *The Story of Philosophy*. New York: Pocket Books, 1957.
Feuer, Lewis S. *Spinoza and the Rise of Liberalism*. Boston: Beacon Press, 1958.
Greene, Marjorie, ed. *Spinoza: A Collection of Critical Essays*. Garden City, NY Doubleday, 1973.
Hampshire, Stuart. *Spinoza*. Harmondsworth: Penguin Books, 1951.
Jaspers, Karl. *The Great Philosophers*, Vol. 2. New York: Harcourt, Brace & World, Inc., 1966.
Levin, Dan. *Spinoza: The Young Thinker who Destroyed the Past*. New York: Weybright and Talley, 1970.
Yovel, Yirmiyahu. *Spinoza and Other Heretics*. 2 vols.; Princeton: Princeton University Press, 1989.

## Notes

1. Bertrand Russell, *A History of Western Philosophy* (New York: Simon & Schuster, 1945), 569.
2. Dan Levin, *Spinoza: The Young Thinker who Destroyed the Past* (New York: Weybright and Talley, 1970), 47.
3. Jean-Maximilian Lucas, *The Oldest Biography of Spinoza*, ed. A. Wolf (New York: Dial Press, 1927), 67, quoted in Levin, *Spinoza*, 50.
4. Levin, *Spinoza*, 62.
5. Levin, *Spinoza*, 217.
6. Levin *Spinoza*, 264.
7. Levin, *Spinoza*, 260-261.

8. Brad S. Gregory, ed., *Baruch Spinoza: Tractatus Theologico-Politicus*, trans. Samuel Shirley (Leiden: E. J. Brill, 1989), 30, quoted in David Laird Dungan, *A History of the Synoptic Problem* (New York: Doubleday,1999), 257.

9. Stuart Hampshire, *Spinoza* (Harmondsworth: Penguin Books, 1951), 46.

10. William A. Earle, "The Ontological Argument in Spinoza," in Marjorie Greene, ed., *Spinoza: A Collection of Critical Essays* (Garden City, NY: Doubleday, 1973), 214.

11. Spinoza, *Short Treatise*, Part I, chapter 1 and chapter 2, in Morgan, *Spinoza*, 39 and 41.

12. Spinoza, *Ethics*, Part I, Prop. 29, *Scholion*, in Morgan, *Spinoza*, 234. This distinction is somewhat similar to that between *logos endiathetos* and *logos prophôricos*, the unspoken and the inwardly spoken Word of God; *verbum* and *sermo*, as Tertullian would say, or "light from light" (*Apologeticum* XXI, 11-13), without implying any external duality.

13. William A. Earle, "The Ontological Argument in Spinoza:Twenty Years Later," in Greene, *Spinoza*, 223.

14. Hampshire, *Spinoza*, 65.

15. Spinoza, *Ethics*, Part II, Prop. 23, in Morgan, *Spinoza*, 260.

16. Spinoza, *Ethics*, Part II, Prop. 32, in Morgan, *Spinoza*, 263.

17. Ibid., Prop. 35, in Morgan, *Spinoza*, 264.

18. Hampshire, *Spinoza*, 48. See Spinoza, *Ethics*, Part I, Prop. 33, in Morgan, *Spinoza*, 235.

19. Friedrich Nietzsche, *The Antichrist*, 1, in *The Portable Nietzsche*, ed. Walter Kaufmann (New York: Viking Press, 1968), 570.

20. Spinoza, *Ethics*, Part V, Preface, in Morgan, *Spinoza*, 363-365.

21. Ibid., Part V, Prop. 6, in Morgan, *Spinoza*, 367.

22. Friedrich Nietzsche, subtitle to *Ecce Homo* , transl. Walter Kaufmann (New York: Vintage, 1967).

23. Gerard Manley Hopkins, "As Kingfishers Catch Fire," *Poems and Prose* (New York: Alfred A. Knopf, 1995), 18.

24. Spinoza, *Ethics*, Part IV, Prop. 18, *Scholium*, in Morgan, *Spinoza*, 330-331.

25. Spinoza, *Theological-Political Treatise*, Chapter 3, in Morgan, *Spinoza*, 416.

26. Spinoza, *Theological-Political Treatise*, chapter 6, in Morgan, *Spinoza*, 444.

27. Spinoza, *Ethics*, Part IV, Preface, in Morgan, *Spinoza*, 321.

28. Spinoza, *Ethics*, Part III, Preface, in Mason, *Spinoza*, 278.

29. Spinoza, *Ethics*, Part III, Preface, in Mason, *Spinoza*, 278.

30. Spinoza, *Ethics*, Part III, Prop. 6, in Morgan, *Spinoza*, 283.

31. Spinoza, *Ethics*, Part III, Prop. 7, in Morgan, *Spinoza*, 283. Hampshire, *Spinoza*, 76-77, 122. There are echoes of Spinoza's *conatus* in Schopenhauer's "Will-to-live" and in Freud's *libido* (the raw force of the *Id*). Psychologist Gordon Allport, in his book *Becoming* (New haven, CT: Yale University Press, 1955), considers "propriate striving" as the essence of the human psyche.

32. Spinoza, *Ethics*, Part III, Prop. 39, Scholium, in Morgan, *Spinoza*, 298-299.

33. Spinoza, *Ethics*, Part IV, Prop. 24, in Morgan, *Spinoza*, 333; Part V, Prop. 3, in Morgan, *Spinoza*, 366.

34. Spinoza, *Ethics*, Part V, Prop. 18, Scholium, in Morgan, *Spinoza*, 372.

35. Spinoza, *Ethics*, Part V, Prop. 36, in Morgan, *Spinoza*, 378-379.

36. Spinoza, *Ethics*, Part V, Prop. 42, Scholium, in Morgan, *Spinoza*, 382.

37. Spinoza, *Ethics*, Part IV, Appendix 32, in Morgan, *Spinoza*, 362.

38. Spinoza, *Ethics*, Part II, Prop. 49, Scholium, in Morgan, *Spinoza*, 273-277.

39. Ibid.

40. Hampshire, *Spinoza*, 163.

41. Spinoza, *Ethics*, Part I, Def. 7, in Morgan, *Spinoza*, 217.

42. Spinoza, *Treatise on the Emendation of the Intellect*, 9, in Morgan, *Spinoza*, 5.

43. Spinoza, *Short Treatise*, Part II, chapter XIX, in Morgan, *Spinoza*, 89.

44. Spinoza, *Short Treatise*, Part II, chapter XXII, in Morgan, *Spinoza*, 94. See Hampshire, *Spinoza*, 166.

45. Spinoza, *Ethics*, Part IV, Prop. 42, in Morgan, *Spinoza*, 343.

# 14

# IMMANUEL KANT

## (1724-1804)

Kant, wrote Lord Russell, "is generally considered the greatest of modern philosophers. I cannot myself agree with this estimate, but it would be foolish not to recognize his great importance."[1] Others disagree with Russell, whose judgments of people are not always fair. Either way we have Kant, the little big man of modern philosophy: he was barely five feet tall, and stooped, at that; but his mind packed a wallop that made the modern world reel.

He was born on April 22, 1724, the fourth of eleven children. His father, Johann Georg Cant, was a harness maker whose own father had migrated to Prussia from Scotland. His mother, Ann Reuter, was a pretty woman of simple faith, whose religious devotion had a profound influence on young Immanuel.

The Cant family lived in Königsberg, a flourishing city where German businessmen hobnobbed with English merchants, and the bustle of everyday life stood in marked contrast to the religious Pietism of family and church. Pietism emphasized the inner life and an emotional approach to religion, and it did not put stock on theology and its dogmatisms. The young boy imbibed this piety and was influenced by it during the early part of his life. Perhaps there is a tribute to his religious upbringing in his *Dreams of a Spirit-seer* (1766), which discusses the doctrines of the visionary Swedenborg. But there were other influences from Romantic sources, the most conspicuous being, perhaps, the "Profession of Faith of the Savoyard Vicar" in Rousseau's *Émile*.

Kant attended the local *Collegium Fredericianum* from age eight to sixteen (1740), when he entered the University of Königsberg. There he distinguished himself as a brilliant student, and in 1746 he was invited to enter the Lutheran ministry, but he refused.

In 1755 (he was thirty-one) he obtained his doctorate and a license to teach as *Magister legens* or *Privatdozent*—that is, as an unsalaried lecturer who could charge lecture fees, which were not sumptuous. To make a living he lectured a lot—as many as twenty lectures a week—and on a variety of subjects: logic, ethics, geography, anthropology, and metaphysics. He also tutored the children of several aristocratic families. By all accounts he seems to have been a stimulating and entertaining lecturer. He continued in this fashion for fifteen years.

During these early years, most of his writings were either scientific or of a general nature. His *General History of Nature and Theory of the Heavens* (1755) was quite original in that it sought to vindicate Newton philosophically (a position he changed later). More importantly, he explained the origin of the solar system through a "nebular hypothesis," a theory later developed by Laplace.

Twice during this time he applied for a full faculty position, and twice he was rebuffed. Finally, in 1770 (he was forty-six) he was appointed to a chair of logic and metaphysics. His inaugural lecture, *De Mundi sensibilis et intelligibilis Forma et Principiis* contained in germ (but in Latin) the tenets of his later critical thinking.

Perhaps it was the financial security of his new post that enabled him to work on a complete revision of his earlier views and to initiate his "critical" philosophy. At any rate, in 1781, he published the *Critique of Pure Reason*, followed two years later by the *Prolegomena to any Future Metaphysics* (1783). The other critiques came out in due time, *Critique of Practical Reason* in 1788 and *Critique of Judgment* in 1790. Other major companion pieces were *Fundamental Principles of the Metaphysic of Morals* (1785) and *The Metaphysics of Morals* (1797).

Kant's work was no walk in the woods, but he was read and discussed, and not always favorably. However, under Frederick the Great of Prussia he felt free and encouraged to publish. The king favored the Enlightenment and even contributed to it. Such protection was welcome when the *Critique of Pure Reason* appeared in 1781, for it was one of the most devastating attacks ever delivered on theology and religion. But ideal circumstances did not last forever. Kant's publication of *Religion within the Limits of Reason Alone* (1793) offended the new king of Prussia, Frederick William II, nephew of *Der Alte Fritz*, who had died in 1786. By 1788, Wöllmer, who was in charge of religious affairs in Frederick William's government, issued a *Religionsedikt* which effectively disestablished religious toleration, established censorship, and threatened penalties on dissenters. In 1794 Frederick warned Kant personally and in writing, and threatened "unpleasant consequences" if he persisted in his rationalistic critiques. Kant was forced to promise not to publish anything in matters of religion, but he was unhappy with his capitulation. In a private note he wrote:

> Repudiation and denial of one's inner conviction are evil, but silence in a case like
> the present one is the duty of a subject; and while all that one says must be true,

this does not mean that it is one's duty to speak out the whole truth in public.²

Fortunately, as soon as Frederick William died in 1797, his successor, Frederick William III repealed the *Religionsedikt*, and Kant resumed his publication. It was his strong belief that one should have the courage to use one's own understanding.³ Kant retired from lecturing in 1797, but he continued writing. He enjoyed social life and conversation, and had many friends, even among the English merchants. Strangely, he never left Königsberg, and because of a somewhat weak physical disposition, he lived in a very orderly fashion: he went to bed at ten and rose at five, and had his dinner at one in the afternoon. Legend has it that the housewives set their clocks by the regularity of his daily afternoon walk.

As he aged, his mental powers weakened. He had never married (though twice he came close to it), and by 1800 one of his pupils had to look after him. He fell seriously ill for the first time in 1803, and died on February 12, 1804. He was eighty years old.

At his funeral, the citizens of Königsberg followed his coffin to the Cathedral (where he is buried), aware that, in his own way, he had been a champion for freedom of thought and expression. On his tomb, to this day, are engraved the words from the *Critique of Practical Reason*: "the starry heavens above, and the moral law within."

.oOo.

Kant owed a double debt to Hume. First of all, it was in the context of Hume's empiricism that Kant constructed his critical philosophy. Secondly, it was Hume's relentless criticism of ordinary ways of talking about causality as well as of unphilosophical transitions from facts to moral obligation that woke him, as he wrote in the introduction to the *Prolegomena to any Future Metaphysics*, from his dogmatic slumber.

Hume had reduced experience to the reception of impressions. Ideas followed such impressions according to certain rules of continuity and repetition. Further, he showed how necessary connections such as that alleged to exist between cause and effect were not given to us in experience. Such ideas were mere generalizations from experience, where experience dictated the extent or the limits of the idea. Hume's analysis forced one to see the limits of reason, and to accord experience a primary, initiatory role.

If experience dictated certain limits to thinking, what was one to do with the idea of essence, for example, or substance? Aristotle had made a distinction between a thing's essence and its existence, implying that it was possible for reason to arrive by induction from particular existents at a generalization applicable to all of them. That was their essence, and even though it was the result of the work of reason, it was not just a figment of the mind, an *ens rationis*, but had an objectivity to it which was merely discovered by the human mind. And the same applied to the distinction between substance and accident; that is, between the traits that are constitutive of a thing and those that are merely accidental predicates, such as for a man to have a beard, or to be six feet tall. Again, even though the distinction was the mind's, substance was real, not just imaginary.

But although substance and essence can be inferred by the mind, they are not perceivable. What is perceivable is the whole complex of substance and accidents as it actually exists. In a sense, and maintaining the traditional terminology, what is perceived is how the substance appears to us in its accidents. Assuming that there is, indeed, a substance, we never perceive it in itself, for its accidental accretions stand between it and us. We only perceive it as it appears to us. In fact, we cannot know what it really is in itself, because any inference we may make arises from its appearance, from how it appears to us.

Now, this was what Kant argued. The thing in itself (*Ding an sich*) he termed the *noumenon*, and the appearances he called *phenomena*. We have no access to the *noumenon*, he said, only to *phenomena*.

It seems clear that in the *Critique of Pure Reason* Kant held the *noumenon* to be real, not just imaginary. It was unknowable, but still real. However, some statements of the *Opus Postumum* raise the issue whether he maintained this view until his death. For example, in the *Opus Postumum* he says, "the thing-in-itself is not a real thing";[4] and again: "the thing-in-itself (*noumenon*) is a mere *Gedanken-ding* (*ens rationis*), in the representation of which the subject posits itself."[5] On the face of it, these statements deny any objective reality to the *noumenon*. But it is possible to interpret them, in light of the more careful writing of the *Critique of Pure Reason*, as meaning that the existence of the *noumenon* is discoverable by reason, and that any interpretative description reveals more the interpreter's imagination than the thing itself.

Kant was also influenced by Leibniz, whose *New Essays Concerning the Human Understanding* had appeared in 1765. In them Leibniz had taken exception to Locke's "There is nothing in the mind which did not come from the senses" with the rejoinder, "Except the mind itself." This rejoinder allowed Kant to envisage an explanation for ideas that Hume, and the Empiricists generally, could not account for very well within the ambits of their philosophies. Such were, for instance, the notions of time and space. Are time and space real entities in the world? Are they objective properties of things? If not, how do we come by them?

Taking the hint from Leibniz, Kant maintained that space and time were the mind's way of apprehending the world. They were not ideas, but rather structures of the mind. Given its own structure, the mind always apprehended objects as being in time and in space, and it could not do otherwise. Time and space were not properties of objects but filters of the mind. However, there *was* a substance filtered, the world *was* real. To use another metaphor, time and space are like red tinted glasses that can never be taken off, so that to the seer the world will always seem red; but there *is* a world.[6]

For Kant, time and space were categories of perception. But beyond perception one sought to understand, and here, too, the mind functioned according to its own innate structures—categories of understanding: cause, effect, quality, quantity, relation, and so forth. Hume had been right in maintaining that cause and effect were not "given" to us in experience, but he was wrong in stating that they were merely generalizations based on experiences of constant conjunction. Cause and effect, said Kant, are structures which the mind imposes upon the data of experience as it seeks to understand them.

To Kant it seemed as if he was achieving a Copernican revolution in reverse. Scholasticism had made the object the focus of attention, and truth was *adaequatio mentis ad rem*, the adaptation of the mind to the thing. But he was reversing the relation: things conformed to the mind, rather than the other way around. Objectivism had de-emphasized the subject in favor of the thing; Kant was re-emphasizing the subject almost at the expense of the thing. Scholasticism was Copernican; Kant's view was Ptolemy's redux.

Now, the mind and its structures are so constituted before any experience affects them. This is the *pure* mind, unsoiled by things. What is the range of this pure mind? Can the structures of the subject's mind be applied beyond experience, beyond the phenomena, to the thing-in-itself, to the *noumenon*? To answer this question is the task of the *Critique of Pure Reason*. The categories, Kant maintains, are applicable only to the *phenomena*, for that is what is within our reach. Therefore the traditional objects of metaphysical knowledge—God, freedom, and human immortality (to mention the most important ones)—remain unknowable. Put differently, the traditional metaphysical claims about them cannot be substantiated. This unknowability is also due to the fact that the concept of beings such as God contains the notion of necessary existence. But necessity is a purely *a priori* element of thinking, totally unrelated to actuality. Such an element cannot be used to transcend the limits of experience, because its very nature as an *a priori* structure of the mind imposes unbreakable restrictions. The situation, in a nutshell, is that we have to deal with the world by means of a mind whose innate structures are limited to what is given immediately in experience, nothing more.

This limitation applies also to the moral realm. Kant accepts the traditional view that distinguishes two functions of the mind, one theoretical (Pure reason), the other practical (Practical reason). At the theoretical level, reason exercises itself about matters of fact, about what is. At the practical level, reason is concerned with the production of moral choices; it decides what ought to be. The question is, What are the grounds for moral decisions and choices?

Put differently, practical reason is not concerned with how humans behave, but with how they ought to behave. But from where does this "ought" originate? From where does it derive its strength, so that even if all people behaved immorally—if all, for example, told lies—it would still be justifiable to state that one should always tell the truth?

By asking the question this way Kant was obviously implying that the power of the "ought" arises *a priori*. It is rooted in the structures of the mind. It does not depend ultimately on God, whose existence is not demonstrable; neither does it rest on the authority of the church, for the church's authority, being derived from God, is equally unfounded. No heteronomy can be satisfactory after the *Critique of Pure Reason*. The *Critique of Practical Reason* (and its companion writings) is a search for the *a priori* element of moral reasoning, for the formal aspect of moral choice, which, when joined to the material (the specific, empirical circumstances), gives us the totality of morality.

From a moral point of view, an action is morally good if it flows from a good will. But when is a will good? Certainly not when the consequences of its choice are good, for that would give goodness a heteronomous criterion. Neither can the goodness of the will depend on external possessions, such as wealth, fame, power, for these are fortuitous and therefore conditional upon favorable circumstances. By "good" Kant means unconditional good. A will is unconditionally good when it acts purely and exclusively out of a sense of duty. Not just according to duty, nor because acting out of duty is pleasing; a will is unconditionally good if, and only if, it acts for the sake of duty.

When does a will act for the sake of duty? When, says Kant, it acts out of pure respect for moral law. And what does it mean to act out of respect for law? It means, answers Kant, to act in such a way that one's act is universalizable. Why so? Because the formal characteristic of law, what constitutes law as such, is that it is universalizable—that is, that it is universally applicable without exceptions. An example of the universality of law is physical law, the law(s) of nature. Gravity, for example, applies throughout the universe without exception. As McGill puts it,"just as a theorem of geometry about equilateral triangles must be (a) rationally irresistible and (b)valid for all equilateral triangles, so a moral law must be *a priori* certain, i.e., incontrovertible and without exceptions."[7]

Now, physical beings, including humans, conform to the laws of physics without even thinking about them; but humans are capable, besides, of acting consciously out of respect for the law. Hence the parallel between "the starry heavens above, and the moral law within." Acting for pure respect for the law, then, is acting consciously in a universalizable way. Putting duty and universalizability together, Kant framed what he calls "the first formulation of the categorical imperative," the imperative, that is, without exception. It is this: "Act only according to a maxim by which you can at the same time will that it should become a universal law." Again: "Act as though the maxim of your action were by your will to become a universal law of nature."[8] Once more: Act as though you could will your action to become a universal law of action.

But does such a categorical imperative exist? Is there an end or goal that must be willed universally, without exception? Is there something which has in itself absolute value, so that it can be willed only as an end in itself? Kant answers that there is such an absolute value. It is "rational nature"; that is, the human person. Why? Because rational nature is the source of value and the end (the goal) of value. It is an end in itself and it applies to all human beings. Therefore it can be—it *must* be—willed universally, in us and in others. Putting this absolute value (namely, human nature) together with the maxim of universalization, Kant arrives at "the second formulation of the categorical imperative," the supreme practical (moral) principle or law: "Act so that you treat humanity, whether in your own person or in that of another, always as an end and never as a means only."[9] When a human will wills in this fashion, in a purely formal way, it is perfectly good, because there is in it no admixture of extraneous considerations, no possibility of self-seeking. Hence Kant can claim, "Nothing in the world—indeed nothing even beyond the world —can possibly be conceived which could be called good without qualification except a good will."[10]

.oOo.

It is against this background that Kant considers the notion of happiness. He defines happiness as "the state of a rational being in the world with whom in the totality of his existence everything goes according to his wish and will."[11] Again: "A rational being's consciousness of the pleasantness of life uninterruptedly accompanying his whole existence is happiness."[12] Still more detailed: "Happiness is the satisfaction of all our desires; *extensive*, in regard to their multiplicity; *intensive*, in regard to their degree; *protensive*, in regard to their duration."[13]

These definitions are entirely consonant with the Western philosophical tradition. In a general sense, all would agree with them, though there would be differences in specifying what constituted satisfaction of desires, and whether or not there was a hierarchy among them. But Kant sets himself against this tradition, not in denying what happiness *is*, but in denying that it is the ultimate goal of human life.

Defined so broadly and comprehensively, happiness can never be achieved on earth, a fact that led Augustine and Aquinas to project its fulfillment to heaven. But heaven is a noumenal reality for Kant, and therefore not to be taken into account. If happiness, unattainable as it is, were the ultimate goal of human life, one would have to maintain that human nature has as its goal a naturally unattainable objective. This makes little sense.

Furthermore, the experience of happiness is contingent on a number of factors outside our control. Therefore, to make happiness the ultimate goal is to make the attainment of life's purpose hinge on what does not depend on us, for we can aim at happiness, but this does not mean that happiness will "happen" to us.

Moreover, a question arises as to the means of pursuing happiness. Is happiness to be pursued only by virtuous means? Wouldn't this entail that only the virtuous are happy? But this is contrary to fact, for we often see that the virtuous are unhappy, and, conversely, that villains prosper and are happy.

Again, if happiness were the goal of life, how would one handle the problems of an ethics of happiness? What would it mean to say that one ought to pursue happiness, especially considering the fact that it is not certain what actions will assure us of happiness? And if happiness is the natural goal of humanity, can its pursuit be commanded? Can one command someone to be five feet tall, or not to be hungry?

The point of Kant's various arguments is that to make happiness the ultimate goal is to make humans tend toward something which is not within their power to achieve. Happiness is, therefore, a *conditioned* goal; its attainment depends on conditions and factors external to the human will. The very English term "happiness" (from *hap*, what "happens" by luck or good fortune; like the Latin *fortunatus*, fortunate) seems to convey its conditional nature: happiness is that it happens to us. Therefore, argues Kant, the ultimate goal of human striving must be placed in something that depends on us alone, on something unconditional and unconditionally good. But the only unconditioned good is the good will. Therefore the good will is the ultimate goal. Humanity's paramount goal is to be moral.

What, then, becomes of happiness? It may or it may not happen to us. Our goal, however, is to be *worthy* of it. This we achieve by being moral. Not that we pursue morality for the sake of being happy; we are moral for the sake of being moral, and take happiness if and when it comes. In a somewhat ideal situation, the moral would be happy, too, and that is, indeed, the *summum bonum*. But in that most perfect amalgam the only unconditionally good element would still be the good will

.oOo.

# Additional Readings

## Sources

*Kants Gesammelte Schriften.* 22 vols.; Berlin: G. Reiner, 1902-1942.
*Kants Sämmtliche Werke.* 10 vols.; Leipzig: Felix Menier, 1921-1940.
*Immanuel Kants Werke.* 11 vols.; Berlin: Bruno Cassirer, 1912-1922.
Hans Reiss, ed., *Kant's Political Writings.* Cambridge: Cambridge University Press, 1970.
Robert Paul Wolff, ed., *Kant: Foundations of the Metaphysics of Morals.* New York: Bobbs-Merrill Co., Inc., 1969.

## Commentaries

Lewis White Beck, *A Commentary on Kant's Critique of Practical Reason.* Chicago: University of Chicago Press, 1960.
Ernst Cassirer, *Rousseau, Kant, and Goethe: Two Essays.* Princeton: Princeton University Press, 1963.
Ernst Cassirer, *Kant's Life and Thought.* New Haven: Yale University Press, 1981.
Frederick Copleston, *A History of Philosophy.* Garden City: Doubleday Image, 1960, Vol.6.
A.R.C. Duncan, *Practical Reason and Morality.* Edinburgh: Thomas Nelson & Sons, 1957.

A.C. Ewing, *A Short Commentary on Kant's Critique of Pure Reason.* Chicago: University of Chicago Press, 1938.

A.D. Lindsay, *Kant.* London: Oxford University Press, 1934.

Vivian J. McGill, *The Idea of Happiness.* New York: Praeger,1967.

H.J. Paton, *The Categorical Imperative. A Study in Kant's Moral Philosophy.* Chicago: University of Chicago Press, 1948.

W.D. Ross, *Kant's Ethical Theory.* Oxford: Oxford University Press, 1954.

Bertrand Russell, *A History of Western Philosophy.* New York: Simon & Schuster, 1945.

Hans Vaihinger, *The Philosophy of "As If."* New York: Harcourt Brace, 1924.

## Notes

1. Russell, *A History of Western Philosophy* (New York: Simon & Schuster, 1945), 704.

2. Quoted in Hans Reiss, *Kant's Political Writings* (Cambridge: Cambridge University Press, 1970), 2.

3. Kant, "An answer to the question: 'What is Enlightenment?'" [1784], in Reiss, *Kant's Political Writings*, 54.

4. *Opus Postumum*, in *Gesammelte Schriften*, Vol.22, 24.

5. Ibid., 36.

6. Copleston, *A History of Philosophy* (Garden City: Doubleday Image, 1960), Vol. VI/1, 240-241.

7. McGill, *The Idea of Happiness* (New York: Praeger, 1967), 95.

8. *Foundations of the Metaphysics of Morals* II; *Gesammelte Schriften*, Vol. IV, 421.

9. Ibid., 429.

10. Ibid., 392-393.

11. *Critique of Practical Reason; Gesammelte Scriften*, Vol. V, 224.

12. *Critique of Practical Reason* I. I. 3.

13. *Critique of Practical Reason* II. II.

# 15

## JEREMY BENTHAM

### (1748--1832)

Bentham was the eccentric founder of Utilitarianism. He was a precocious child who studied Latin at age four, but who found schooling distasteful and unsatisfying. Later in his life he would propose a new system of education in the *Chrestomathia* (1816). He studied law and was admitted to the Bar, taking up residence at Lincoln's Inn, where he eventually became a bencher. But he did not enjoy legal practice. Rather, he devoted his energies to the analysis of the legal and penal codes, of the religious and political institutions of his day, of jurisprudence and of economic practices. He wrote much and rewrote even more, leaving at his death a mass of manuscripts which have not yet been published in their entirety.

He traveled widely, to Italy, Russia, and France, where he was made a citizen. There Étienne Dumont published some of Bentham's works as well as his own commentaries. In England, Bentham surrounded himself with a select group of devoted friends and disciples, among whom were Lord Shelburne, Bowring (later his editor and plagiarist), James Mill, and John Stuart Mill.

Theoretical inquiry gave way to proposals for radical reform of courts and jails. In 1776 he published his *Fragment on Government* attacking Sir William Blackstone; from Russia he penned a *Defence of Usury* (1787); in 1791 he pub-lished his blueprint for prison reform, the *Panopticon*, and in 1817 his *Catechism of Parliamentary Reform*. Among his many other works, the *Introduction to the Principles of Morals and Legislation* (1789) and the *Deontology or Science of Morality* (published posthumously in 1834) are especially relevant to any discussion of his ethical views.

Bentham specified that at his death his body be dissected for the benefit of science. It was reconstructed afterward and mummified, as he had directed. To this day it sits upright, with the head by his feet, in a case at University College, London.

.oOo.

Here we are concerned exclusively with Bentham's ethics; specifically, with his theories of happiness and utility. He defined ethics as "the art of directing men's actions to the production of the greatest possible quantity of happiness, on the part of those whose interest is in view."[1] This art of producing happiness he founded upon a principle which for him was an "impregnable truth"—the principle of utility. In ethics, this principle had for him the same force as experience in matters of fact. He considered it his fundamental ethical assumption:

> This then I assume as a *postulatum*: and this, in matter of censure and approbation, is the only *postulatum* I do assume . . . . For matter of fact I appeal to the experience or observation of those in whose cognizance it lies. For matter of censure or approbation I appeal solely to this principle.[2]

Bentham claimed that he had discovered the principle of utility in the works of the ancient Hedonists, Epicurus and Carneades. Horace, Helvétius, and Beccaria were also contributors to it, as well as Hume, whose "Why Utility Pleases"[3] Bentham had read. It was, however, in 1768, that he chanced to read Dr. Joseph Priestley's *Essay on Government*, which contained the phrase "the greatest happiness of the greatest number."[4] After a few years the connection between utility and happiness was established: utility became the touchstone of virtue and the tool of happiness. He wrote: "I learnt to see that utility was the test and measure of all virtue; of loyalty as much as any: and that the obligation to minister to general happiness was an obligation paramount to and inclusive of every other."[5]

Bentham maintained that we all calculate, albeit not formally or carefully or with inclusion of all relevant factors. The virtuous person is a good calculator; evil is in error. "Vice may be defined to be a miscalculation of chances; a mistake in estimating the value of pleasures and pains. It is false moral arithmetic."[6]

Much writing and rewriting would alter the application of the principle and refine the meaning of the phrase "the greatest happiness of the greatest number." But the essential insight remained.

.oOo.

Bentham saw happiness as the primary and fundamental goal of human living. For him, to be or not to be was not the question. Rather, it was to be happy or not at all. The unhappy life was not worth living. For this, two conditions are necessary: "1. That . . . he should be exempt from those horrors—from those pains of mind .

. . infused . . . by the opium of the existence of man in a life to come. 2. That in regard to pleasures, he should not . . . be debarred from . . . reaping . . . any pleasure which he exercises without producing thereby pain to a preponderant amount . . . either in his own person or the person of any other."[7] Accordingly, "Happiness consists of . . . enjoyment of pleasures, security from pains."[8] Pleasure and pain are the universals of human existence. They pervade all experience, and fundamentally divide life into opposing camps.

For Bentham, it is obvious that "Nature has placed mankind under the governance of two sovereign masters, pain and pleasure. . . . The principle of utility recognizes this subjection, and assumes it for the foundation of that system, the object of which is to rear the fabric of felicity by the hand of reason and of law. Systems that attempt to question it, deal in sounds instead of sense, in caprice instead of reason, in darkness instead of light."[9]

> But, it may be said, "Your principle of utility is useless; it will not excite to virtuous action, it will not restrain from vicious." If it will not, there is no help for it; no other principle will stand in its stead . . . . What motives can be furnished by any other system—what motives which are not borrowed from this? Men may wear out the air with sonorous and unmeaning words; those words will not act upon the mind; nothing will act upon it but the apprehensions of pleasure and pain."[10]

By pleasure Bentham meant what a person wills to do—volitions—even though it may not necessarily bring enjoyment with it. On the other hand, pain is simple aversion.[11] "What is pleasure, and what is pain? Does every man form the same estimate? Far from it. That is pleasure which a man's judgment, aided by his memory, recommends and recognizes to his feelings *as* pleasure. No man can allow another to decide for him as to what is pleasure, or what is the balance, of the amount of pleasure."[12] Pleasure and pain, volition and aversion, are the fundamental ingredients of the ethical life. They are the human concern *par excellence*.

> The first inquiry, then, should be directed to that conduct which concerns the individual alone, and which has no influence upon the pains or pleasures of others; that is to say, the purely self-regarding. Where the influence of conduct does not reach beyond the individual,—where his thoughts, or tastes, or actions do not affect others,—his line of duty is plainly marked. He must provide for his own personal enjoyment, weighing one pleasure against another, taking into account all corresponding pains, and then draw that balance of happiness which will best stand the test of thought and of time. . . . In those relations with others where a man's own happiness is involved, those relations which may be deemed of extra-regarding prudence, Deontology will teach him to apply the same happiness-producing and misery-avoiding rules of conduct, and to watch the flux and reflux of his deportment towards others on his own individual well-being.[13]

Now, happiness is not directly synonymous with pleasure; it is the maximum of pleasure and the minimum of pain. This is so because pain and pleasure, even though theoretically self-exclusive, factually run into each other and are often indistinguishable. "A pleasure is single—happiness is a blended result."[14] Happiness "is the possession of pleasure with the exemption from pain. It is in proportion to the aggregate of pleasures enjoyed, and of pains averted."[15]

Bentham did not have in mind a mere theoretical definition of happiness, but a concrete and livable one. In fact, his concern was happiness rather than its definition. Concretely, happiness would always have to include both pain and pleasure. Happiness, as Plato might have said, is "of the whole." Bentham saw this as he fastened his inquiry around the statement "the greatest happiness of the greatest number." To pursue the greatest balance of pleasure over pain for oneself —to pursue one's happiness—was certain to have an effect upon the similar pursuit of happiness of one's neighbors. The point, then, was to produce an overall state of happiness, and to judge actions in terms of their positive or negative effect on the happiness of all.

Eventually Bentham moved from the concern for the happiness of "the greatest number" to that of *all* the individuals in a group. He felt that if the amount of happiness available was a relatively fixed quantity, then any redistribution of it in favor of "the greatest number" (that is, of the majority) would have to be done at the expense of the minority, thus lessening the amount of happiness altogether for the group as a whole. He argued this point with mathematical precision in a number of examples, one of which will suffice here:

> Be the community in question what it may, divide it into two unequal parts, call one of them the majority, the other the minority, lay out of the account the feelings of the minority, include in the account no feelings but those of the majority, the result . . . to the aggregate stock of happiness in the community [will be] loss not profit . . . .[16]

Now, utility was the quality Bentham felt was necessary in all actions directed toward the greatest happiness of the greatest number. As an ethical principle (i.e., as a reason for behaving morally) he gave it a deontological value. He saw it as the only reason that can ultimately justify moral behavior.

> By the principle of utility is meant that principle which approves or disapproves of every action whatsoever, according to the tendency which it appears to have to augment or diminish the happiness of the party whose interest is in question: or, what is the same thing in other words, to promote or to oppose that happiness. whatsoever; and therefore not only of every action of a private individual, but of every measure of government. . .
>
>   An action then may be said to be conformable to the principle of utility, or, for shortness sake, to utility . . .when the tendency it has to augment the happiness of the community is greater than any it has to diminish it . . . .
>
>   Of an action that is conformable to the principle of utility, one may always

say either that it is one that ought to be done, or at least that it is not one that ought not to be done. One may say also, that it is right it should be done; at least that it is not wrong it should be done, that it is a right action; at least that it is not a wrong action.[17]

In order to make utility concretely applicable, Bentham developed a set of considerations for measuring pleasure and pain. This is the "felicific" calculus:

To a person considered *by himself*, the value of a pleasure or pain considered *by itself*, will be greater or less, according to the four following circumstances:
    1. Its *intensity*.
    2. Its *duration*.
    3. Its *certainty* or *uncertainty*.
    4. Its *propinquity* or *remoteness*.
These are the circumstances which are to be considered in estimating a pleasure or a pain considered each of them by itself. But when the value of any pleasure or pain is considered for the purpose of estimating the tendency of any act by which it is produced, there are two other circumstances to be taken into the account; these are,
    5. Its *fecundity*, or the chance it has of being followed by sensations of the *same* kind, that is, pleasures, if it be a pleasure: pains, if it be a pain.
    6. Its *purity*, or the chance it has of *not* being followed by sensations of the *opposite* kind: that is, pains, if it be a pleasure, pleasures, if it be a pain.
These two last, however, are in strictness scarcely to be deemed properties of the pleasure or the pain itself; they are not, therefore, in strictness to be taken into the account of the value of that pleasure or that pain. They are in strictness to be deemed properties only of the act, or other event, by which such pleasure or pain has been produced; and accordingly are only to be taken into the account of the tendency of such act or such event.
To a *number* of persons, with reference to each of whom the value of a pleasure or a pain is considered, it will be greater or less, according to seven circumstances: to wit, the six preceding ones; viz.
    1. Its *intensity*.
    2. Its *duration*.
    3. Its *certainty* or *uncertainty*.
    4. Its *propinquity* or *remoteness*.
    5. Its *fecundity*.
    6. Its *purity*.
And one other; to wit:
    7. Its *extent*; that is, the number of persons to whom it *extends*; or (in other words) who are affected by it.

Not long after the publication of the first edition of the *Introduction*, Bentham framed the following verses as a mnemonic aid:

        *Intense, long, certain, speedy, fruitful, pure--*
        Such marks in *pleasures* and in *pains* endure.

Such pleasures seek, if *private* be thy end:
If it be *public*, wide let them *extend*.
Such *pains* avoid, whichever be thy view:
If pains *must* come, let them *extend* to few.[18]

The calculus was specifically designed to serve a legislator or a judge in apportioning happiness equally to all without respect of persons. It was not intended for private use, though nothing prevents its being used thus. The calculus, above all, could not dispense with discernment, "the art of judging of individual capacity,"[19] which he thought both rare yet impossible to supersede. The application of the calculus is very tedious, complex, and time consuming, but it can hardly be denied that, if properly applied, it would be effective in establishing what can best lead to the happiness of most members in a community.

.oOo.

# Additional Readings

## Sources

*The Works of Jeremy Bentham*, ed. John Bowring. Edinburgh: William Tait, 1843.
Jeremy Bentham, *Deontology, or the Science of Morals*, ed. John Bowring. 2 vols. London: Longman et al., 1834.
———. *An Introduction to the Principles of Morals and Legislation*, ed. J. H. Burns & H. L. A. Hart. London: The Athlone Press, 1970.
———. *Original Manuscripts*.
  -University College Collection, London.
  -Additional Manuscripts, British Museum.
  -Keynes Collection, King's College, London.

## Commentaries

C. M. Atkinson, *Jeremy Bentham*. London: Methuen & Co., 1905.
P. Baumgardt, *Bentham and the Ethics of Today*. Princeton: Princeton University Press, 1952.
Mary P. Mack, *Jeremy Bentham*. New York: Columbia University Press, 1963.
Leslie Stephen, *The English Utilitarians*. 3 vols. London: Duckworth & Co., 1900.

## Notes

1. Bentham, *Introduction to the Principles of Morals and Legislation* XVII, 282.

2. Bentham, *The Limits of Jurisprudence,* 115- 116.

3. David Hume, *Enquiry Concerning the Principles of Morals* [1751].

4. Mary Mack, *Jeremy Bentham* (New York: Columbia University Press, 1963), 102-103.

5. Bentham, *Fragment on Government. Works*, I, 269.

6. Bentham, *Deontology*, Vol. I, 131.

7. "J. B.'s Instruction for Living Happily or Not At All" [1831]. *Additional Manuscripts*, British Museum, 33551, 327-328.

8. *Introduction to the Principles of Morals and Legislation*, VII, No.1, 74.

9. *Introduction*, I, No.1, 11.

10. *Deontology*, Vol.2, 10-11.

11. Mack, *Bentham*, 220.

12. *University College Collection*, Box 149, 358; *Deontology,* Vol. I, 29.

13. *Deontology*, Vol. 2, 5-7.

14. *Works*, Vol. X, 585.

15. *Deontology*, Vol .I, 17.

16. "A Short History of Utilitarianism," *University College Coll*ection Box 13; *Deontology*, Vol. I, 328 *ff.*

17. *Introduction*, I, No. 2, 3, 6, 8, 10, 11-13.

18. *Introduction*, IV, No. 2, 3, 4, and note.

19. *Works*, II, 19.

# 16

## ARTHUR SCHOPENHAUER

### (1788-1860)

On that year Goethe would publish *Egmont* and Kant his *Critique of Practical Reason*; Mozart's three "great" symphonies (in E-flat, G-minor, and the "Jupiter") would be heard for the first time, and the Marquis de Laplace's *Laws of the Planetary System* would explain the regularity of the celestial orbs; people would riot in France for bread, while pretty flowers (hortensias and fuchsias) would be imported to Europe from Perú. The year was 1788, and in it, on February 22, Heinrich Floris Schopenhauer, wealthy merchant and trader of Danzig, and his wife, Johanna Henrietta, beheld their first born, a son, and named him Arthur.

For the next eight years Arthur was the sole center of attention—at least of Johanna, whose fun-loving and artistic leanings were in marked contrast to her husband's business sense. Then, in 1796, a sister, Adele, was born, and she joined Arthur in the idyllic peace of the family's countryside farm. There most of their childhood was spent, under the care of Frau Schopenhauer; daddy was much too busy with his business in the city.

Schooling was leisurely and diverse for Arthur: two years in Paris and Le Havre; three years in private school in Hamburg. Then, suddenly, he was fifteen, and Herr Schopenhauer pushed the business life on him, relented, compromised: serious study if Arthur wanted to pursue a literary career, or travel to learn the world before settling into business. Arthur chose the latter alternative, and after two years of travel (1803-1805) he returned to Hamburg and took a job as clerk to a merchant named Jenisch. Two months later, in April, 1805, Herr Schopenhauer was found dead, face down, in a gutter in Danzig, accident or suicide no one could determine, though the family suspected the latter.

Frau Schopenhauer closed the business in Danzig, invested the money, and moved with her daughter to Weimar, where she became a minor literary celebrity, wrote books, ran a salon which even Goethe attended now and then, and earned the undying jealousy of her son. Arthur, in the aftermath, remained chained to his desk in Hamburg, hating every minute of his business life, but bound by the promise to his father. Finally, in 1807, his mother convinced him that two years of misery was enough to keep a promise, and released him to the life of the mind.

During a brief sojourn in Weimar Arthur made the acquaintance of Goethe and Wieland, and felt encouraged by them to engage in study. In 1809 he received his inheritance and forthwith departed for the University of Göttingen to study medicine, but by his second year he had shifted to philosophy. By 1811 he was at the University of Berlin listening to Fichte and Schleiermacher, and in 1813 he earned his doctorate at the University of Jena and published his doctoral thesis, *On the Fourfold Root of the Principle of Sufficient Reason*. He was twenty-five years old. Curiously, Goethe noticed the work, and in profuse gratitude, Schopenhauer published *On Vision and Colors* (1816), in which he defended Goethe against Newton, but interpreted vision differently from Goethe.

Schopenhauer moved to Dresden, then, and set to work on his major work, *The World as Will and Idea*, which appeared in 1818, to scant review by the intellectual community. To rest from his labors Schopenhauer toured Italy, where he met Byron, and on his return (1820), he decided to become a lecturer at the University of Berlin. With what was becoming characteristic arrogance and stubbornness he set as the time for his lectures the very one in which Hegel taught his main course. Few students showed up to listen to the unknown upstart, who closed shop after only one semester.

Deterred from teaching but not from writing, he persisted in his studies until the plague drove him from Berlin in 1831. After some peregrinations he settled in Frankfurt-am-Main, and there, from 1833 until his death twenty-seven years later, he followed the same daily routine without exception. His routine, however, left ample time for wenching, writing, and playing the flute. He hated women, loved writing, and indulged the flute as well as lunch at the Englischer Hof. He was more an aesthete than an ascetic; he lived Book III though he thought Book IV of *The World as Will and Idea*. He kept a poodle named Atma, but his only offsprings were books: *On the Will in Nature* (1836), *The Two Fundamental Problems of Ethics* (1841), and *Parerga und Paralipomena* (1851), a collection of essays and apho- risms on, among other things, the miserable character of life. Engaged in such gloomy endeavors but a peace with himself he died of a heart attack on September 21, 1860.

.oOo.

Our philosophical garb is tailored from the rags of our experience. Schopen- hauer's pessimism reflects his poor relationship with his family, with women, and with the academic world—his frustrations with his world; his will- to-live was but the sublimation of his own stubbornness. A case in point: in 1819, the Danzig business in which he, his mother, and his sister had invested a lot of their money after Herr Schopenhauer's death, went bankrupt. The company offered its creditors thirty percent of their investment, and Frau Johanna and Adele accepted. Not Arthur. He demanded seventy percent on the spot or else one hundred percent. For two years he fought a legal battle with the defunct company, and in the end he did collect one hundred percent plus interest!

"My philosophy starts from Kant's," says Schopenhauer in the Preface to the second edition of *The World as Will and Idea*.[1] Indeed, it does. Kant's work was largely an answer to Hume's demonstration that causality cannot be perceived, and therefore is nothing but a generalization from perceived sequences and contiguities. In rebuttal, Kant maintained that cause was a category of the understanding imposed on the manifold of experience resulting from our perception of the world in the context of space and time. Cause was one of many categories, and their imposition by the mind upon the data of experience was what properly constituted the activity of thinking. While Kant described time and space as categories of perception, and cause, quality, quantity, and the rest, as categories of the understanding, Schopenhauer reduced all the latter to causality, tied this to time-space, and made their application to experience an involuntary, automatic matter.

The effect of thinking—that is, of the application of the categories of cause and space-time to experience—is the creation of the perceived world, the phenomenon. The world is for us a perceived world: "the world is my Idea,"[2] says Schopenhauer. Not my concept of it, but what I perceive it to be. What is constituted as my world is but a series of perceptions of it. The world exists only for a knowing subject; the sum total of experience is an object for a subject; in a sense akin to Berkeley's, the world's *esse* is its *percipi*. Or, as the Vedantins whom Schopenhauer studied would put it, existence is *mâyâ*, i.e., phenomenon.

Beyond Idea or Representation (*Vorstellung*), however, lies existence as it is in itself, independent of perception. This is the "thing-in-itself" (*Ding an sich*), the Kantian *noumenon*. But for Schopenhauer this *noumenon* is Will, will-to-exist: "Thing-in-itself signifies that which exists independently of our perception, in short that which properly is. For Democritus this was formed matter. It was the same at bottom for Locke. For Kant it was = X. For me it is Will."[3] The world, then, is Will *and* Idea, reality *and* appearance. But how is this known? Through the little window of the self: we are an analogy of the world.

There is to every self an objective side, a perceived dimension, namely, the body. The body is the self as perceived, as phenomenon. The body, we could say, is our Idea; that is, the body is constituted by the whole series of perceptions of it. But there is also an inner experience, imperceptible, subjective: impulses, stirrings, strivings, desires. This unreachable level of existence is the *noumenon* which Schopenhauer termed the Will.

For the individual, body and will are one.[4] The body is the phenomenal form, or the sensuous appearance of the will, while the will is the *noumenon* of the body. Body is representation; will is *Ding an sich*.

This identity is known in that the self's willing is nothing but bodily action: will is willing action. Says Schopenhauer: "the action of the body is nothing but the act of the will objectified, i.e., translated into perception."[5] The duality that is true in us is true also in the world. Moreover, the will in us is the same as the will in nature. The *noumenal* world, in other words, is one. It is the natural life force, striving toward the highest possible objectification, i.e., toward concrete existence and toward eventual phenomenalization. Conceiving the world as Idea is the ultimate phenomenalization of the Will, and it is achieved in and through us. In us the world as Will becomes Idea; the world's *esse* becomes *perceptum*. "In all Ideas . . . it is *one and the same Will* that reveals itself, i.e., enters the form of representation, enters objectivity."[6]

The Will's essence is blind "will-to-live." In Höffding's words, it is "the blind impulse towards existence which, working up from stage to stage, pressing knowledge into its service, and finally awaking to the full consciousness of its misery, is present in all things."[7] Will is the overarching strife to be and to persevere in existence. It knows no boundaries, and it seeks all possible advantage. In fact, in its effort to persist it gives rise to consciousness as a tool that renders the human more fit for survival than the animal. Nor is survival an individual achievement; our own individual striving for existence is really the Will's urge to preserve itself in and through us. Says Schopenhauer: "Every grade of the Will's objectification fights for the matter, the space, and the time of another . . . eagerly striving to appear, snatch the matter from one another, for each wishes to reveal its own Idea. This contest can be followed through the whole of nature; indeed only through it does nature exist."[8] And he quotes a saying of Empedocles preserved by Aristotle: "If strife did not inhere in all things, no difference would exist."[9] Will to live is experienced in a negative fashion, not as joy but as pain. For Schopenhauer, "only pain and want can be felt positively; and therefore they proclaim themselves; well-being, on the contrary, is merely negative."[10] What we really experience is strife, not peace. If anything, peace is lack of strife. Satisfaction of desire is a respite, not the mainstream. Only the deluded optimist thinks so, mistaking the faint flicker of one flame at night for reality when all around the darkness pervades everything; or thinking gold plate more real than the coarse metal underneath. "Certainly," he says, "human life, like all inferior goods, is covered on the outside with a false glitter; what suffers always conceals itself."[11]

However, some temporary respite from strife is achieved through art. From Schopenhauer Nietzsche learned that art can save us from the truth. This happens when intuition, i.e., pure perception, disengages us from the relentless harshness of the Will, and in a purely contemplative, disinterested mood, we forget, momentarily, that we are part of it. Some of us can do this better than others. As Höffding puts it, "men of genius are endowed in a high degree with the faculty of enjoying artistic representations of that which, in its naked reality, they flee."[12] This artistic deliverance, nevertheless, is never complete or permanent. Lasting salvation is achieved only through negation of the will-to-live. Salvation is *nirvâna*, and Schopenhauer does not hesitate to use the term in its Buddhist meaning. This, too, is the resignation of St. Francis who not only needed very little, but even the little that he needed, he needed very little. But what remains of the Will after it wills no more, Schopenhauer, any more than Buddha, cannot say. He writes:

> The denial of the Will to live does not in any way imply the annihilation of a substance; it means merely the act of nonvolition: that which previously *willed*, *wills* no more. This *will*, as thing in itself, is known to us only in and through the act of *volition*, and we are therefore incapable of saying or of conceiving what it is or does further after it has ceased to perform this act: thus this denial of the will to live is *for us*, who are phenomena of volition, a transition to nothingness.[13]

.oOo.

For Schopenhauer, there is no purpose to life. The will-to-live is blind. Nevertheless, the immense majority of people are convinced that there *is* a purpose to life, that there *is* a goal to be achieved, whether here or hereafter, and that this goal is happiness. From ancient times the conviction endures. What people consider happiness to be may be controverted, but that all want happiness is not. For Schopenhauer, this is an error: "There is only one inborn error, and that is the notion that we exist in order to be happy."[14]

The error arises from thinking that happiness is satisfaction because it momentarily extinguishes desire. The fact is, however, that any satisfaction is temporary, and that it is merely a pleasant interlude in an otherwise dreary series of desires. We need to be sober about this matter. A deliberate look at life cannot but expose the error of thinking that happiness is the goal of existence: "Suffering expresses itself clearly enough to the whole of human existence as its true destiny. Life is deeply steeped in suffering, and cannot escape from it; our entrance into it takes place amid tears, at bottom its course is always tragic, and its end is even more so."[15]

Further, the illusion that the goal of life is happiness is dispelled when we consider that happiness itself is always negative. It is the *negation* of pain, the *cessation* of desire, the *elimination* of displeasure, the *interruption* of pain, the *pacification* of strife.[16] All his arguments are based on the fact, he writes, "that the will, whose objectification is human life like every phenomenon, is a striving without aim or end."[17]

If happiness is negative (the negation of pain), then pain is the only positive experience; not positive in the sense of "good," but in the sense of "real." Pain, want, need, strife, are the only qualities of experience that can be really felt directly. Perhaps more exactly, the life force that is the will-to-live is experienced directly only as a striving, a desiring, a wanting, a paining. Therefore cessation of desire itself must be the ultimate good.

How is the cessation of desire achieved? Through resignation. Personal suffering awakens in the sufferer a knowledge of the futility of looking for respites, for momentary lulls in the unending strife, for the temporary stillness that comes when a want has been satisfied by the possession of the wanted object. The realization that the strife always returns, that desire is always reawakened, leads the wise sufferer to acquiesce to the fact of life, the indomitable energy of the will-to-live. With resignation comes, finally, salvation.

Schopenhauer called this stage *nirvâna*. *Nirvâna* is happiness, but clearly in a Buddhist sense. It is stillness, nothingness; but also unutterableness. And whether it is a presage of the future or merely the end of the present it is impossible to say. His advice? "He will be least afraid of becoming nothing in death who has recognized that he is already nothing now, and who consequently no longer takes any interest in his individual phenomenon, since in him knowledge has, so to speak, burnt up and consumed the will, so that there is no longer any will, any keen desire for individual existence, left in him."[18]

.oOo.

# Additional Reading

## Sources

Arthur Schopenhauer, *Essays and Aphorisms*, trans. & ed. R. J. Hollingdale. Baltimore: Penguin, 1970.
———. *On the fourfold Root of the Principle of Sufficient Reason*, trans. K. Hillebrand London, 1907.
———. *The Basis of Morality*, trans. A.B. Bullock London, 1903.
———. *The World as Will and Representation*, trans. E. F .J. Payne 2 vols.; Indian Hills, CO: The Falcon Wing's Press, 1958.

## Commentaries

Frederick Copleston, *A History of Philosophy*. 10 vols.; New York: Doubleday, 1963.
Frederick Copleston, *Arthur Schopenhauer, Philosopher of Pessimism*. London, 1946.
Harald Höffding, *A History of Modern Philosophy*. 2 vols.; New York: Dover Publications, 1955.
V. J. McGill, *Schopenhauer, Pessimist and Pagan*. New York, 1931.

## Notes

1. Schopenhauer, *The World as Will and Representation*, Vol. I, xxxi.
2. Ibid., Book I.1, 3.
3. Schopenhauer, *Parerga und Paralipomena*, in Copleston, *History of Philosophy* (New York: Doubleday, 1963), VII, Part 2, 30.
4. *World as Will and Representation*, Book II. 18, 102.
5. *World as Will and Representation*, Book II. 18, 100.
6. *World as Will and Representation*, Book II. 27, 143.
7. Höffding, *A History of Modern Philosophy* (New York: Dover Publications, 1955), II, 221.
8. *World as Will and Representation*, Book II. 27, 146-147.
9. Aristotle, *Metaphysics* II. 5 [$1000^b$ 1].
10. *World as Will and Representation*, "Supplement," IV, Ch. 46, 575.
11. *World as Will and Representation*, IV. 59, 325.
12. Höffding, *A History of Modern Philosophy*, II, 234.
13. *Parerga und Paralipomena*, in *Essays and Aphorisms* (Baltimore: Penguin, 1970), 61. Also *World as Will and Representation*, "Supplement," IV, Ch. 48, 609.
14. *World as Will and Representation*, Vol. II, Ch. 49, 634-635.
15. *World as Will and Representation*, Vol. II, Ch. 49, 635-636.
16. *World as Will and Representation*, Vol. I, Ch. 58, 319-320.
17. *World as Will and Representation*, Vol. I, Ch. 58, 320-321.
18. *World as Will and Representqtion*, Vol. II, Ch. 48, 609.

# 17

## MAX STIRNER

### (1806-1856)

Stirner was born in Bayreuth and christened Kaspar Schmidt, but the name was too plebeian. His classmates called him "Stirner" ("Bald Patch") because of his wide forehead. He saw in this nickname a forecast of genius. In 1826 he would matriculate at the University of Berlin as Max Stirner.

His father died when he was six months old. His mother, who married a second time, went progressively insane and was eventually committed in 1837. Stirner completed high school and moved on to higher learning, attending lectures by Hegel and Schleiermacher, and studying for a time in Königsberg. He struggled through his studies and finally passed his exams in 1834. His thesis, *Über Schulgesetze*, was enough to earn him a license to teach at the Gymnasium level, but not more.

Stirner married twice, in 1837 and in 1843. His first wife, Agnes Clara Kunigunde Burtz died during childbirth. His second wife, Marie Dähnhardt, left him. He seems to have been fond of them, but unable to share life with them.

Professionally, Stirner taught for a while at the Königliche Realschule in Berlin, and from 1839 at Madame Gropius' institute for the education of young ladies. He resigned in 1844. During the early 1840s he began to frequent the meetings of the Young Hegelians who called themselves *Die Freien*, "The Free Ones." There he met the likes of Ruge, Marx, Bruno Bauer, Otto Wigand, Köppen, and others, as well as his second wife, Marie. This group seems to have provided some kind of nursery for the development of his ideas—although he did not share them generously before they appeared in print. Several short pieces came out at this time, including two articles published by Marx in the *Rheinische Zeitung*. But the major event in his life was the publication of *The Ego and His Own* (1845). That the book was received seriously is proved by the fact that several members of *Die Freien* reacted to it immediately and in many cases with fervor: Marx and Engels alone devoted two thirds of *The German Ideology* to a satirical rebuttal of *The Ego*.

After this publication Stirner faded out of existence rapidly. The two volumes of *Die Geschichte der Reaction* (1852) were hardly noticed. He died ignominiously, stung by a poisonous fly, on June 25, 1856.

.oOo.

Stirner argues the position of the extreme individualist. In the wake of the Hegelian deification of the Universal Spirit, Stirner affirms the primacy of the particular and the material, the Ego of flesh and blood. Against the worship of the collective, Stirner preaches the cult of the individual. No liberal humanistic fiddle-faddle for him; his concern is only for the concrete self. No commitment to cause, no loyalty to humankind, religion, reason, or God. For Stirner, all this entails enslavement, the subordination of the individual to what is not it. What matters is the self. "Man has killed God in order to become now—'sole God on high.'"[1] From now on, "the divine is God's concern; the human, man's."[2] Our motto is to be *homo homini Deus*—humans are humanity's God.[3]

Stirner's creation is the egoist, "a man who, instead of living to an idea, that is, a spiritual thing, and sacrificing to it its personal advantage, serves the latter."[4] His concern is only with himself, with his concrete, corporeal self and with the enjoyment it can have. The egoist is not concerned with humankind, which is an abstraction. Stirner writes, "He who is infatuated with *Man* leaves persons out of account so far as that infatuation extends, and floats in an ideal, sacred interest. *Man*, you see, is not a person, but an ideal, a spook."[5]

The egoist is concerned only with its own, with its "property." Stirner assumes that in our heart of hearts we all desire only one thing, to possess and count everything as our property, to have everything in our power, to control everything. This ownership is for Stirner a matter more of will than of riches, of mastery rather than of actual accumulation. It is a matter of decision. Everything, therefore, is mine if I will it to be. Nothing stands in my way. "The only thing I am not entitled to is . . . what I do not entitle myself to."[6]

Thus the world, as Stirner envisages it, would ideally be populated by self-assertive egoists enjoying themselves in freely chosen cooperation. The norm of morality is "*egoistic right*: it is right for me, therefore it is right."[7] The name of such a society is "The Union of Egoists."[8] Its motto is, "The *people* is dead. —Up with *me*!"[9]

Clearly, for Stirner the *zoön politikon* is a spook. The only human reality is that of the individual affirming its right without regard for anyone else. Individual self-possession: *that* is the point. The fact that there may be other egos in the world is not its concern at all. The ego's ego is affirmed and enjoyed solely for itself. It is unique: "I am not an ego along with other egos, but the sole ego: I am unique. Hence my wants too are unique, and my deeds; in short, everything about me is unique. And it is only as this I that I take everything for my own, as I set myself to work, and develop myself, only as this. I do not develop men, nor as man, but, as I, I develop—myself. This is the meaning of the—*unique one.*"[10]

Stirner is aware of the narrowness of this claim, as much as he is aware of his own mortality. The values of the unique one arise and cease with it, they do not pre-exist, nor do they have endurance beyond the ego's life. The ego is their sole creator, and it creates them out of nothing. Borrowing a line from Goethe, Stirner exults, "I have founded my affair on nothing."[11]

.oOo.

Given the individualistic orientation of Stirner's philosophy, it is obvious that his concern for happiness is going to be centered around the individual, not the group, or the collective, or humankind. Happiness, for him, means enjoyment. He gives this term a connotation of pleasure. By pleasure he means a certain abandon in the enjoyment of life that is concerned only with the present moment and has no thought for the future. We spend too much time longing for joy and not enough enjoying life:

> If the enjoyment of life is to triumph over the longing for life or hope of life . . . it must crush spiritual and secular poverty, exterminate the ideal end—the want of daily bread . . . . He who must expend his life to prolong life cannot enjoy it, and he who is still seeking for his life does not have it and can as little enjoy it; both are poor, but "blessed are the poor."[12]

The individual pursuit of happiness does not entail living the life of a solitary, but it does require the pursuit of a love that remains centered around the self. No altruism here, but an open and unabashed self-seeking that safeguards one's self regardless of what one shares with others. As far as the other is concerned, "it constitutes my pleasure and my happiness to refresh myself with his happiness and his pleasure. But *myself, my own self,* I do not sacrifice to him, but remain an egoist and—enjoy him."[13]

.oOo.

# Additional Readings

## Sources

Max Stirner, *The Ego and His Own*, ed. S. T. Byington. London: Fifield, 1912.
———. *Über Schulgesetze*. Dresden: Verlag des dritten Reiches, 1920.
———. *Die Geschichte der Reaction*. Berlin: Allgemeine Deutsche Verlags-Anstalt, 1852.
———. *Kleinere Schriften*. Treptow: Bernard Zack, 1914.

## Commentaries

John Henry Mackay, *Max Stirner, Sein Leben und sein Werk*. Berlin: Schuster und Loeffler, 1898.
R. W. K. Paterson, *The Nihilist Egoist, Max Stirner*. London: Oxford University Press, 1971.
Karl Marx and Frederick Engels, *The German Ideology*. London: Lawrence and Wishart, 1965.
Martin Buber, *Between Man and Man*. New York: Macmillan, 1967.

## Notes

1. *The Ego and His Own*,, 202.
2. *The Ego*, "Preface."
3. *The Ego*, 75.
4. *The Ego*, 37.
5. *The Ego and His Own*, 101.
6. *The Ego and His Own*, 247.
7. *The Ego and His Own*, 248.
8. *The Ego and His Own*, 278.
9. *The Ego and His Own*, 284.
10. *The Ego and His Own*, 483.
11. *The Ego and His Own*, 490.
12. *The Ego and His Own*, 428.
13. *The Ego and His Own*, 385-386.

# 18

## JOHN STUART MILL

### (1806--1873)

John Stuart Mill was born in London, on May 20, 1806. He was the eldest son of philosopher James Mill, a friend, disciple, and collaborator of Bentham. Mill's mother's name was Harriet. She was beautiful but dull. Her husband despised her, and John found himself unable to be loved by her. The love came, instead, from Sarah Austin, a neighbor of the Mills's and of Bentham's, wife of professor John Austin, who became substitute mother, friend, confidant, and intellectual companion.

Young John was educated by his father in all manner of subjects, and prepared to become Bentham's spokesman. Today we would call James Mill an extreme behaviorist, convinced as he was that all differences among humans are the result of nurture. Hence his complete control of the education of his son according to the principles of Helvetius.

By the time he was eight years old, John had read Aesop's *Fables* in the original Greek, which he began to study at age three. This was the lightest of his readings. The heavier stuff included Xenophon's *Anabasis*, *Cyropaedia*, and *Memorabilia*, the whole of Herodotus, some Lucian, some of the accounts of Diogenes Laërtius, some speeches of Isocrates, and six dialogues of Plato.[1] He read, besides, Hume, Gibbon, the historians Millar, Burnet, Watson, Robertson, Hooker, Plutarch, as well as accounts of journeys to various parts of the globe. Also *Robinson Crusoe, Arabian Nights, Don Quixote*, and some more pedestrian tales.

At eight he began the study of Latin and of geometry, Euclid's *Elements* being his main text for the latter. To these he added the *Iliad* (in Pope's translation), the

*Odyssey*, some plays of Sophocles, Euripides, and Aristophanes; Thucydides, Demosthenes, Aischines, and the *Rhetoric* of Aristotle. Soon followed the *Bucolics* of Virgil, the *Aeneid*, most of Horace, Phaedrus, Sallust, Ovid, Terence, Lucretius, and some of Cicero's speeches.

At the age of twelve he began to study Aristotelian logic, both in the original and in the Scholastic commentaries. This was followed by studies of contemporary political economy, Adam Smith and David Ricardo. Later on he would study French, psychology, chemistry, botany, and Roman law.

His formal education came to an end when he began work for the East India Company, in 1823, at the young age of seventeen. He was promoted to assistant examiner in 1828, and from 1836 to 1856 he supervised the Company's relations with the Indian states in which it operated. He became Examiner in 1856.

In 1826, at the age of twenty, John felt that the wonderful education he had received in his youth had given him a sort of artificial knowledge, all pre-packaged and dispensed by his father. He thought of himself as "a mere reasoning machine,"[2] and he resented the thought. A crisis ensued, as a result of which he set out to re-educate himself, beginning with the reading of Wordsworth, for he was determined now to include the cultivation of feelings in his transformation.

The crisis—a nervous break-down—was both intellectual and emotional. On the emotional side, Mill "blamed both his parents: his father for the absence of genuine paternal love, which stultified his capacity for forming normal personal relationships; his mother for being intellectually limited, unimaginative, and obsessed with domesticity."[3] On the intellectual side, one of the major departures for him at this time was from the rigid calculations of Bentham's hedonism. First of all, he understood that happiness is not attained simply because it is sought. As he put it,

> It occurred to me to put the question directly to myself: "Suppose that all your objects in life were realized; that all the changes in institutions and opinions which you are looking forward to, could be completely effected at this very instant: would this be a great joy and happiness to you?" And an irrepressible self-consciousness distinctly answered "No!" At this my heart sank within me: the whole foundation on which my life was constructed fell down. All my happiness was to have been found in the continual pursuit of this end.[4]

As is clear, the attainment of all the conditions that would seem to accompany the appearance of happiness, did not seem to him sufficient for happiness itself. Pursuit of the happiness of all (Bentham's idea) did not guarantee one's own happiness. This conclusion seems to have entailed a second point, namely, that feelings, or non-quantifiable states of mind, were an intimate aspect of happiness, and therefore had to be reckoned with.[5]

In 1830, in the midst of this crisis, Mill met Harriet Taylor (née Hardy). He was twenty-four and she one year younger and married to John Taylor, a prosperous wholesale druggist, honorable and amiable, but by all accounts indeterminate and dull. That first meeting sealed their friendship. Carlyle, who was not present but had the account from first hand witnesses, wrote how Mill, "who up to that time, had never so much as looked at a female creature, not even a cow, in the face, found himself opposite those great dark eyes, that were flashing unutterable things while he was discoursin' the utterable concernin' all sorts o' high topics."[6] She was the light that Mill needed to get himself out of his tunnel.

From then on their friendship blossomed, despite criticisms from his family and friends. The young friends were aided by John Taylor's agreement, under duress, to maintain the marriage in appearance only, and to allow Mill access to "Harry" whenever he pleased. Thus the relationship continued until Taylor's death in 1849.

The crisis eventually subsided, and Mill embarked in a political career on the side, as it were, since his "job" continued to be at the East India Company. His involvement took place through his writings and through his active membership in various political and philosophical organizations. Thus, a part-time journalist of sorts, Mill contributed through his writings to various political reforms.

In 1851, Mill married Harriet. At the wedding he legally renounced any power, control, and rights over her and her finances. Neither his own mother (his father had died in 1836), his brothers, or his sisters, were invited to the wedding. With the marriage he broke with the rest of his family, with whom his relations had always been strained.

All his life Mill was a supporter of women's rights. In his late teens he had been an advocate of birth control. Against Comte he had maintained that the apparent inferiority of women was due to social restrictions and the denial of their rights rather than to lower innate capacities.[7] Harriet herself, with his encouragement, wrote a pamphlet, "The Enfranchisement of Women" (1851). Later, in *On Liberty* (1859), he recommended the institution of equal education for girls and boys.

Because of his known advocacy of women's rights, he drew the support of women's groups in his successful run for a Parliament seat from Westminster, in 1865, and lost little time in submitting a Petition on women's suffrage, ably speaking on its behalf on May 20, 1867, though the measure failed to carry. But the conservative tide waxed stronger, and he lost his bid for re-election to Parliament in 1868. In 1867, together with other political liberals, Mill founded what became known as the National Union of Women's Suffrage Societies, and for them he published, in 1869, *The Subjection of Women*, which he had penned in 1861.

Harriet died suddenly in 1858, and so did the East India Company. But while the dissolution of the latter left him a good pension of £1,500 that guaranteed his leisure to write and travel, the death of his wife plunged him in melancholy. Through his later years he spent more and more time at Avignon, where she had died, and where he was accompanied by his loving stepdaughter, Helen Taylor. There he died of a virulent attack of erysipelas, at seven o'clock in the morning of Wednesday, May 7, 1873. His last words, to his stepdaughter Helen, were, "You know that I have done my work."[8]

.oOo.

The work that established Mill as a philosopher was the *System of Logic* (1843), which was both hailed by friends and criticized by opponents, whom he answered through the eight editions published during his life. There followed *Essays on Some Unsettled Questions of Political Economy* (1844), *Principles of Political Economy* (1848), *On Liberty* (1859), *Dissertations and Discussions*, where he collected his best essays, and which comprised four volumes in the posthumous edition of 1875, *Considerations on Representative Government* (1861), *Utilitarianism* (first *seriatim* in 1861, then as a whole in 1863), and *An Examination of Sir William Hamilton's Philosophy* (1865), which gave him the opportunity both of criticizing his opponents and of developing further ideas first presented in *System of Logic*. There followed still *The Subjection of Women* (1869). *Autobiography* (1873) and *Three Essays on Religion* (1874) were published by his stepdaughter Helen after his death.

For Mill, logic is not merely a system for guaranteeing the formal validity of reasoning; it is the systematization of the rules for obtaining truth: it is "the science of *proof or evidence*,"[9] and it is necessary because most knowledge is obtained through inference from empirical data. Though intuition is a valid source of truth, Mill considers it a legitimate method only for intra-psychic events or self-knowledge. As far as the external world is concerned, only inference can give us truth.

Mill was writing before Russell, symbolic logic, and computers; but also after Bacon and Locke. Logic, he thought, had to be grounded on experience, but in true Aristotelian fashion, he thought it moved in the realm of words; therefore the precise use of language was necessary to guarantee the perfection of the instrument:

> Language is evidently . . . one of the principal instruments or helps of thought; and any imperfection in the instrument or in the mode of employing it is confessedly liable to . . . confuse and impede the process and destroy all ground of confidence in the result.[10]

One of Mill's major tasks, therefore, is an analysis of "names" and of propositions which, again with a bow to Aristotle, he admits as being either affirming or denying (*ponens/tollens*).

What kinds of conclusions or truths could logic help one attain? Having rejected the possibility of intuitive or *a priori* knowledge of the external world, and having affirmed the grounding of all knowledge on experience, Mill rejects what Kant called "synthetic *a priori*" propositions. Logic, therefore, he thought, if properly applied, could guarantee only the truth of propositions inferred from observed or experienced phenomena, nothing more. But in a fashion that anticipated the conclusions of Gödel a hundred years later, he admitted that there might be propositions that are true but unprovable within the system, though he thought their affirmation was the result of psychological necessity, not the compulsion of objective truth.

One of the characteristics of Mill's *System* is the importance given to the syllogism. He distinguishes, as was the custom, two main types of syllogism, deductive and inductive. Deductive reasoning, the syllogistic descent from the general to the particular, he considers but an explanation or elucidation of the truth contained in the major premise. Deduction does not give rise to any new knowledge. The truth of the conclusion, if the syllogism has been properly constructed, is already contained in the major premise. Inductive reasoning, on the other hand, the generalization achieved from the observation of similar instances or occurrences, produces new knowledge and is, therefore, the only true inference. In fact, one of the major functions of inductive reasoning is to arrive at generalizations which can in turn become major premises for deductive reasoning. From this point of view, deduction is not useless, since it particularizes again the generalizations that, through induction, had originally been made from the particular.

The significance of the re-assertion of the importance of reasoning—even syllogistic reasoning—can hardly be overestimated. Despite the various criticisms that may be leveled at his whole system or at aspects of it, this surely stands out as an important contribution to the furtherance of scientific inquiry in the modern world. For Mill understood well that empirical observation and experimentation alone are not sufficient for the advancement of science; that is, for increasing our knowledge of the world. It is the reasoning we do with the data accumulated through observation and experiment that eventually gives us knowledge:

Of great significance, too, was Mill's extension of the logic of what today we would call the physical sciences to the realm of human affairs, what he called "the moral sciences," which included psychology, moral development, sociology, and history. Here, two animadversions are important. The first is that Mill sought through his writings to extricate these studies from a crass empiricism—mere observation, experimentation, and collection of data—into which, even then, they had been allowed to flounder. He thought this task the more important because the study of human affairs is by far worthier than the study of the physical universe. And with relish, he quoted Pope: "The proper study of Mankind is Man."[11] The second point, equally important, concerned the exactitude with which Mill thought this study could be conducted. Here, Mill argued that the science of human affairs could not be an exact science because the data needed for such certitude could never be found altogether, at the same time, or in similar circumstances. In this case, he argued, one must be satisfied with approximation, but this is sufficient for the purposes of political and social sciences.[12] Thus Mill rounded out his *System* by applying to the social sciences the same logic he had applied to the physical ones, though with different degrees of certainty in each case. The starting point for both was experience; the goal was correct action; the thesis, as Nagel summarized it, that "sound action is possible only on the basis of sound theory, and sound theory (whether in the natural or in the social sciences) is the product of a sound logic."[13]

.oOo.

In his *Autobiography*, Mill writes how upon his return to England after a short visit to France when he was sixteen, he read and studied Bentham in great detail, and accepted Bentham's utilitarianism as the cornerstone of his own thinking: "The 'principle of utility' understood as Bentham understood it, and applied in the manner in which he applied it . . . fell exactly into its place as the keystone which held together the detached and fragmentary component parts of my knowledge and beliefs. It gave unity to my conception of things."[14]

Following Bentham, Mill took utility as the principle for determining when an action is moral. The goal of life is happiness, which Mill interpreted as pleasure and the absence of pain. The goal of morality is to render people happy. The principle of utility states "that actions are right in proportion as they tend to promote happiness; wrong as they tend to produce the reverse of happiness."[15] The pursuit and procurement of happiness, therefore, is embedded into a system of ethics. The question, then, is not one merely of determining what is happiness, but equally of deciding how happiness should be pursued. To strive for happiness is to strive to be moral, and vice versa. The criterion, both of happiness and morality, is utility; that is, the tendency of one's acts to promote or hinder happiness.

The principle of utility had been formulated by Bentham, but Mill's use of it is in no way identical. In fact, Mill is very critical of Bentham, on several grounds. Mill accepts in a psychological sense that human actions are determined by pleasure and pain. This formula is an echo of the old definition of good, *bonum est quod omnia appetunt* ("the good is what is desired by all"). The echo, expressed differently, maintains that everything is desired *sub specie boni*: we are unable to will evil *per se*. But while accepting this, Mill criticizes Bentham for claiming that our actions are prompted by the prospect of pain or pleasure that may accrue *as a consequence*. Mill counters that pain and pleasure, as motives, are not always consequent, but are often antecedent; that is, they precede and induce action. Moreover, Mill contends that in enumerating the motives for action Bentham fails to reckon with conscience, with the feeling of duty.[16] Finally, as was mentioned above, Mill thinks that Bentham failed to account for feelings, such as the emotions of music and poetry, and that it was the exclusion of such a realm of human experience and endeavor that had allowed him to view the quantification of pleasure as the paramount method of ethics.

For Bentham, the meaning of pleasure seems to be univocal. If pleasure alone is happiness, then the more pleasure, the greater the happiness. But people have preferences as to pleasures. Therefore happiness consists in the greatest possible enjoyment of the preferred pleasures. In terms of social policy, this must be understood as the procurement of the greatest pleasure for each person or group according to its preference. There is here a minimum involvement of quality as preference, and it is possible to admit this without introducing any kind of hierarchy among pleasures. In fact, if pleasure *alone* is the criterion of happiness, then the greater the amount of the preferred pleasure, the greater the happiness. This seems to have been Bentham's point of view.[17]

But Mill seems to go beyond mere preference when he admits "the superiority of mental over bodily pleasures," and even that "some kinds of pleasure are more desirable and more valuable than others."[18] Obviously, Mill is introducing here a criterion other than the mere quantity of pleasure. There is a question of quality here, of gradation, that is not merely quantitative but, rather, pertains to the quality of each pleasure. At the same time there seems to be a qualitative hierarchy among pleasures.

Mill dismisses the usual justification of the higher worth of intellectual pleasures, in vogue since Aristotle, as merely "circumstantial." He needs an *intrinsic* criterion, something within pleasure itself that will allow for qualitative distinctions. He thinks he has found it in the fact that humans are higher beings than animals, and *therefore* enjoy more those pleasures which are more connected with what makes them human—that is, different from animals. "A being of higher faculties requires more to make him happy," he writes.[19] And elsewhere: "I regard utility as the ultimate appeal on all ethical questions; but it must be utility in the largest sense, grounded on the permanent interests of man as a progressive being."[20]

Now it is clear that Mill here is adding a qualitative consideration to pleasure that at the same time introduces a hierarchy among pleasures, so that the Benthamite calculus can no longer be applied rigidly to a mere sum of pleasures. That Mill is conscious of this is clear, too, from his criticism of Bentham. In his essay, "Bentham" (1838), he writes: "Man is never recognized by him [Bentham] as a being capable of pursuing spiritual perfection as an end; of desiring, for its own sake, the conformity of his own character to his standard of excellence, without hope of good or fear of evil from other source than his own inward consciousness."[21]

But the question is whether or not in doing this Mill is introducing into his system a criterion of happiness extraneous to pleasure, and whether or not this criterion is human nature in its widest acceptance. Bradley thought so already in Mill's time.[22] Copleston also thinks so,[23] and his view may be true if one considers pleasure purely from a theoretical point of view. But Mill does not do that. For him, "happiness is not an abstract idea but a concrete whole."[24] In the concrete, he sees the determination of what is pleasure as a determination made by human beings aware of their humanness. This means, for him, that the higher the being, and the more developed the being's capacities for all kinds of pleasures, the greater (and higher) the total sum of pleasure will be. In other words, in the abstract, all pleasures are equal, so the more of them the better; in the concrete, "more" depends on an enlarged potential for diverse pleasures, with a corresponding qualitative distinction among them. When this happens, Mill finds that consistently people prefer the pleasures of contemplation to those of eating strawberry ice cream. Moreover, he argues that their being capable of more pleasures enlarges quantitatively the total amount of their pleasure (as well as the total amount of pleasure altogether), even though it may also render them aware of the final finitude of all human happiness: "It is better to be a human being dissatisfied than a pig satisfied; better to be Socrates dissatisfied than a fool satisfied. And if the fool, or the pig, are of a different opinion, it is because they only know their own side of the question. The other party to the comparison knows both sides."[25]

.oOo.

# Additional Readings

## Sources

John Stuart Mill, *Collected Works*. 31 vols. Toronto: University of Toronto Press, 1963—.
———. *Autobiography*. New York: P. F. Collier & Son, 1937.
———. *On Liberty*, in vol.43 of *Great Books of the Western World*, ed. Robert M. Hutchins. Chicago: Encyclopaedia Britannica, Inc., 1952.
———. *Utilitarianism*, ed. Oskar Piest. Indianapolis: Bobbs-Merrill Co., Inc., 1957.
———. *Philosophy of Scientific Method*, ed. Ernest Nagel. New York: Hafner Publishing Co., 1950. (This is an abridged version of the *System of Logic*, and includes selections from other works).

## Commentaries

Robin Barrow, *Utilitarianism*. Brookfield, VT: Edward Elgar Publishing Co., 1991.
Fred R. Berger, *Happiness, Justice, and Freedom*. Berkeley: University of California Press, 1984.
Francis H. Bradley, *Ethical Studies*. London: Oxford University Press, 1927.
Frederick Copleston, *A History of Philosophy*. 10 vols. New York: Doubleday, 1966.
Josephine Kamm, *John Stuart Mill in Love*. London: Gordon & Cremonesi, 1977.
Michael St. John Packe, *The Life of John Stuart Mill*. New York: Macmillan, 1954.
Geoffrey Scarre, *Logic and Reality in the Philosophy of John Stuart Mill*. Dordrecht: Kluwer Academic Publishers, 1989.
Leslie Stephen, *The English Utilitarians*. 3 vols. New York: A.M. Kelley, 1968.
Thomas Woods, *Poetry and Philosophy*. London: Hutchinson & Co., 1961.

## Notes

1. Mills, *Autobiography* I (New York: P. F. Collier & Son, 1937), 9-10

2. *Autobiography* IV, 71.

3. Kamm, *John Stuart Mill in Love* (London: Gordon & Cremonesi, 1977), 27.

4. *Autobiography* V, 86.

5. Copleston, *A History of Philosophy* (New York: Doubleday, 1966), 8/1, 43.

6. Quoted in Kamm, *John Stuart Mill in Love*, 32.

7. Ibid., 83.

8. Kamm, *John Stuart Mill in Love*, 204; Packe, *The Life of John Stuart Mill* (New York: Macmillan, 1954), 507.

9. *System of Logic*, "Introduction," 2, 11.

10. *System of Logic* I, 1, 1, 13.

11. *System of Logic* VI, 1, 1, 309.

12. *System of Logic* VI, 3, 2, 312-313.

13. Nagel, *Philosophy of Scientific Method*, xxvii.

14. *Autobiography* III, 45.

15. *Utilitarianism* II, 10.

16. "Remarks on Bentham's Philosophy," *Collected Works* X, 12 *ff.*

17. Copleston, *A History of Philosophy* 8/1, 47.

18. *Utilitarianism* II, 12.

19. Ibid., 13.

20. *On Liberty* I, 272.

21. *Collected Works* X, 95 = *Dissertations and Discussions* I, 359.

22. Bradley, *Ethical Studies* (London: Oxford University Press, 1927), 85-141.

23. Copleston, *A History of Philosophy* 8/1, 47-49.

24. *Utilitarianism* IV, 47.

25. *Utilitarianism* II, 14.

# 19

## KARL MARX

### (1818-1883)

It was definitely not a good thing to be Jewish in Germany at the beginning of the Nineteenth century, so Hirschel Levi, son of the rabbi of Trier, decided to become a Christian. He changed his name to Heinrich Marx. The move was harder on his wife, the former Henriette Pressburg, who claimed a long rabbinical line among the Jewish community in Holland. She acquiesced (though she delayed her baptism until 1825). The year was 1817. One year later, on May 5, 1818, their first child was born. They named him Karl Heinrich.

From 1830 to 1835 young Karl attended the Trier High School, where he learned his Latin, Greek, French, Mathematics, and History, which he didn't like yet. In 1835 he entered the University of Bonn ostensibly to study law. In fact, he spent his time writing poetry, squandering money, drinking, disturbing the peace, dueling, and presiding over the student body. Much of the poetry dealt with pretty Jenny von Westphalen, daughter of Baron von Westphalen, a friend of the Marx family and Karl's intellectual mentor since his high school days. Years later Karl would dedicate his doctoral thesis to the Baron who had inspired him "to perceive, behind the veils that hide it, the shrine that burns at the heart of this world."[1]

In 1836 Karl transferred to the University of Berlin, but not before having become secretly engaged to Jenny von Westphalen in August. Here again, poetry took up his interest—three volumes worth of it, all dedicated to Jenny, and none of which have survived. Probably they did not deserve to survive. At any rate, their art was not up to Jenny's deserts, as he would write to his father in 1837.

Poetry gave way to philosophy. Marx had initially espoused the Romantic idealism of Fichte and Schelling, and disparaged Hegel. But he read Hegel in great detail, something many of Hegel's bitterest opponents never do, and suddenly found himself, as he put it, "converted to the enemy." His intellectual fervor brought him in touch with Karl Friedrich Köpen and history, Bruno Bauer and theology, Eduard Gans and law, as well as lesser luminaries like Adolf Rutenberg, who taught geography.

In 1838 Marx's father died, and faced with the necessity of earning a living, Marx began work on his doctoral thesis, which he submitted in April, 1841, to the University of Jena. The degree was granted *in absentia*. He then went to Trier for a while and joined Bauer in Bonn. Their plans for joint publication of antireligious tracts did not totally materialize, but the association was well known. When Bauer was dismissed from his teaching post in March, 1842, Marx gave up all hope for a university career and devoted himself, instead, to political journalism.

His initial articles dealt with freedom of the press and presented a strong critique of censorship. They were published mainly in the *Rheinische Zeitung* (Cologne), of which Marx became editor-in-chief in October, 1842. In November of the same year he met Engels for the first time. More articles against censorship followed, and in April, 1843, the *Rheinische Zeitung* was suppressed by the Government. Removed at least temporarily from the whirl of politics, Karl married Jenny in Kreuznach, on June 10, assured of an editorial position in Ruge's *Deutsch-Französische Jahrbücher*. For this he had to move to Paris in October.

Marx's stay in Paris was a fruitful one in many ways. His daughter Jenny (Jennychen) was born on May 1, 1844. The first—and last—issue of the *Jahrbücher* contained two articles by him, "Critique of Hegel's Philosophy of Right," and "On the Jewish Question." He met Bakunin, Proudhon, and, for the second time, Engels. He worked on the *Economic and Philosophical Manuscripts of 1844*, and he earned an order of expulsion from France.

In February, 1845, he moved to Brussels. Here he published (with Engels) *The Holy Family* and wrote "Theses on Feuerbach" (1845) and *The German Ideology* (1846); published *The Poverty of Philosophy* and *Wage Labor and Capital* (1847), and *The Manifesto of the Communist Party* (1848). In the midst of all this a second daughter, Laura, was born (September 26, 1845), and his first son, Edgar (December 17, 1847). He also dutifully earned a decree of expulsion from Belgium.

He returned to Cologne via Paris, and immediately began plans to publish a *Neue Rheinische Zeitung*. But the Government denied him citizenship, and after a trial for incitement to rebellion (for which he was acquitted—February, 1849), he was again expelled from Prussia. After a sojourn of a few months in Paris he was expelled from France and left the continent for London, where he arrived in September, 1849.

His last children were born in London—Heinrich Guido on November 5, 1849; Franziska on March 21, 1851; and Eleanor on January 16, 1855. Between the last two there was an illegitimate son, Frederick Demuth, who was born on June 23,

1851. Edgar, Heinrich, and Franziska died very young. His oldest daughter, Jenny, died of cancer on January 11, 1883. Laura and Eleanor survived their father. Both committed suicide—Laura on November 26, 1911, and Eleanor on March 31, 1898. The lone survivor was Frederick: he outlived Marx's all other children, and died on January 28, 1929.

Marx's years in London were not particularly eventful. He visited daily the library of the British Museum. There he conducted his extensive studies on political economy. He contributed articles to the *New York Daily Tribune*, and he wrote *The Eighteenth Brumaire of Louis Bonaparte* (1852), *Critique of Political Economy* (1859), the first volume of *Das Kapital* (1867), *The Civil War in France* (1871), *Critique of the Gotha Programme* (1875), as well as hundreds of articles in sundry journals.

His health began to deteriorate. Hemorrhoids, carbuncles, sciatica, tumor in the lungs, toothaches, earaches, and so forth. He and his wife Jenny, also in ill health, sought the cure at various European spas, but to no avail. Yet his work continued unabated.

Jenny died of cancer on December 2, 1881. Marx was too ill to attend the funeral. He sought the cure for bronchitis and pleurisy in Algiers, but his lungs were too far gone. He died at his home in London, attended by Helen Demuth (the family's longtime domestic and mother of his Frederick), sitting in his easy chair, at 2:45 in the afternoon of March 14, 1883. He was buried in the family grave at Highgate Cemetery.

.oOo.

At Marx's funeral Engels chose to mention what he considered to be Marx's two most significant discoveries, the law of the development of human history, and the theory of surplus value. A brief consideration of the first may provide a context for Marx's view of happiness.

Marx, said Engels, discovered "the simple fact . . . that mankind must first of all eat, drink, have shelter and clothing, before it can pursue politics, science, art, religion, etc."[2] In *The German Ideology*, Marx and Engels had written that "the first premise of all human existence and, therefore, of all history [is] . . . that men must be in a position to live in order to be able to 'make history.' But life involves before everything else eating, drinking, housing, clothing and various other things. The first historical act is thus the production of the means to satisfy these needs, the production of material life itself."[3] Syllogistically, one might express it this way:

> First be, then philosophize.
> But to be is to labor.
> Therefore first labor, then philosophize.

To be is to be concretely; that is, to eat, drink, mate, and so forth. Eating, drinking, etc. —concrete being in the world—is what Marx understands as labor.

Labor is, in a sense, the short form for human conscious existence as it occurs concretely in human feeding, loving, protecting, etc. Labor is human action as it humanizes the world and renders it suitable for human habitation. Seen in this light, it is obvious that labor is a natural condition of human life. It is the natural necessity imposed by life upon all beings that must interact with their environments with awareness in order to survive.[4] It is also clear that labor (that is, conscious activity) defines the human reality. We are what we do and as we do: "As individuals express their life, so they are. What they are, therefore, coincides with their production, both with what they produce and with how they produce. Hence what individuals are depends on the material conditions of their production"[5] Again, syllogistically:

> We are made by the world.
> But we make the world.
> Therefore we make ourselves.

We do not make ourselves by thinking, or by wishing, but by and through labor. Hence the emphasis placed by Marx on the socio-economic and political conditions in which we humans live: they make us be what we are. But we have made them. Therefore we make ourselves through them.

The structure is simple, and if everything were in a perfectly developed state, it would be easy to understand the human condition But things are otherwise. Humans have not always put their humanness ahead of everything. Through thousands of years of labor, they have created environments that are no longer humanizing. Just the contrary. The socio-economic world in which we live—which we have made—does not cater to our specifically human needs. Rather, it creates artificial needs and seeks to satisfy them above everything, ignoring the more fundamental human needs. We do things "to keep up with the Joneses," or "because of fashion," or "because we have the money," not because they satisfy an innate human need. A situation is thus created in which the artificial takes over the natural and subdues it. As a holograph of reality, the artificial stands by itself, removed from the truly concrete human, and alien to it. The phenomenon of the "seeming" human is thus created. Alienation takes over: "Man's own deed becomes an alien power opposed to him, which enslaves him instead of being controlled by him."[6]

Alienation is a rift between our human needs—the need for love, security, acceptance, wellbeing—and the needs created by the particular historical moment in which we live—the need to own huge automobiles, the need to be tanned, the need to join "the Pepsi generation," and so forth. Humanity is threatened when it becomes more important to have gone to "the right college" than really to know; when money talks, not real worth; when the muzzle of a gun is more cogent than moral suasion; when profits are more important than the conditions of life.

Marx spent a great deal of time exposing alienation, describing its historical rise, and suggesting ways of eliminating it. His inquiries took him into the study of political economy, for he never once allowed himself to forget that alienation is not a mere concept but a concrete experience. It is an illness, and like all illnesses, it is not cured by sweet talk but by real medicine.

The proliferation of socio-economic details in Marx's writings has often obliterated Marx's central concern for the human—the human, indeed, in its concrete socio-economic setting, but nonetheless the human. His primary objective was the restoration of the human in all its richness and fullness. He saw this as the most radical of all activities. As he put it, "to be radical is to grasp things by the root. But for man the root is man himself. [Hence] . . . the categorical imperative to overthrow all those conditions in which man is an abased, enslaved, abandoned, contemptible being."[7]

.oOo.

For Marx, happiness is a human experience as well as an ideal. By this he means that happiness belongs to humans as humans, regardless of their social status, rank, power, or riches. Such happiness, therefore, must be universal, not restricted to just one class, or one race. This does not mean that humans would enjoy the same type of happiness. Marx does not deny individuality. What he opposes is the restrictions imposed upon individuals in the pursuit of their happiness, restrictions based on class, race, or other artificial factors. Happiness, therefore, must satisfy essential human needs, physical and psychological, and must become possible for all men and women. This possibility is denied in our present-day societies.[8]

The reality of a true human experience is denied by alienation, the divorce between oneself and one's actions and the results of those actions, between oneself and on's fellows, between oneself and one's world. Happiness becomes demeaned: fun, revelry, wantonness, getting ahead, having a good time. Activities associated with happiness become apportioned according to class, status, and money. Happiness becomes associated with what money can buy. In fact, happiness itself becomes defined as that which money can buy.[9] True human happiness cannot exist within an alienated society. In such circumstances, what is generally called happiness is a false, inadequate sort of experience, a delusion created by the particular society. Marx brings this point out in his critique of religion, which creates a similar illusion:

> The abolition of religion as the *illusory* happiness of men, is a demand for their *real* happiness. The call to abandon their illusions about their condition is *a call to abandon a condition which requires illusions*. The criticism of religion is, therefore, *the embryonic criticism of this vale of tears* of which religion is the *halo*.[10]

Marx is clearly after an experience of human happiness that would satisfy the complete human being completely and concretely. It is not that Marx despises the imagination. On the contrary. But he is aware of the fact that the imagination has been used in order to divert human beings from the concrete pursuit of their happiness here and now, and to settle for a merely imaginary form in a future extraterrestrial life. To make happiness concrete the human context of human life must be made human. Only then can the expectations, desires, needs, that characterize us as human beings be fulfilled—that is, only then can happiness be achieved.

The true experience of happiness can take place only in a society in which human beings deal with each other and with their world in a purely human fashion, where "love can only be exchanged for love, trust for trust, etc.," where "if you wish to enjoy art you must be an artistically cultivated person; if you wish to influence other people you must be a person who really has a stimulating and encouraging effect upon others."[11] This human happiness is possible only in a communistic society such as might exist in the future.

.oOo.

# Additional Readings

## Sources

Karl Marx and Frederick Engels, *Collected Works* . New York: International Publishers, 1976.
Karl Marx, *Early Writings*, ed. T. B. Bottomore. New York: McGraw-Hill, 1964.
————. *The Poverty of Philosophy*. Moscow: Progress Publishers, 1973.
Karl Marx and Friedrick Engels, *The German Ideology*. Vol.5 of the *Collected Works*. New York: International Publishers, 1976.
————. *The Holy Family*. Moscow: 1956.
————. *Selected Works in One Volume*. New York: International Publishers, 1972.

## Commentaries

Louis Dupré, *The Philosophical Foundations of Marxism*. New York: Harcourt, Brace & World, Inc., 1966.
Erich Fromm, *Marx's Concept of Man*. New York: Ungar, 1969.
David McLellan, *Marx Before Marxism*. New York: Harper Torchbooks, 1970.
Robert Tucker, *Philosophy and Myth in Karl Marx*. Cambridge: Cambridge University Press, 1969.
Joel Carmichael, *Karl Marx*. New York: Charles Scribner's Sons, 1967.

## Notes

1. David McLellan, *Marx Before Marxism* (New York: Harper Torchbooks, 1970), 40.

2. *Karl Marx's Funeral*, in Fromm, *Marx's Concept Of Man* (New York: Ungar, 1969), 258.

3. *The German Ideology*, I, "Feuerbach," 41-42.

4. *Capital* I/1, Ch.1, 50.

5. *The German Ideology*, I, "Feuerbach," 31-32.

6. *The German Ideology* I, "Feuerbach," 47.

7. "Critique of Hegel's Philosophy of Right," in Fromm, *Marx's Concept of Man*, 52.

8. *The German Ideology*, I, "Feuerbach," 46-47.

9. *Economic and Philosophical Manuscripts*, Third Manuscript, 192-193.

10. "Contribution to the Critique of Hegel's Philosophy of Right," in *Early Writings*, ed. T. B. Bottomore (New York: McGraw-Hill, 1964), 43- 44.

11. *Economic and Philosophical Manuscripts*, Third Manuscript, 193-194.

# 20

# FRIEDRICH NIETZSCHE

## (1844-1900)

Nietzsche was born in 1844 at Röcken. His father, a Lutheran minister, died when the young boy was merely five years old, leaving him to be raised by a coterie of women, mother, sister, grandmother, and two maiden aunts. Little is known of his childhood except for the later reminiscences of his sister, and these cannot be trusted.

The young boy began his formal schooling at the age of fourteen, as a boarder at Schulpforta. He remained there for six years, and then proceeded to the University of Bonn (1864-1865) and later to Leipzig (1865-68), where he studied theology and classical philology. Upon the glowing recommendation of Professor Friedrich Ritschl, his mentor, he was appointed to a professorship at Basel, Switzerland, even though he had not completed his residency requirement. In his letter of recommendation Ritschl remarked that, even though Nietzsche was trained as a philologist with specific interest in Greek philosophy and literature, "he will simply be able to do anything he wants to do."

Nietzsche taught at Basel for ten years, with the sole interruption of volunteer service as a medical orderly during the Franco-Prussian War (1870). But this brief respite from academic life seems to have had a decisively bad effect on his health. In 1879 he had to resign his teaching post because of it, though he continued to receive a pension.

During his tenure at Basel, he was the colleague of the historians Jacob Burkhardt and Franz Overbeck, and he became the friend and admirer—at least for a time—of Richard Wagner. Nietzsche taught regularly every year. His courses varied from Latin Grammar and Greek Lyrical Poetry to Plato's Life and Doctrines and Pre-Platonic Philosophers. Enrollment was not great, but he averaged between 10 and 12 students per course.

After his retirement, Nietzsche spent most of his life commuting between Italy (during the winter) and Switzerland (during the summer). His ill health made it difficult for him to sustain his work. Often he went through periods when he could not read at all—but he thought a lot. Some of his ideas seem to have come upon him with great force and suddenness. Such was the case with the idea of eternal recurrence, which came to him in August, 1881, "6000 feet beyond man and time."[1] He hoped in vain for a disciple and intimate friend, but beyond the servile though useful help of Peter Gast and the detached interest of Frau Lou Salome, his hope was denied.

In January, 1889, Nietzsche collapsed on a street in Turin. Overbeck went there to fetch him and brought him to Basel, where he was hospitalized briefly. He also spent some time in an asylum in Jena, but was released and taken home to Naumburg by his mother, who cared for him until her own death in 1897. His sister Elizabeth Förster then transferred him to Weimar. The last eleven years of his life were without fruit. His mind was in abeyance most of the time, though he often had lucid bouts during which he engaged in conversation. He died on August 25, 1900.

By the time he died, Nietzsche was famous. Georg Brandes had been teaching courses on Nietzsche's philosophy at the University of Copenhagen since 1888. His fame rested on his books, none of which had anything to do with philology, Nietzsche's official specialty. In fact, except for some articles written while still a student, and fragments never published (like "Homer's Contest," and "Philosophy in the Tragic Age of the Greeks"), he never wrote anything specifically on philology. Even the fragments are not technical in the usual sense. His first book, *The Birth of Tragedy* (1872) created a big uproar partly because it was not scholarly in the traditional sense. What Nietzsche thought of the scholar can be gleaned from many passages in his writings, especially from *Schopenhauer as Educator* (1874).

Between 1873 and 1876 Nietzsche published a series of four books under the general title of *Untimely Meditations* (*David Strauss Confessor and Writer* [1873]; *On The Uses and Disadvantages of History for Life* [1873]; *Schopenhauer as Educator* [1874]; and *Richard Wagner in Bayreuth* [1876]). Then followed a period of tremendous productivity, during which he published a new book every year (plus revised editions of old ones). Thus, in succession, came *Human, All-too-Human* (1878), *The Dawn* (1881), *The Gay Science* (1882), *Thus Spoke Zarathustra* (1883-1885), *Beyond Good and Evil* (1886), *The Genealogy of Morals* (1887), and *The Wagner Case* (1888). After his break down and subsequent commitment, a number of books written before 1889 were published: *Twilight of the Idols* (1889), *The Antichrist* (1895), *Nietzsche Contra Wagner* (1895), and *Ecce Homo* (1908). The latter, a literary and personal autobiography, had been finished in 1888. *The Will to Power*, consisting of notes (both used and unused in previous works) was first assembled by Elizabeth Förster and later issued in complete form in 1911.

.oOo.

The central core of Nietzsche's mature philosophy is his conception of "the Will to Power." Power here has little, if anything, to do with what people usually understand by it: political power, the power of money, armaments, and demagoguery. To have power—rather, to strive for power—is to strive to overcome oneself, to be master over oneself without losing any of one's innate dynamisms. Speaking of Goethe as a great human being (an example of the *Übermensch*), Nietzsche wrote, "what he wanted was *totality*; he fought the mutual extraneousness of reason, senses, feeling, and will . . . ; he disciplined himself to wholeness, he *created* himself . . . he said Yes to everything that was related to him."[2] All his life Nietzsche struggled to find a concept that would allow him to integrate what in his youth he had called the Apollonian, and the Dionysian, reason and instinct, into a unit that would not sacrifice one for the other. He did not want reason to subdue passion into a harmless whimper. Neither did he wish passion to be senseless debauch. In Freudian terms, he did not want the Reality Principle so to triumph over the Pleasure Principle that the latter would be totally emasculated. Neither did he want the two united in some kind of *détente* or uneasy truce, as in the Freudian equivalent of the Nirvana Principle. He wanted to achieve a unity of tension that would incorporate a great deal of power to control because the impetus requiring control was developed to the utmost. He wished for an Id strengthened to its farthest limits, and equally for an Ego with power enough to channel it. Great power, he felt, is not shown if what is to be controlled is weak and irrelevant. As Camus would comment, there is no great virtue in being "naturally" good. On the contrary. Therefore Nietzsche wrote: "I assess the power of a will by how much resistance, pain, torture it endures and knows how to turn to its advantage."[3] And again, "It is only a question of strength, to have all the morbid traits of the century, but to balance them through a superabundant, recuperative strength. The strong man."[4] It is in this sense that one must understand Nietzsche's aphorism, "What does not destroy me, makes me stronger."[5]

Nietzsche found what he was looking for in the will to power. It is the will to become all that one is capable of becoming. This is the truly Dionysian striving. Kaufmann's definition is appropriate: it is "a creative striving that gives form to itself."[6]

It is around the notion of the will to power that Nietzsche develops his conception of happiness. Aristotle and Aquinas had made the distinction between the fact of the universal striving or desire for happiness, and the specific definitions they gave of happiness. They could thus grant that everyone desired happiness, but insist that what happiness was understood to be by them differed considerably from person to person, and was often mistaken. They agreed that happiness was the ultimate state desired by all, and then tried to define what the specific state might be like.

Nietzsche makes a similar distinction with regard to power. He claims that essentially all human beings seek power. He finds evidence for this in the fact that all human activities are expressions of a will to overcome. However, each one understands (or *misunderstands*) by power something specific, like pleasure, or political dominance. In so far as they make power synonymous with any one thing, they err. Power is essentially self-overcoming, regardless of specific field.

For Nietzsche, pleasure (like joy for St. Augustine) is merely a concomitant of power. "*Not* for pleasure does man strive, but for power," he wrote.[7] Pleasure is merely "an aspect of the possession of power."[8] At the conscious level people may think they are striving for pleasure, but in reality they are striving for power.[9]

More importantly, Nietzsche argued that what human beings strive for ultimately is truly indifferent to pain and pleasure. Pain and pleasure, as St. Thomas Aquinas would say of joy, of friends, and so forth, are accidental to human striving.[10] "*Pleasure*," he says, "appears where there is the feeling of power. *Happiness*: in the triumphant consciousness of power and victory."[11]

Happiness, then, is "the most alive feeling of power."[12] Happiness is associated with striving, with "willing": it must be an achievement.[13] Nietzsche is aware that such a view of happiness is not easily accepted, since it would place the attainment of happiness exclusively within the realm of the strong:

> What is bad? Everything that is born of weakness.
> What is happiness? The feeling that power is growing, that resistance is overcome.[14]

In summary, let me quote Kaufmann: "If happiness is defined as the state of being man desires; if joy is defined as the conscious aspect of this state; and if pleasure is defined as a sensation marked by the absence of pain and discomfort, then Nietzsche's position can be summarized quite briefly: *happiness is the fusion of power and joy*."[15] But ultimately, as Zarathustra explains, even happiness must be overlooked: "What matters happiness?" Zarathustra asks: "I have long ceased to be concerned with happiness; I am concerned with my work."[16]

.oOo.

# Additional Readings

## Sources

*The Portable Nietzsche*, ed. Walter Kaufmann. New York: Viking, 1968.

Friedrich Nietzsche, *Philosophy in the Tragic Age of the Greeks*. South Bend: Gateway Editions, 1962.

————. *The Birth of Tragedy* and *The Case of Wagner*. New York: Vintage, 1967.

————. *Schopenhauer as Educator*. Chicago: Gateway, 1965.

————. *The Gay Science*. New York: Vintage, 1974.

————. *Thus Spoke Zarathustra*. New York: Viking, 1966.

————. *Beyond Good and Evil*. Chicago: Gateway, 1955.

————. *On the Genealogy of Morals and Ecce Homo*. New York: Vintage, 1967.

————. *The Will to Power*. New York: Vintage, 1967.

————. *Unpublished Letters*. New York: Philosophical Library, 1959.

## Commentaries

Karl Jaspers, *Nietzsche*. Chicago: Gateway Editions, 1965.

Walter Kaufmann, *Nietzsche: Philosopher, Psychologist, Antichrist*. New York: Vintage, 1968.

Robert Solomon, ed., *Nietzsche*. New York: Doubleday Anchor, 1973.

Rudolf Steiner, *Friedrich Nietzsche*. New York: Steiner Publications, 1960.

## Notes

1. *Ecce Homo*, "Thus Spoke Zarathustra," 1, 295.
2. *Twilight of the Idols*, IX, 49.
3. *The Will to Power*, 382.
4. *The Will to Power*, 1014.
5. *Twilight* I, 8.
6. Kaufmann,*Nietzsche* (New York: Vintage, 1968), 282.
7. *The Will to Power*, 434.
8. Kaufmann, *Nietzsche*, 269.
9. *The Will to Power*, 688.
10. *Thus Spoke Zarathustra* IV, 1.
11. *The Will to Power*, 1023.
12. *The Dawn*, 113.
13. *The Will to Power*, 288.
14. *The Antichrist* I, 1-2, 569-570.
15. Kaufmann, *Nietzsche*, 278.
16. *Thus Spoke Zarathustra*, IV, 1, 237-240.

# 21

# SIGMUND FREUD

## (1856-1939)

Sigmund Freud was born in Freiberg, Moravia (then in Austria, now in the Czech Republic), on May 6, 1856. His parents were Jews, and Freud remained one all his life, a factor of importance, especially when the Nazis rose to power during the 1930s. When he was four years old his family moved to Vienna. There he attended the Gymnasium, emerging regularly as the top student in his class. In 1873 he entered the University of Vienna, where he studied under the physiologist Ernst W. von Brüke, and where he first faced the full force of anti-Semitism.

Since his school days, Freud had been interested in the theoretical study of science. However, not being independently wealthy, he took a degree in medicine (1881) and joined the Allgemeine Krakenhaus, a general hospital, in 1882. It was during these years that his experiments with cocaine took place. While his interest in cocaine was truly scientific, Freud also used cocaine as an antidote to his depressions, and he even sent some to his fiancé, Martha Bernays, "to make her strong and give her cheeks a red color."[1] The publication of several monographs on the anatomy of the brain led to an appointment to a lectureship in neuro-pathology at the University, and eventually to the award of a traveling fellowship for research (1885). Freud decided to go to Paris and to study under Jean Charcot, the neurologist, then teaching at the Sorbonne. He returned to Vienna in 1886 and married Martha. They had six children, of whom, Anna, the youngest, became a famous psychoanalyst in her own right.

Freud's main interest was still in the theoretical aspects of research. But once married and with a growing family, he had to be practical. He therefore took up practice as a specialist in nervous diseases. He used as a therapeutic tool the techniques of hypnosis he had learned under Charcot, and he began a close collaboration with Dr. Josef Breuer. Together they published *Studies in Hysteria* (1895). Soon after, Freud took the step that launched the career of psychoanalysis. He substituted the technique of free association for that of hypnosis. Two years later, in 1897, he applied his newly acquired knowledge to an examination of his own psyche. From this experience arose the tradition that all aspiring psychoanalists undergo self-analysis under the supervision of an experienced practitioner.

By 1900 Freud had accumulated enough data to publish *The Interpretation of Dreams*, which he considered his best work. Soon after came *The Psychopathology of Everyday Life* (1904), and the "Freudian slip" was born. By 1908 there were enough professionals interested in his work and following his approach to assemble in Salzburg for the first International Congress of Psycho-Analysis. In 1910 Freud visited the United States as guest of Clark University, and delivered a series of lectures later published as *The Origin and Development of Psycho-Analysis* (1910). That year, too, saw the establishment of the Psychoanalytic Association, and Freud devoted a great deal of his time and effort to its direction as well as to editing its journals. Both in 1915 and 1917 he gave lectures on psycho-analysis at the University of Vienna. These were later published as *A General Introduction to Psycho-Analysis* (1917).

During these later years Freud continued to work as an analyst and to write technical monographs, such as *The Unconscious* (1915), *Beyond the Pleasure Principle* (1920), *The Ego and the Id* (1923), and *Inhibitions, Symptoms, and Anxiety* (1926). But he also managed to devote himself to the more theoretical and philosophical aspects of research which had been his first love. Thus, *Totem and Taboo* (1913), *The Future of an Illusion* (1927), and *Moses and Monotheism* (1939), explored the phenomenon of religion; *Thoughts for the Times on War and Death* (1915) was a sober meditation on the reasons for war at a time when Europe was immersed in it; and *Civilization and its Discontents* (1929) was a broad appraisal of the successes and failures of culture from a psychoanalytic point of view.

In 1923, at the age of 67, Freud contracted cancer of the palate and jaw. He was a heavy smoker—twenty cigars a day!—a fact which must have had its effect on his health. He tried repeatedly to stop, or at least curtail, his smoking, but was unable to do so even when smoking caused him angina pains. During the next sixteen years Freud underwent some thirty-three operations for cancer of the jaw and mouth, but to no avail.

In 1938 the Nazis invaded Austria. Freud's works were burned, the Psychoanalytische Verlag was destroyed, and his passport was confiscated. Ill and wasted by his ailments he was eventually permitted to leave for England, where he died on September 23, 1939.

.oOo.

It is impossible to capture in a few pages the richness of insight that characterized Freud's work as an analyst. His brilliance shines most profusely when, after describing in minute detail the case histories of patients, he presents his own interpretation and diagnosis. Since this is impossible, I will content myself with a brief exposition of the main elements of Freud's view of the structure of the human psyche.

One of Freud's most interesting ideas is his view of the human psyche as a quantum of energy. There is nothing mysterious about this energy. It is of the same kind as every other energy in the universe, except that it is appropriated or reserved for use by the psyche. Psychic energy, therefore, is simply the amount of (physical) energy that is needed for psychic processes such as thinking, willing, desiring, calculating, etc. One of Freud's greatest accomplishments was the exploration of the ways in which this energy is used.

In his early work, Freud had been guided by the division of the psyche into the *conscious* (encompassing perception, thinking, analysis, etc.), and the *unconscious*, which contained the residues of past experiences, especially from childhood, of which one was no longer aware, but which were still active in one's psychic life. The unconscious was subdivided into the *latent unconscious*, the repository of names, etc., merely forgotten but capable of being recalled to consciousness with comparative ease; and the *repressed unconscious*, containing those aspects of experience whose recollection would be too painful and traumatic, and whose exploration could take place only through dream analysis and the techniques of free association.

This bipartite view of the psyche was never abandoned completely by Freud. But in his later work he felt the need for another structure to explain the various movements of repression, sublimation, impulse, control, etc. The tripartite division of the psyche into Id, Ego, and Superego provided the components necessary for explaining dynamically the various psychic interactions while still incorporating the categories of the conscious and the unconscious.

For Freud, the primary repository of psychic energy is the Id. The Id is the totality of the specific channels of energy which Freud termed instincts. Instincts are specific innate tendencies of living matter.[2] Hunger, sex, aggression, are examples of instincts. All the instincts bundled together make up the Id.

It is in the nature of an instinct, when stimulated or excited, to seek its object blindly. When excited, the hunger instinct seeks food; the sexual instinct, orgasm. If the material object is not immediately available, the instinct is directed to an image of the object. Such images are first formed through what Freud called *Primary Processes*, which take place when the physical objects are not readily obtainable. Thus, instincts always tend automatically toward things or the images of things. They are object-directed. Such a movement Freud termed *object-cathexis*.

However, it is obvious that hunger is not ultimately satisfied by the mere image of food. When satisfaction is not obtained, energy from the Id is transferred out, as it were, and the Ego is formed. The Ego encompasses the activities of discrimination, judgment, reasoning, and so forth. In a sense, the Ego is the eyes of the Id. It scouts about for the object it knows will satisfy the instinct, until it finds it. This activity Freud called *Secondary Process*. As the object is apprehended, the Ego directs the total organism toward it. Such a movement is termed *ego-cathexis*.

Clearly, the reason for the formation of the Ego is the satisfaction of the instincts. The more successful the Ego becomes at this task of satisfying the instincts, the more energy is shifted to it for its own specific functions. The more economically and efficiently the Ego manages to satisfy the instincts, the more energy it will have left as surplus, energy it can use for thinking, attending, learning, etc., for their own sake.

The Ego, therefore, works pretty much as an administrator. It must redirect, shift, thwart temporarily (*anti-cathect*) the object-cathexes of the Id even though eventually the instincts must be satisfied. So long as the Ego manages things properly, the personality functions smoothly. If the anti-cathexes are overdone or not planned properly, the object-cathexes may overflow their channels and overwhelm the Ego, resulting in a temporary loss of control.

The Ego achieves part of its control by incorporating some of the outside, social controls into its own structure. Fear of punishment (*conscience*) and desire of reward (*ego-ideal*) from parents form the third aspect of the intrapsychic structure, the Superego. The Superego functions also as anti-cathexis; only it is more stringent than the Ego.

The intricate interactions among these parts help explain the various processes and eventualities of psychic life. Id-(object)-cathexes scream, Now! Superego anti-cathexes counter, No! Ego-cathexes counsel, Delay! Wait! To the wants of the Id and the shoulds/should nots of the Superego, the Ego proffers restraint and compromise. If the bulk of the energy is controlled by the Id, the person is impulsive; if it is controlled by the Superego, the person is moralistic; if it is controlled by the Ego, the person is realistic.

.oOo.

In his later writings, Freud made a consistent effort to place the details of the intrapsychic structure within a larger context of more general principles. He constructed, as it were, a more philosophical view of the personality and placed it in close relation to the rest of the cosmos.

The First Law of Thermodynamics states that the amount of energy in any system remains constant in all its transformations. There is thus at the core of the physical universe a tendency to maintain an equilibrium of forces. Moreover, in moving toward equilibrium, the amounts of energy transferred become increasingly smaller, until equilibrium is regained. A certain amount of energy is thus dissipated (*entropized*) within the system. This fact is covered by the Second Law of Thermodynamics.

Freud saw these two principles of inorganic matter replicated at the organic level. He saw a tendency within all organisms to return to a state of inertia. Living organisms, having evolved from matter, could not be exempt from those universal laws. Thus Freud saw birth as a departure from equilibrium, and death as a return to it. Life, therefore, is but a roundabout way to death.[3] This general tendency toward homeostasis Freud called the *Nirvâna Principle*, since for Buddhism, *nirvâna* entails the cessation of all activity.

Accordingly, Freud discovered within the psyche an innate tendency toward homeostasis, an instinct that he termed "a tendency innate in living organic matter impelling it toward the reinstatement of an earlier condition." This is "the manifestation of inertia in organic life."[4] He called this tendency the death instinct (*Thanatos*).

This entropy of the psyche is counterbalanced by the Life instincts (*Eros*), instincts that represent tendencies of excitation, leading to the disruption of homeostasis. The *Libido* is the form of psychic energy used by the Life instincts.

Thus life and death, reproduction and extermination, love and hate constitute two great groups of instincts; they are manifestations, at the level of the living organism, of the laws that rule inorganic matter.[5]

Implicit in Freud's formulations is a quasi-moral judgment that considers homeostasis as desirable. On the other hand, imbalance and excitation are troublesome in that they represent a departure from the prevailing equilibrium. Such excitations may seem necessary and even desirable, but they are so only in the short term. In the long run they are merely episodes within a prevailing state of quiescence, like temporary eruptions of mostly dormant volcanoes. Thus, if the excitation of hunger and the desire for food may seem necessary for the preservation of the life of the individual living organism, individual life itself is but a transitory moment between non-being and death.

From this perspective it should not be difficult to understand Freud's notions of *pleasure* and *pain*. Pain is the experience of increased excitation. More generally, pain is any departure from equilibrium. On the other hand, pleasure is any decrease of excitation and approximation to the original homeostasis. The fullness of pleasure, therefore, is obtained only by a complete return to quiescence. This is what satisfaction means.[6]

In the same way as the Second Law of thermodynamics encompasses the general tendency of inorganic matter to return to inertia, so at the level of living organisms, the *Pleasure Principle* denotes the tendency of the (*Death*) instincts to reduce tension, or at least the amount of tension. As Freud put it, "the pleasure principle seems directly to subserve the death-instincts."[7]

Such a return to quiescence is not always immediately possible. Realistically, some thwarting and postponement by the Ego may be necessary before the pleasure or satisfaction of extinction is gained. In fact, therefore, and even though the Pleasure Principle must eventually prevail, human life is ruled from day to day by the *Reality Principle*. Realistically, a life of sheer unexcitement is not possible. The pleasure of rest must always be postponed—except for the final rest of all, death, which, as Shakespeare says, "will come when it will come."

.oOo.

In the context of Freud's understanding of pleasure and pain, it is not difficult to see how the question of happiness would inevitably arise. But the search for an answer is pursued in more concrete terms than is usual—in actual human behavior. The search for happiness is identified with the search for pleasure: people "strive after happiness; they want to become happy and to remain so. This endeavor has two sides, a positive and a negative aim. It aims, on the one hand, at an absence of pain and unpleasure, and, on the other, at the experiencing of strong feelings of pleasure. In its narrower sense the word 'happiness' only relates to the last.[8]

This pursuit of happiness is individual: each one of us desires to be happy. But side by side this individualistic desire for happiness runs the desire to socialize. The human need to love and be loved is operative here.[9] We yearn to be part of a group, part of a culture, even though, at the same time, the claims of individual happiness conflict with those of society and culture, resulting in all kinds of conflicts.[10] To these interpersonal conflicts must be added the naturally occurring disturbances of nature, hurricanes, earthquakes, epidemics, and the pains caused by our own decaying bodies. It is as if "the intention that man should be 'happy' is not included in the plan of 'Creation,'" says Freud.[11]

Such difficulties in obtaining pleasure—that is, happiness—introduce a shift from the Pleasure Principle to the Reality Principle. This shift does not affect the individual alone, but humankind as a whole. To obtain even a modicum of pleasure we must become "reasonable."[12] From explicit and positive search for happiness, one must move to avoidance of pain. Thus, too, are born the many techniques supposedly conducive to attaining happiness. Popular literature abounds with examples of such techniques. However, at bottom, they are only methods of lessening suffering and pain. Their approach is negative.

The harsh reality of the world—body, nature, and society— necessitates the abandonment of the direct and positive pursuit of happiness. Such a refusal of pleasure leads to the construction of "ideas" of happiness, phantasies and day-dreams, artistic, religious, and otherwise, which in some way compensate for the loss of actual happiness. But even though a full happiness is not obtainable, Freud insists that the pursuit of happiness must be maintained, and that each one of us must learn how to maximize the possibilities of experiencing happiness: "There is no golden rule which applies to everyone; every man must find out for himself in what particular fashion he can be saved. All kinds of different factors will operate to direct his choice. It is a question of how much real satisfaction he can expect to get from the external world, how far he is led to make himself independent of it, and, finally, how much strength he feels he has for altering the world to suit his wishes. In this, his psychical constitution will play a decisive part, irrespectively of the external circumstances."[13]

.oOo.

# Additional Readings

## Sources

Sigmund Freud, *The Standard Edition of the Complete Psychological Works of Sigmund Freud.* 24 vols.; London: Hogarth Press and Institute of Psycho-Analysis, 1953— .
Sigmund Freud, *Collected Papers.* 5 vols.; London: 1924-1950.

## Commentaries

Ernest Jones, *Sigmund Freud: Life and Work.* 3 vols.; New York: Basic Books, 1953.
Alasdair MacIntyre, *The Unconscious.* New York: Humanities Press, 1962.
Herbert Marcuse, *Eros and Civilization: A Philosophical Inquiry into Freud.* New York: Vintage, 1955.
John Rickman, ed., *Sigmund Freud: A General Introduction.* London: Hogarth Press, 1954.
Philip Rieff, *Freud: The Mind of the Moralist.* New York: Doubleday Anchor Books, 1961.

## Notes

1. Ernest Jones, *Sigmund Freud: Life and Work* (3 vols.; New York: Basic Books, 1953), Vol. 1, 81.
2. Freud, *Beyond the Pleasure Principle,* V, in *Standard Edition,* Vol.18, 36.
3. *Beyond the Pleasure Principle,* V, in *Standard Edition,* Vol.18, 38.
4. *Beyond the Pleasure Principle,* V in *Standard Edition,* Vol.18, 36.
5. Freud, *The Ego and the Id,* Ch.4.
6. *Beyond the Pleasure Principle,* I, in *Standard Edition,* Vol.18, 7-8.
7. *Beyond the Pleasure Principle,* VII, in *Standard Edition,* Vol.18, 63.
8. *Civilization and its Discontents,* II, in *Standard Edition,* Vol.21, 75-76.
9. "Thoughts for the Times on War and Death," I, in *Standard Edition,* Vol.14, 282-283.
10. *Civilization and its Discontents,* VIII, in *Standard Edition* Vol.21, 140.
11. *Civilization and its Discontents,* II, in *Standard Edition,* Vol.21, 76-77.
12. *Introductory Lectures on Psycho-Analysis,* Lecture XXII, in *Standard Edition,* Vol.16, 356-357.
13. *Civilization and its Discontents,* II, in *Standard Edition,* Vol.21, 83-84.

# 22

# HERMANN HESSE

## (1877-1962)

"I was born toward the end of modern times, shortly before the return of the Middle Ages, with the sign of the Archer on the ascendant and Jupiter in favorable aspect. My birth took place at an early hour of the evening on a warm day in July."[1] Thus Hesse, about his birth in Calw, in Württenberg. His father and mother had been missionaries to India, and they continued the association with the mission throughout their lives. His maternal grandfather was the famous missionary and Indologist Hermann Gundert.

Hesse attended elementary school in Calw (1886-1889), and then the Latin school in Göppingen, in order to prepare himself for the *Landesexamen*, which he passed in July, 1891. Of these early years he would write:

> Not by parents and teachers alone was I educated, but by higher, more arcane and mysterious powers as well, among them the god Pan, who stood in my grandfather's glass cabinet in the guise of a little dancing Hindu idol. This deity, and others too, took an interest in me during my childhood years, and long before I could read and write they so filled me with age-old Eastern images and ideas that later, whenever I met a Hindu or Chinese sage, it was like a reunion, a homecoming. And yet I am a European.[2]

The Europeanization of Hesse was about to begin in earnest at the seminary in Maulbronn. He began his classical studies and liked them immensely. Then "suddenly from inside me a storm arose that led to flight from the monastery school,

punishment by strict imprisonment, and dismissal from the seminary."[3] There
followed counseling and exorcism, an attempt at suicide, confinement in an asylum,
and commitment, this time to the Gymnasium at Bad Cannstat (1892). But he stayed
there only for about a year and a half. He just could not take it. On January 20,
1893, he wrote to his mother:

> I am interested in nothing. Day after day I am talked at, about languages, con-
> stitutions, wars, nations, statistics, hypotheses, experiments, emperors, forces,
> electroscopes, and whatever the garbage is called—and I listen; some things I
> retain, others I don't, and the whole business couldn't mean less to me. . . . This
> afternoon . . . I grabbed some books at random and sold them in Stuttgart for—a
> revolver. And now I am sitting here again and the rusty weapon is lying in front
> of me.[4]

His mother rushed to his aid and calmed him for a while, but by October he left
school for good and became an apprentice in Perrot's Clockworks Factory in Calw.

In 1895 he was apprenticed to J. J. Heckenhauer's Bookshop in Tübingen.
Here, at last, he found some peace and time to write. At thirteen he had vowed to
himself "to be either a poet or nothing at all."[5] Having tried the nothing twice,
writing was the only thing left to do.

So he wrote. *Romantische Lieder* appeared in 1898; *An Hour Beyond Midnight*
the next year. He moved to Basel and worked as a stock clerk in a bookstore. And
he continued to write: *Hermann Lauscher* (1901), *Gedichte* (1902), and *Peter
Camenzind* (1904), upon whose success he acquired enough money to marry Maria
Bernoulli and to move to a farm house in Gaienhofen, on Lake Constance. In 1905
his first son, Bruno, was born; a second, Heiner, in 1909; and a third, Martin, in
1911. Interspersed were *Beneath the Wheel* (1906), *Diesseits* (1907), *Nachbarn*
(1908), *Gertrude* (1910), *Unterwegs* (1911), *Umwege* (1912), *Aus Indien* (1913),
and *Rosshalde* (1914). At this point his world caved in around him. The War began;
his father died; his youngest son, Martin, was gravely ill; his wife's mind began to
unhinge (eventually she had to be committed). Several works were published at the
time, among them *Knulp* (1915), but Hesse experienced a nervous breakdown and
entered a sanatorium in Sonnmatt, near Lucerne. There he underwent psychotherapy
with Dr. Joseph B. Lang, a pupil of Jung's. The crisis abated, Hesse moved to
Montagnola, Ticino, and resumed writing: *Zarathustra's Wiederkehr*, *Märchen*, and
*Demian*, all in 1919; *Klingsor's Last Summer* (1920), and *Blick ins Chaos* (1921),
which so impressed T.S. Eliot that he went to visit Hesse personally.

At this point Hesse underwent further psychoanalysis with C.G. Jung, and his
writing continued: *Siddhartha* (1922), *A Guest at the Spa* (1925), *The Journey to
Nürenberg* and *Steppenwolf* (1927). Having finally divorced his first wife, he
married Ruth Wenger in 1924, and was divorced by her in 1927. *Crisis* and
*Reflections* were published in 1928, and *Narcissus and Goldmund* in 1930. In 1931
he married Ninon Dolbin. Then came *Journey to the East* (1932), a series of col-

lections of poetry, and finally *The Glass Bead Game* (1943), followed by more poetry. The Nobel Prize and the Goethe Prize were awarded to him in 1946, and the Peace Prize of the German Booksellers' Association in 1955. He died on August 9, 1962.

Or did he? In his conjectural autobiography he wrote of a picture he had painted on the wall of the jail cell to which he foresaw he would have been confined as a non-conformist. In the middle of it "there ran a very small railroad train. It was going straight toward the mountain and its head was already buried in it like a worm in an apple, the locomotive had already entered the little tunnel out of whose dark mouth sooty smoke was pouring. . . ."

One day, he continued,

> I called to mind the Chinese formula, stood for a minute with suspended breath .
> . . made myself small and stepped into my picture, got aboard the little train, and
> rode in the little train into the little black tunnel. For a while sooty smoke
> continued to be visible, pouring out of the round hole, then the smoke dispersed
> and disappeared and with it the entire picture and I with the picture.[6]

.oOo.

Hesse was not a philosopher. To have been called one would have probably made him shudder. But few individuals in the history of humankind have been given the opportunity to be witnesses to as much suffering and achievement as he was. When he was born, the automobile did not exist; when he died, jet airplanes were commonplace and Sputnik had beep-beeped its way around the globe. He lived through two World Wars, through the dawn of Communism and its spread around the world, through the rise and fall of Nazism. And he wrote about it all. His first novel, *Schweinigel* (the manuscript has not been found) was written in 1899; his last poem in 1962 on the eve of his death—sixty-three years of voluminous production. Surely, there is much here to learn.

In 1932 Hesse published an essay, "A bit of Theology," that stated very clearly his philosophical view of the human world. He saw human development as proceeding through three stages. The first is the stage of innocence, symbolized in mythology by accounts of paradise and primeval unity with nature. This is the stage of childhood, the stage of Adam and Eve before the Fall, the stage of Enkidu before the courtesan seduces him. Here there is undifferentiated unity, the thetical stage of the Hegelian dialectic. The path leads to a second stage where the world is this and that, good and evil, sacred and profane, beautiful and ugly. Affiliations are formed; there is "we" and there is "they," rich and poor, the children of light and the children of darkness, Christ and Antichrist, God and Satan, saved and damned, Jerusalem and Babylon. Transcendentally, there is spirit and matter, the one and the many, permanence and flux, eternity and time, being and nothingness. Psychologically, individuality blooms. The "I" intrudes upon the psychic world as different from the "Thou," and identity is formed amidst the masses. Reflection arises, the objectification of the self by the self. This is the stage of alienation in which the world—inner, outer, cosmic—is dismembered. The center no longer holds, and mere chaos may be loosed upon the world. It is a period of *Sturm und Drang*, and many succumb in it. For many this stage leads to disillusionment and defeat. The puzzle has been scrambled, and who can reassemble it? Humpty-Dumpty has had a great fall, and who can put him back together again? Questions arise: where is truth? Where is love? We live a few hours away from nihilism and despair.

Some, however, says Hesse, manage to move on. They enter the third stage, beyond good and evil, beyond beautiful and ugly, where time is transcended, the alien is made friend, the broken is made whole, flux and permanence combine, male and female are androgynized, the sick are made sane, dismemberment is remembered, and a light dawns that obliterates every darkness. This is *nirvâna*, heaven on earth as it is in heaven; Hegel's synthesis, in which there is no below and no above, and the universal spirit, whose sparks we are, stands in majesty with itself alone. Therein is happiness.

.oOo.

Hesse sees the present as a stepping stone to a glorious future where all turmoils will be resolved. Throughout his writings there is a millenarian or chilliastic idea constantly at work, and it gets defined as the work progresses. This millenarism is most clearly delineated in his writings beginning with *Demian*. The spiritual dimension envisioned in *Demian* is the realm of innocence experienced in childhood.

> This realm was familiar to me in almost every way—mother and father, love and strictness, model behavior, and school. It was a realm of brilliance, clarity, and cleanliness, gentle conversations, washed hands, clean clothes, and good manners. This was the world in which morning hymns were sung and Christmas celebrated. Straight lines and paths led into the future: there were duty and guilt, bad conscience and confession, forgiveness and good resolutions, love, reverence, wisdom and the words of the Bible. If one wanted an unsullied and orderly life, one made sure one was in league with this world.[7]

Those who believed in this world, and those who belonged to it, were marked with a sign, like Cain. They were special people because they "knew." They were the ones destined to take possession of this realm once the opposing forces of evil had been vanquished and destroyed. Salvation was around the corner. The War—the First World War—was but the beginning of the end, the beginning of the millenarian age to which Nature was impelling humankind.

But the kingdom did not come yet! The years following the War were dark years, indeed. It is a Hesse in his late forties who turns to the matter again in

*Steppenwolf.* The duality of the world, both inner and outer, is depicted here in more cogent, realistic, even despairing terms. But the realm of the spirit is also more clearly defined. It is a realm of love, beauty, nature, and music—the realm of the "Immortals." It is an ever present realm, accessible to us all through drunkenness and opium dreams, through the magic of play in "the Magic Theater," and through music. And it is clear that this realm represents what Hesse understands happiness to be. Describing the meaning of the word "Glück," (happiness, joy), he writes:

> Around this lovely short glowing golden word there has gathered everything I have felt at its sound since my childhood days. Then the feeling was certainly stronger, the response of all the senses to the sensual qualities of the appeal of the word were sharper and louder, but if the word had not been so profound, so basic and so world-embracing, my conception of the eternal present, of the "golden clue" (in *Goldmund*) and the laughter of the Immortals (in *Steppenwolf*) would not have crystallized around this word.[8]

The eternal present, however, the realm in which all seeking ceases and all quests are satisfied, is obtainable finally only after death. Many of Hesse's major characters attain a glimpse of the reality and the content of this realm only at the moment of their deaths. For us, here and now, freedom and happiness consist in transcending the dualities of past and future, of here and there, and so forth, as he proclaims beautifully and with great clarity in *The Journey to the East*, and more prosaically, in the following words:

> I believe in nothing in the world so deeply, no conception is so holy to me, as unity, the conviction that everything in the world forms a divine whole, that the "I" takes itself too seriously. I had suffered much pain in my life, had done much that was stupid and unpleasant, but again and again I had managed to free myself, to forget my "I" and yield to the feeling of oneness, to recognize that the division between inner and outer, between "I" and the world, is an illusion and to enter willingly with closed eyes into the unity. It had never been easy for me, no one could have less talent for he holy than I; nevertheless, again and again I had encountered that miracle to which the Christian theologians have given the beautiful name of "grace," that divine experience of reconciliation, of ceasing to rebel, of willing agreement, which is indeed nothing other than the Christian surrender of the "I" and the Hindu realization of unity.[9]

The experience of happiness, then, is to be found in the transcendence of all opposites. Put differently, it is the experience of the coincidence of all opposites. Such an experience requires that one be able to transcend the kind of life and existence in which dichotomies and contrarieties are considered true.

> By *Glück* [happiness, joy] I understand something completely objective, to wit, the totality itself, timeless existence, the eternal harmony of the world, that which others at times have called the music of the spheres or the smile of God.

This epitome, this unceasing music, this deep resounding golden gleaming eternity is pure and absolute present, it knows no time, no history, no before and after. Eternally the countenance of the world shines and laughs, all human beings, generations, nations, empires rise, flourish, and sink back again into the shadows and into nothingness. Eternally life plays its music, dances its roundelay, and whatever joy, comfort, capacity for laughter falls by chance to the lot of us transitory, weak, endangered mortals is a ray from that source, is an eye full of brightness, an ear full of music . . . .

To exist in the perfect present, to join in the chorus of the spheres, to dance in the roundelay of the world, to join in the eternal laughter of God, that is our share in *Glück*. Many have experienced it just once, many only a few times. But he who has experienced it has not only been happy for an instant, he has also had given him some of the splendor and music, some of the light of timeless joy, and everything by way of love that has been brought into the world by lovers, everything by way of comfort and cheer that has been created for this world by artists and after centuries glows as brightly as on its first day--all this comes from that source.[10]

.oOo.

# Additional Readings

## Sources

Hermann Hesse, *Gesammelte Schriften*. Frankfurt: Suhrkamp, 1957.
————. *Autobiographical Writings*. New York: Farrar, Straus & Giroux, 1972.
————. *Reflections*. New York: Farrar, Straus & Giroux, 1974.
————. *My Belief*. New York: Farrar, Straus & Giroux, 1975.

## Commentaries

Mark Boulby, *Hermann Hesse, his mind and art*. Ithaca: Cornell University Press, 1967.
George W. Field, *Hermann Hesse*. New York: Twayne, 1970.
Volker Michels, ed., *Hermann Hesse, A Pictorial Biography*. New York: Farrar, Straus & Giroux, 1977.
Joseph Mileck, *Hermann Hesse: Life and Art*. Berkeley: University of California Press, 1978.
Anna Otten, ed., *Hesse Companion*. Frankfurt: Suhrkamp, 1970.
Ernst Rose, *Faith from the Abyss*. New York: New York University Press, 1965.
Theodore Ziolkowski, *The Novels of Hermann Hesse*. Princeton: Princeton University Press, 1965.

## Notes

1. Hesse, "Life Story Briefly Told" [1925], in *Autobiographical Writings* (New York: Farrar, Straus & Giroux, 1972), 43.

2. "Childhood of the Magician" [1923], in *Autobiographical Writings*, 3.

3. "Life Story Briefly Told," in *Autobiographical Writings*, 47.

4. Quoted in George W. Field, *Hermann Hesse* (New York: Twayne, 1970), 26.

5. "Life Story Briefly Told," in *Autobiographical Writings*, 45.

6. "Life Story Briefly Told," in *Autobiographical Writings*, 60-62.

7. Hesse, *Demian* (New York: Bantam, 1970), 5.

8. "Happiness," in *My Belief* (New York: Farrar, Straus & Giroux, 1975), 264.

9. "A Guest at the Spa," in *Autobiographical Writings*, 121-122.

10. "Happiness," in *My Belief*, 263.

# 23

# PIERRE TEILHARD DE CHARDIN

## (1881-1955)

Pierre Teilhard de Chardin was born on May 1, 1881, in Sarcenat, France, the fourth of eleven children. His parents were sincere, pious Christians, who influenced their children through their loyalty to tradition, their kindness, and their spiritual life. Pierre was a normal little boy. He had a pleasant disposition. The rich natural environment in which his home was located served as a stimulus to his curiosity, and his father took pleasure in ensuring that his children understood and appreciated the beauties and mysteries of their piece of the earth. Young Pierre was fascinated by the durability of matter, and he has left us a description of his childish interests:

> You should have seen me as in profound secrecy and silence I withdrew into the contemplation of my "God of Iron," delighting in its possession, gloating over its existence. A God, note, *of Iron* . . . . and why *Iron*? . . . Because in all my childish experience there was nothing in the world harder, tougher, more durable than this wonderful substance.[1]

Pierre studied at the Jesuit school of Villefranche, and eventually joined his teachers in their religious life. He was eighteen when he entered the Jesuit novitiate at Aix-en-Provence, in 1898, and after two years he proceeded to Laval to study the classics. When the Jesuits were expelled from France in 1902 he went to England, to the Isle of Jersey, to study philosophy. There he experienced a spiritual crisis: "I seriously considered the possibility of completely giving up the 'Science of Rocks,' which I then found so exciting, in order to devote myself entirely to so-called 'supernatural' activities."[2] The crisis was transcended with the help of his spiritual adviser, Père Paul Troussard. Teilhard finished his philosophy studies and then went to teach for three years at the Jesuit school in Cairo. He returned to Hastings, England, in 1908, to study theology, and was ordained a priest in 1911. The Great War awaited him at the end of his final year of training. He served as stretcher bearer with the Eighth Regiment of Moroccan Tirailleurs, and was decorated twice for bravery.

At the end of the War he went to Paris to study anthropology under Marcellin Boule. In 1922 his doctoral thesis was accepted, and he became a professor of geology at the Institut Catholique.

Between 1923 and 1946 he was in China, with sorties to India, the Gobi dessert, Mongolia, and visits to France. But in France, his theology was *non grata*, his thought was considered to be too bold, his personality too appealing to the young, too charismatic. He was forbidden to teach, and so China became for him an exile. There he was a member of the expedition that discovered the remains of *Sinanthropus* in Chou-kou-tien (1928).

On his return to France in 1946 he suffered his first heart attack. It took him two years to recover fully, and then he traveled to South Africa to inspect sites possibly associated with the Australopithecines. In 1951 he was elected to the Académie des Sciences, and then moved to New York as a member of the Wenner Gren Foundation. He resided there until his death, of a heart attack, on April 10, 1955. It was Easter Sunday.

.oOo.

Teilhard's work is quite extensive. It contains some two hundred articles and books, most of them available in English. Most of it was not published during his life time. The ecclesiastical authorities in Rome forbade the publication even of *The Phenomenon of Man*. Many of his manuscripts, however, circulated in clandestine dittoed sheets even among theological students. When his works finally became available after his death, Rome issued a *Monitum* forbidding seminarians to read them, a warning that has been lifted only recently.

Teilhard was pained by this narrow-mindedness, but he understood. In a letter to the Jesuit Superior General, Father Janssens, in 1951, he wrote: "I fully recognize. . . that Rome may have its own reasons for judging that, in its present form, my concept of Christianity may be premature or incomplete and that at the present moment its wider diffusion may therefore be inopportune." But he was not about to revolt. He was bound by the vow of obedience and he was resolved to remain "a child of obedience."[3]

What was it, in his writings, that offended the ecclesiastical sensibilities? There was, first of all, Teilhard's appreciation of the material world. This seemed to jar the traditional spiritual character of Christianity. There was also the fact that, in true mystical fashion, he saw God in everything, a vision that conjured up accusations of pantheism. He advocated an asceticism of right use rather than of renunciation, and he found the justification for this in the letters of St. Paul at a time when theology had not yet uncovered its Biblical roots. His optimism scandalized the somber dignitaries of the Roman Curia, whose ruling principles seemed to be original sin rather than grace, and the death of Christ rather than the resurrection.

There was also the frank confrontation with the data of science and the acceptance of evolution, all of which smacked too much of modernism and secularism. There was nothing unorthodox here; but the issue was not truth as much as power, the power to fetter ideas by controlling the minds that produce them. In the end the censorship proved of no avail. Teilhard's works were eventually published, and they kindled an enlightenment the likes of which may not be repeated for a long time to come.

.oOo.

At the core of Teilhard's thought there is an essential intuition about the relation between matter and spirit. From childhood he had had the feeling of the interpenetration between the human and the physical, as well as of the goodness of the physical. Similarly, he was intimately aware of the possibility of the world's disappearance—and of *our* disappearance with it. He found in this awareness, which he thought was pervasive though subconscious, the cause of anguish in the modern world.

Startling though they seemed to many, Teilhard's ideas were part of a long tradition of opposition to the mechanistic views of nature espoused originally by Hobbes and Descartes, and consecrated eventually by Newton. This mechanistic view, according to which nature, including the human body, functions simply like a sophisticated machine, had been opposed by a number of thinkers such as Leibniz, the Van Helmonts, Lady Anne Conway, Goethe, Schopenhauer, Nietzsche, and more recently Bergson. For, as Conway herself put it, "as touching the Cartesian Philosophy, this says that every body is a mere dead mass, not only void of all kind of life and sense, but utterly uncapable thereof to all eternity; this grand error also is to be imputed to all those who affirm body and spirit to be contrary things, and inconvertible one into another, so as to deny a body all life and sense."[4]

Conway saw matter and spirit as two aspects of one and the same substance, and so did Teilhard. Essentially, he maintained, there is no opposition between matter and form, or body and soul, science and art, technology and the spirit. The relationship between these two dimensions is conceived in terms of a dialectic *sui generis*. Matter, the "without," is the principle of complexity and multiplicity. Spirit, the "within," is the principle of unification and order. The real may be conceived as a fundamental quantum of energy which disperses itself tangentially through matter and yet holds itself together radially in spirit. The real, which is the universe, concentrates itself in thought (through us) and disintegrates itself in matter. Matter and spirit are like two foci of an ellipse. They are the two dimensions of the real. The world, therefore, is a psycho-physical reality.

We are used to the study of the physical world in scientific terms. The regularities of the physical dimension are encapsulated in the complex laws of thermodynamics, entropy, and so forth. The spirit also has its "laws," described in the mystical literatures of the world and in the treatises of logic. The relation between these two dimensions is formulated by Teilhard as a law, the Law of Complexity-Consciousness. This law expresses the dialectical interaction between matter and spirit: the more complex the matter, the more concentrated and heightened the spirit will be; the less complex the matter, the weaker its psychic lining. Thus, a crystal's material complexity is sufficient to support only a primitive type of "psychic" organization. The physical structure of a plant is more complex, and therefore it can support life; the physical organs of animals, especially the brains of the mammals and the primates, are enormously more complex, and therefore can support a higher degree of psychic concentration manifested in instinct and sensation. The material organ we humans possess in our brain is the most complex piece of matter, and therefore it is lined by the highest form of psychism known in the universe, reflection. But essentially, the organization of the crystal, life, instinct and sensation, and thought, are simply graduated manifestations of the same psychic dimension of reality. The same continuity applies to the material level between crystal and human brain.

The same continuity and parallelism is applied to the force that holds the two dimensions together. At the level of the atom we speak of a "glue," unspecified yet real, that holds the most inner components of matter so closely together that their sundering ensues in an awesome explosion. At the human level, that "glue" is love. Love, however, is continuous with the force of attraction that holds together the universe.

Teilhard's reasoning for this is simple yet startling: Nothing appears at any one stage of evolution that was not there before in less developed fashion.[5] What we call thought and love at our level, therefore, existed before in less obvious and developed fashion in the animal, the vegetable, and the mineral worlds. Everything that is now has evolved.

Teilhard accepted evolution very early in his career as the only hypothesis capable of explaining all the data available to us. He saw the universe in a state of steady progression toward more and more complex states of matter, culminating in the human brain and the birth of thought. From an evolutionary point of view he saw the universe as a process of developing ever more complex organs with which to support the ever-increasing concentration of spirit. Conversely, he saw humanity as the acme of the evolution of the universe: we are the universe become conscious of itself.

Evolution has not stopped. The universe continues to fashion ever more complex material structures in order to support a more heightened power of reflection. Teilhard, like McLuhan, saw the modern advances of technology—especially telecommunication (TV, radio, satellite networks, telephones, computers, etc.)—as extensions of the human brain. On them is being built the higher awareness of humankind as a global phenomenon. Consciousness, supported by technology, has now become deployed all over the earth—planetized—and it envelops the earth as a sphere of mind—the noösphere—just as air envelops it, too.

Evolution has not stopped. It continues, and it continues *on this earth*. Teilhard finds this significant, that evolution should take place on this earth, a spheroid planet floating along in the Milky Way. Evolution on a globe is different from evolution on a cube, or on a cylinder, or on a cone. The reason is simple: a sphere is a closed space. On the surface of a sphere, a group of beings can be said to expand only up to a point—just as one can enter a forest only up to a point. Beyond that certain point expansion turns to contraction. One can enter a forest only up to the middle; beyond that point one exits. An example might illustrate this matter. If four human beings started walking northwards from the South Pole along equidistant meridians of 90 degrees, they would be constantly moving farther apart while they walked as far north as the Equator. From the Equator onwards, their paths would begin to converge as they moved toward the apex of the North Pole. This is due simply to the nature of a sphere. Similarly, according to Teilhard, as human consciousness appeared first upon the earth, it followed a movement of expansion. It sought to encompass the earth. Now we are beginning to converge, to move closer to one another—for we live on a sphere. Expansion is not limitless; there is no other place to go.

This convergence poses problems: our privacy is invaded; our territorial instincts are aroused and we fight to protect ourselves, our homes, our nations; we fear "the other"; we are wary of the masses that revolt and encircle us, and we see no alternative but to fight for the right of elbow room or give up and lock ourselves up in isolation. Much of today's thought is tinged by this prospect. Teilhard, however, holds up another possibility, that of finding a brother in the neighbor, and not a spy; that of love and cooperation, not competition; that of a unity that differentiates without isolating us into monads. It is in this context that he discusses his view of human happiness.

.oOo.

The evolutionary thrust of the universe, imbedded in the original quantum of energy, tends toward a goal. Evolution is not haphazard but teleological. This teleology is manifested in various ways in the different types of beings that make up the universe. At the purely physical level, teleology is encompassed by the laws of gravitation; at the level of the vital, the goal is well-being in whichever form it may be found; at the human level, the goal is happiness. At the human level, however, the pursuit of the goal is qualitatively different, for it involves choice.

The beasts of the field may trust blindly to instinct, without thereby diminishing or betraying themselves, because they have not *seen*. But for us, because our eyes have been opened, even though we seek hurriedly to close them, the question will continue to burn in the darkest corner of our thought. We cannot recapture the animal security of instinct. Because, in becoming men, we have acquired the power of looking to the future and assessing the value of things, we cannot do nothing, since our very refusal to decide is a decision in itself. We cannot stand still.[6]

Three options confront modern humanity. They implicate one another, so that the choice of one immediately raises further questions that necessitate the consideration of the second; and so forth. The first option is that between optimism and pessimism. Those who choose pessimism might well be left to themselves. But those who choose optimism are faced by a further option: withdrawal or commitment? "Withdrawal, or evolution proceeding ever further. This is the second choice that human thought encounters in its search for a solution to the problem of action."[7]

A third option still awaits those who would march forward with the world evolving: plurality or unity? What is better, dispersion or cohesion? the ant-hill or the community? "Fulfillment of the world by divergence, or fulfillment of the same world by convergence?"[8]

The same options apply to the pursuit of happiness, for we cannot pursue happiness in total disregard of the context in which we live, move, and have our being. Teilhard, therefore, distinguishes three types of happiness arising respectively out of the choices made by individuals on this earth. These three types are the happiness of the tired, those without ambition; the happiness of the hedonist, or the pleasure seeker; and the happiness of those who seek to grow and simply find happiness as an added bonus to their striving.

These, then, are the alternatives. How to choose among them? Is it merely a matter of individual taste, temperament, or upbringing? Is it a matter of whim?

For Teilhard, the only reasonable alternatives are optimism, and a commitment to the world in the establishment of unity. In short, his choice is happiness of growth. But it is legitimate to ask, Why? Why should this be the only reasonable alternative? The answer, simply stated, is because only this alternative offers a chance of survival—that is, of enhanced life. Why? Because whenever this alternative was "chosen" by evolution in the past, the world continued to evolve and prosper.

For us human beings, then, the only way to be happy is "as the world is happy, and with the world."[9] Happiness is essentially an effect or concomitant of growth. To experience it one must be involved in the growth of the world. This requires of us three important commitments; first, to focus on our own development; second, to do so without selfishness and without domineering over others; third, we must center on something higher and greater than ourselves: "We must add one stitch, no matter how small it be, to the magnificent tapestry of life; we must discern the Immense which is building up and whose magnetic pull is exerted at the very heart of our humblest activities and at their term; we must discern it and cling to it--when all is said and done, that is the great secret of happiness."[10]

.oOo.

# Additional Reading

## Sources

Pierre Teilhard de Chardin, *The Phenomenon of Man*. New York: Harper & Row, 1961.
————. *Le Milieu Divin*. London: Collins, 1961.
————. *The Future of Man*. New York: Harper & Row, 1964.
————. *The Appearance of Man*. New York: Harper & Row, 1965.
————. *Building the Earth*. Wilkes-Barre: Dimension Books, 1965.
————. *The Making of a Mind*. New York: Harper & Row, 1965.
————. *Letters from Egypt*. New York: Herder & Herder, 1965.
————. *Letters from a Traveller*. New York: Harper & Row, 1962.
————. *Hymn of the Universe*. New York: Harper & Row, 1965.
————. *Man's Place in Nature*. New York: Harper & Row, 1966.
————. *Writings in Time of War*. New York: London: Collins, 1968.
————. *Human Energy*. New York: Harcourt, Brace, Jovanovich, 1969.
————. *Christianity and Evolution*. New York:
————. *Activation of Energy*. New York: Harcourt, Brace, Jovanovich, 1971.
————. *Toward the Future*. London: Collins, 1975.
————. *The Heart of Matter*. London: Collins, 1978.

## Commentaries

Henri de Lubac, *Teilhard de Chardin: the Man and his Meaning*. New York: Mentor-Omega, 1967.
————. *The Eternal Feminine*. New York: Harper & Row, 1971.
Donald Gray, *The Phenomenon of Man*. Riverdale Studies #2; New York: Riverdale Center for Religious Research, 1976.
Alice Vallé Knight, *The Meaning of Teilhard de Chardin: A Primer*. Old Greenwich, CT: Devin-Adair Co., 1974.
Mary and Ellen Lukas, *Teilhard*. New York: Doubleday, 1977.
Carolyn Merchant, *The Death of Nature*. New York: Harper & Row, 1989.
Emile Rideau, *The Thought of Teilhard de Chardin*. New York: Harper & Row, 1967.

## Notes

1. *The Heart of Matter* (London: Collins, 1978), 18.

2. *The Heart of Matter*, 46.

3. *Letters from a Traveller* (New York: Harper & Row, 1962), 41-44.

4. Conway, *Principles* [1692], 147, in Merchant, *The Death of Nature* (New York: Harper & Row, 1989), 258.

5. *The Phenomenon of Man* (New York Harper & Row, 1961), 71.

6. *The Future of Man* (New York: Harper & Row, 1964), 47.

7. *The Future of Man*, 43-44.

8. *The Future of Man*, 45-46.

9. "Reflections on Happiness," *Toward the Future* (London: Collins, 1975), 116.

10. "Reflections on Happiness," *Toward the Future*, 123-126.

# 24

# BURRHUS F. SKINNER

## (1904-1990)

Burrhus Frederick Skinner was born in Susquehana, PA., on March 20, 1904. His father was a lawyer who achieved some distinction in the field of corporate law. His mother, Grace Madge Burrhus, was, according to the local newspaper, "one of Susquehana's fairest and most accomplished daughters."

Susquehana was a small and peaceful railroad town. It proved to be, in Skinner's own words, "a bountiful world, in which many wonderful things were to be had for the asking."[1] In it Skinner grew up spooked by the violence of fairy tales and with no illusions about Santa Klaus. He went to school there, studied piano, and later took up the saxophone, at which he became quite proficient. He enjoyed literature and Francis Bacon, whom he read while still in eighth grade. He also read Dickens, Scott, Shakespeare, Darwin, Wilde, and *The Autobiography of Benvenuto Cellini*. He enjoyed high school, where he learned, as he put it, "the delight to be found in bringing order out of chaos."[2]

Skinner moved to Scranton with his parents and continued his studies there. He graduate in 1922, second in his class, and proceeded to Hamilton College, Ezra Pound's alma mater. He majored in English literature with a minor in Romance languages. He wrote poetry and short stories, and on the somewhat ambivalent advice of Robert Frost, he decided to become a writer.

He graduated in 1926 and tried for two years to become financially successful as a writer, but with no success. Bertrand Russell's seemingly favorable comments on "behaviourism" convinced him that science would be the art of the twentieth century.[3] Upon this conversion he bought Watson's *Behaviorism* and applied to

Harvard, where he began graduate studies in Psychology in the Fall, 1928.

At Harvard he studied physiology and whatever experimental psychology he could find. He began experiments with rats, constructing his own apparatus for this purpose, as was the custom. He also made the acquaintance of philosophers Ernest Hocking and Alfred North Whitehead, but he preferred the logical positivism of the Vienna Circle. In August, 1929, he met Ivan Petrovitch Pavlov, the psychologist, who delivered the principal address at the International Congress of Psychology meeting at Harvard.

Skinner received his Ph.D. in 1931. He stayed at Harvard for five years as a research fellow, and during that time he achieved a break-through beyond Pavlovian conditioning. During the same period he perfected the "Skinner box," the apparatus he constructed for his experiments with rats.

In 1936 he began teaching. His first appointment was at the University of Minnesota. As he left Boston for Minneapolis he met Yvonne Blue, an attractive young woman from Flossmoor, Illinois. They were married that same year. Their first child, Julie, was born on April, 1938. *The Behavior of Organisms* appeared later that year.

The War began, and Skinner's patriotism led him to develop a system for guiding missiles by means of trained pigeons. The Pentagon did not trust the pigeons, so the project was scrapped. Skinner turned his attention to more personal matters. His second daughter, Deborah, was born in the late summer, 1944, and for her, Skinner built a "baby-tender"—a crib-like enclosure with large picture windows, controlled temperature, filtered air, and sound-absorbing walls. Efforts to promote the invention commercially ended in failure.

In 1945 Skinner moved to Indiana University as Chairman of the Psychology Department, but by 1947 he was back as a faculty member at Harvard, where he would stay for good. The next year saw the publication of *Walden Two*. This was followed by *Science and Human Behavior* (1953) and *Verbal Behavior* (1957), a manuscript he had worked on for more than eighteen years. Other books followed. Eventually he retired and wrote his autobiography, which makes for fascinating reading. If *Walden Two* had been written in the same disingenuous prose as *Particulars of My Life* (1976) it would have sold many more than the million copies it has up to now.

Skinner died in 1990.

.oOo.

Skinner is best known as a psychologist, but his extensive work rests quite self-consciously on certain philosophical assumptions. Skinner's philosophy is, on the one hand, a strict and unrelenting scientific positivism that strives to preclude any mentalistic interpretation of observable phenomena. On the other hand, he is an empiricist in the Humean tradition, bent on experiment and the gathering of empirical data, and on describing as objectively as possible the results arrived at.

It is the application of this method of observation and experiment that characterizes contemporary science. The purpose is to gather data, with the hope, eventually, of constructing explanatory theories on which might be built a more efficient and human control of the world. Thus, for Skinner, behaviorism is not merely a scientific study of human behavior. Rather, it is a philosophy of science concerned with the formulation of the general laws of human behavior (drawn from empirical observations and experiments) as practical tools for social/behavioral engineering.

Human behavior, he maintains, is *caused*, a descriptive term he uses more in a Humean than in a scholastic sense. The causes of human behavior are whatever antecedent conditions exist prior to the behavior. Skinner postulates that human behavior—in fact, *any* organismic behavior (*dependent* variable)—is a function of a set of antecedent conditions (*independent* variables), and that no mental states (*intervening* variables) mediate between stimulus and response. If the behavior occurring in response to the environment is reinforced, it is more likely to reoccur. Organisms are likely to arrange their environments in ways that will encourage behaviors that are satisfying to the organism, and therefore reinforcing. Plato had, of course, envisaged the importance of interaction between organism and environment, and Marx had placed such an interaction at the core of his view of human becoming; Dewey had analyzed the process thoroughly, but only Skinner has dealt with it in a scientific manner. The environment conditions the ways in which we operate upon the environment. But since we manipulate the environment, we can actually be in control of our own operations indirectly, by controlling the environment.

Thus, there is an obvious determinism operative at the level of individual action. Every action has antecedents that condition it and render it at least virtually predictable. But this does not entail that human existence as such is determined, since the antecedent conditions can be altered, and with them, the very behaviors they produce. All organismic behavior is planned, but there is no overall plan or blueprint of behavior. What will be, will be—depending on the environment.

Therefore it is impossible—and irrelevant—to determine what happiness *should* be, though it may be possible to ascertain what it is—that is, what people enjoy and find pleasurable. It may also be possible to make people happy, not by telling them what they should find happiness in, but by arranging the environment in such a way as to produce and reinforce behaviors people find pleasurable.

.oOo.

The criteria for any definition of happiness, Skinner maintains, cannot be justified empirically. He considers the definition of such ethical terms as "good," "bad," "right" and "wrong," to be dependent upon what is advantageous to those who control a social group. Essentially, this position is very similar to Nietzsche's in *The Genealogy of Morals*. Of course, the classifications thus established cannot be justified in any sort of transcendental manner. They arise behaviorally and are changed when the behaviors change due to changes in the environment. Beyond that, behaviorism is of no help to us.

Happiness, one might argue, is a feeling. But that in itself does not give us a justification for a definition. Skinner criticizes the belief that feelings are adequate explanations of behavior. People are said to act one way or another because of their feelings. This error is compounded when the feelings are taken to be values, and are then seen as the reasons for behavior. Thus we often say that people act in a kindly way out of altruistic feelings. But to look for intra-psychic causes of behavior is antiquated and wrong, says Skinner. For that we must look at the environment and the control it exerts on behavior. The environment causes behavior; feelings just accompany it.

> We often feel happy when we behave in ways leading to the possession of good, and we then mistakenly take the possession to be the cause of the feeling. We make the same mistake when we act to make others happy by giving them good things. Whole philosophies of government have been tested on the theory that if goods are distributed "to each according to his need" people will be happy. But happiness is the accompaniment of successful action rather than of what the action brings. It is characteristic of getting rather than possessing. Possession leads to happiness only when it makes further action possible. Whether or not people are happy is of great political significance, but a subjective measure of the quality of life will do little more than tell us whether a given change should be made.[4]

The trouble with definitions of happiness is just that they are definitions. For Skinner, happiness is not a matter of theoretical determination, as was the case with traditional views of happiness. Put differently, Skinner is not concerned with *defining* happiness but rather with *achieving* it. Whether happiness is this or that cannot be determined, according to him, through complex argumentation. Happiness is not deduced into life from some abstract principle. Happiness is an experimental matter, as Frazier explains to Castle:

> the philosopher in search of a rational basis for deciding what is good has always reminded me of the centipede trying to decide how to walk. Simply go ahead and walk! We all know what is good until we stop to think about it . . . . I can't give you a rational justification for any of it. I can't reduce it to any principle of 'the greatest good.' This is the Good Life. We know it. It's a fact, not a theory. It has an experimental justification, not a rational one."[5]

And what are the facts of happiness, the behaviors we encompass under it?

> "For example . . . other things being equal, we choose health . . . Secondly . . . an absolute minimum of unpleasant labor. . . I mean the minimum which is possible without imposing on anyone. We must always think of the whole

group. . . . . The Good Life also means a chance to exercise talents and abilities. . . . sports, hobbies, arts and crafts, and most important of all, the expression of that interest in the world which is science and in the deepest sense. . . . And we need intimate and satisfying personal contacts. We must have the best possible chance of finding congenial spirits . . . . Last of all, the Good Life means relaxation and rest.[6]

These behaviors—the behaviors that constitute the "Good Life"—are not acquired by chance, in a haphazard way. Neither are they induced through preaching. They must be engineered through what Skinner calls "a technology of behavior." Behavioral engineering is accomplished by altering the environment.

Many people, when confronted with the image of what they mistake as a planned happiness, "organized joy," recoil in horror, envisaging automata whose behavior is identical, mechanical, who act as clones in a totally symmetrical environment. Nothing can be farther from the truth. If diversity is treasured, it must be  planned and engineered as any other behavior.[7]

.oOo.

# Additional Reading

## Sources

Burrhus F. Skinner, *The Behavior of Organisms*. New York: D. Appleton-Century Co., 1938.

————. *Walden Two*. New York: Macmillan, 1948.

————. *Science and Human Behavior*. New York: Macmillan, 1953.

————. *Verbal Behavior*. New York: Appleton- Century-Crofts, 1957.

————. *The Technology of Teaching*.New York: Appleton-Century-Crofts, 1968.

————. *Contingencies of Reinforcement*. New York: Appleton-Century-Crofts, 1969.

————. *Beyond Freedom and Dignity*. New York: Knopf, 1971.

————. *Cumulative Record*. 3rd. ed.; New York:                Appleton-Century-Crofts, 1972.

————. *About Behaviorism*. New York: Knopf, 1974.

————. *Particulars of my life*. New York: Knopf, 1976.

————. *Reflections on Behaviorism and Society*. Englewood Cliffs: Prentice-Hall, 1978.

————. *The Shaping of a Behaviorist*. New York: Knopf, 1979.

————. *Upon Further Reflection* Englewood Cliffs: Prentice-Hall, 1987.

## Commentaries

Richard I. Evans, *B.F. Skinner: the Man and his Ideas*. New York: E.P. Dutton, 1968.
Arthur Koestler, *The Ghost in the Machine*. Chicago: Henry Regnery Co., 1967.
Joseph Wood Krutch, *The Measure of Man*. New York: Grosset & Dunlap, 1953.
Ellen P. Reese, *The Analysis of Human Operant Behavior*. Dubuque, Iowa: W.C. Brown Co., 1966.
T. W. Wann, ed., *Behaviorism and Phenomenology*. Chicago: University of Chicago Press, 1964.

## Notes

1. *Particulars of my Life* (New York: Knopf, 1976), 51.
2. *Particulars of my Life*, 146.
3. *Particulars of my Life*, 291.
4. *Reflections on Behaviorism and Society* (Englewood Cliffs: Prentice-Hall Co., 1978), 93.
5. *Walden Two* (New York: Macmillan, 1948), 158-159, 161.
6. *Walden Two*, 159-161.
7. *Beyond Freedom ad Dignity* (New York: Knopf, 1971), 154.

# 25

# AYN RAND

## (1905-1982)

Ayn Rand was born on February 2, 1905, in St. Petersburg, later Petrograd, then Leningrad, and now, again, St. Petersburg. Her given name was Alisa Rosenbaum, which she later changed to Rand in gratitude to her typewriter. Her parents were Jewish, though not particularly religious. Her father was a successful businessman, and Ayn's early years were spent in a comfort that included summer vacations in Switzerland and France. At eight she fell in love with literature and began to write, inventing her own stories, for she thought it was a waste of time to wait for others to create the kind of story she wanted. She extended this view to the writings of philosophers.

The security of her existence was extinguished in 1917 when the Revolution shook Russia. Her father's business was nationalized. Ayn was twelve when she misunderstood Communism as a life of service to the state and was permanently horrified. She found solace in the novels of Victor Hugo and in discussions with her father. At fourteen she decided she was an atheist and that she had no faith at all.

Her father's savings supported the family for a while, but eventually they had to move to the Crimea, where she stayed until 1921 when they returned to Leningrad.

In 1921, Ayn entered the University to major in history. There she discovered Plato, Dostoyevsky and Nietzsche, whom she misunderstood and rejected, and Aristotle and Schiller, whom she misunderstood and loved.

Life became bleak in Leningrad, and living, a struggle. But things improved after a while. Foreign films and operettas made existence bearable. She graduated in 1924 and took a job as a guide in a museum. A year later she left for Chicago, in the United States, where relatives awaited her. By the summer, 1926, she had moved to Hollywood determined to become a screen writer. There she met Cecil B. de Mille, who offered her a job as an extra in *The King of Kings*, and later hired her as a junior screen writer. When de Mille closed down his studio she was out of a job and had to work in other capacities in order to make a living.

In the spring, 1929, she married Frank O'Connor, a handsome bit actor whom she had first met in Hollywood in 1926. She started working as a costumier for RKO, and she wrote in her spare time. Her play, *Woman on Trial*, opened to a successful run first in Hollywood in 1934 and later in New York as *The Night of January 16th*. The success of the play gave her economic independence, though in the years that followed she worked occasionally as a screen writer for various movie companies.

Her novel, *We the Living*, was published in 1936. *Anthem* followed in 1938, and *The Fountainhead* in 1943, which was turned into a movie in 1949. *Atlas Shrugged* was published in 1957, and then *For the New Intellectual* (1961). "The Objectivist Newsletter" began publication in 1962 under her editorship. Selections from it were published in book form as *Capitalism: the Unknown Ideal* (1966). *The Virtue of Selfishness* appeared in 1964. Other philosophical essays followed.

Ayn Rand died in 1982.

.oOo.

Once Ayn Rand was asked to summarize her philosophy while standing on one foot. Her answer:

1. *Metaphysics*: Objective Reality.
2. *Epistemology*: Reason.
3. *Ethics*: Self-interest.
4. *Politics*: Capitalism.[1]

She has officially labeled her philosophy "Objectivism." By this she means that there exists a reality that is independent of the mind's consideration. It is, in other words, objective. The human mind, however, is capable of apprehending the real such as it is in itself. Facts apprehended by the human mind form the basis of our judgments of value.

Rationality is the basis of individuality. "Man is an end in himself," she states; "he must live for his own sake with the achievement of his rational self-interest as the moral purpose of his life."[2] No one, therefore, has the right to force another human being to sacrifice either itself or its interests, or to subordinate itself to others. The paramount human purpose is private, individual happiness. The socio-political context best suited to this pursuit is that of laissez-faire Capitalism.

According to Rand, all societies up to now have been dominated by either of two fundamental principles: (1)self-sacrifice, altruism, regard for "the Common Good"—essentially the principles of Christianity; and (2)brute force, opportunism, the axiom that "might makes right." The two moralities of altruism and force, symbolized respectively by the Witch Doctor and Attila, have characterized all modes of human social living.

These two moralities have in common a disregard for the power of reason. Not that philosophers and intellectuals have been lacking in such societies, but their endeavors have been conducted either totally independently from the social conditions, or in total subordination to them. Philosophy has been either too abstract or too subservient. It has never really addressed itself resolutely to the task of coping with the problems confronted by individual living human beings.

A case in point is the United States. Here, says Rand, an intellectual crisis is apparent. Rigorous rational analysis has given way to "soft" intellectualisms such as Zen Buddhism and concern for the poor and destitute ("bleeding hearts" liberalism), or to abstract speculations that have nothing, or very little to do with daily living. Simultaneously, the business establishment has cut itself loose from any intellectual concerns and has given itself wholly to the pursuit of financial success through the economic equivalent of brute force. In America, Witch Doctor and Attila lead their lives in total disregard for each other. The consequences of this split are observable everywhere.

This sorry state of affairs is the more deplorable because America was the first society that sought to avoid the dichotomy between soul and body, mind and work, mystic and slave. To achieve this, it created Capitalism, a system, she maintains, in which two new types of people make their appearance for the first time: the businessman and the intellectual. The success of Capitalism, she claims, consists largely in its having completely eradicated slavery in both body and spirit, at least in theory and in Rand's novels. The success of Capitalism derives from its having combined the objective value of work with the rationality of its intellectual defenders.[3]

.oOo.

Capitalism, according to Rand, is the only socio-economic arrangement within which human beings can be human—that is, in which they can be consciously themselves as individuals. "Man is the measure of all things," said Protagoras. Rand adds: Not man in general but the Individual. "Collectivism, as a social ideal, is dead, but capitalism has not yet been discovered."[4] This would mean, of course, that any Christian social ethic is dead. Capitalism she defines as "a social system based on the recognition of individual rights, including property rights, in which all property is privately owned."[5] Capitalism is a mixture of reason and power at the service of the individual. Power, instead of being blind and destructive, becomes enlightened and creative. Reason, instead of being abstract and useless, becomes practical.[6]

It is within the context of Capitalism that the search for happiness must take place. In *Anthem* (1966), a marvelous story written in wonderful poetic prose, Ayn Rand describes the search for the individual and for individual happiness. Equality 7-2521 is a strapping young man of twenty-one when the story begins. He is a Street Sweeper, though he would rather be a Scholar. But this kind of desire is forbidden. It is the Sin of Preference, and Equality 7-2521 is conscious of his sin and feels guilty. All his life he has been told that only the Group matters, that the will of the Community must hold sway, that the happiness of All is the only happiness. The sense of community is so strong that he has never thought of himself except as "We."

Slowly, as the weeks and the months pass, Equality 7-2521 becomes aware that there is something wrong with this universalistic credo. He does not know what it is, but he sees it mirrored in the eyes of his fellow workers and manifested in their behavior.

Escape from the community, followed by prolonged meditation, lead him eventually to a profound insight into himself and into the human condition. The words he utters constitute a summary of Ayn Rand's credo, her belief in the supremacy of the individual and of the individual pursuit of happiness.

The emphasis on the individual and on an individualistic pursuit of happiness finds an obstacle in the ages-long insistence on self-sacrifice, compassion, and altruism, characteristic of a true Christianity. Individual happiness must revolt against this collectivistic myth that happiness may be found "together." Howard Roark tells his friend Gail Wynand what he has discovered about the evil effects of a collectivist ideology on the pursuit of happiness: happiness is an entirely private experience, and as such accessible only to the individual.[7] In *Atlas Shrugged* (1957), Rand's statements of her philosophy gain their most powerful expression.

Capitalism conjures up the idea of money, but Rand has in mind a wider understanding of Capitalism. It is not money alone that creates happiness. Money is but a tool at the service of the mind. It can purchase happiness but only if one knows what one wants.

.oOo.

# Additional Reading

## Sources

Ayn Rand, *The virtue of Selfishness*. New York: New American Library, 1964.
————. *Atlas Shrugged*. New York: Random House, 1957.
————. *Anthem*. Caldwell, Idaho: Caxton, 1966.

————. *Capitalism: the Unknown Ideal*. New York: New American Library, 1966.
————. *For the New Intellectual*. New York: Random House, 1961.
————. *The Fountainhead*. New York: Bobbs-Merrill, 1943.
————. *Introduction to Objectivist Epistemology*. New York: Objectivist, Inc., 1967.
————. *The New Left*. New York: New American Library, 1971.
————. *The Romantic Manifesto*. New York: World Publishing Co., 1969.
————. *We the Living*. New York: Random House, 1959.
————. *The Ayn Rand Lexicon: Objectivism from A to Z*. New York: New American Library, 1986.
————. *The Voice of Reason: Essays in Objectivist Thought*. New York: New American Library, 1988.

## Commentaries

James T. Baker, *Ayn Rand*. Boston: Twayne Publishers, 1987.
Nathaniel Branden, *Who is Ayn Rand?* New York: Random House, 1965.
————. *Psychotherapy and the Objectivist Ethics*. New York: N. Branden Institute, Inc., 1968.
————. *Judgment Day: My Years with Ayn Rand*. Boston: Houghton Mifflin, 1989.
Douglas J. Den Uyl & Douglas B. Rasmussen, eds., *The Philosophic Thought of Ayn Rand*. Chicago: University of Illinois Press, 1984.
Albert Ellis, *Is Objectivism a Religion?* New York: Lyle Stuart, Inc., 1968.
Mimi Reisel Gladstein, *The New Ayn Rand Companion*. Westport, CT: Greenwood Press, 2009.
Mimi Reise Gladstein and Chris Matthew Sciabarra, eds., *Feminist Interpretations of Ayn Rand*. University Park, PA: Pennsylvania State University Press, 1999.1
Sid Greenberg, *Ayn Rand and Alienation*. San Francisco: Sid Greenberg, 1977.
Ronald E. Merrill, *The Ideas of Ayn Rand*. Peru, IL: Open Court, 1991.
William F. O'Neill, *With charity toward none*. New York: Philosophical Library, 1971.
Michael Paxton, *Ayn Rand: A Sense of Life*. New York, 1998.
Leonard Peikoff, *Objectivism: The Philosophy of Ayn Rand*. New York: Dutton, 1991.
John W. Robbins, *Answer to Ayn Rand*. Washington, DC: Mount Vernon Pub-lishing Co., 1974.

## Notes

1. "Introducing Objectivism," *The Objectivist Newsletter* I, No.8 [August, 1962], 35.
2. "Introducing Objectivism," 35.
3. Cf. *For the New Intellectual* (New York: Random House, 1961), 23-24.
4. Rand, *For the New Intellectual*, 53.
5. Rand, *Capitalism, the Unknown Ideal* (New York: New American Library, 1966), 11-12.
6. Rand, *The Fountainhead* (New York: Bobbs-Merrill, 1943), 737.
7. Rand, *The Fountainhead*, 659-660.

# 26

# ALBERT CAMUS

(1913-1960)

Albert Camus was born on November 7, 1913, at Mondovi, in French North Africa. He had been preceded into the world by an older brother, Lucien. His father, Lucien Auguste Camus, was an Algerian of French descent, whose ancestors had migrated to Africa in the first half of the nineteenth century. He died October 11, 1914, from wounds suffered in the first Battle of the Marne.

His place as head of the family was taken over by Albert's maternal grand-mother, a cruel and dictatorial woman. Albert's mother, Catherine Sintès, claimed ancestry from Minorca, Spain. Afflicted by some hearing impediment and traumatized by the tragic death of her husband, she became taciturn and resigned, a silent presence with whom little Albert yearned to converse, but whose abstracted gaze did not invite communication.

His childhood, which provided the experiential core for his unfinished last novel, *Le Premier Homme*, transpired in the shadow of his dead father, in the care of his illiterate mother and grandmother, in a house without books, at Belcourt, a working class section of Algiers. Sustenance came from the earnings of his uncle Etienne, who lived with the family, and from the Government pensions awarded to all war orphans.

Albert attended the local kindergarten and primary school and later the *lycée.* He enjoyed swimming, the movies, and soccer (he played goalkeeper), and he read books borrowed from school or from the local public library. Louis Germain, his elementary school teacher, and Jean Grenier, his high school teacher and later mentor and friend, were decidedly important influences at this early stage of his life.

During his last year in high school (1930-31) he had his first bout with tuberculosis. Hospitalized briefly, he was released and went to live with his uncle, Gustave Acault, a butcher of some means and of intellectual leanings, who first introduced Gide's writings to his young nephew. Once recovered, Albert repeated the last year of high school. He passed the baccalaureate exam in June, 1932. During the year 1932-33 he published his first essays in a local literary monthly, *Sud.* He also began to attend classes at the University of Algiers, and he did some more writing, earnestly in search of his own style.

He enrolled officially at the University in the Fall, 1933, and received his license in 1935. He earned his *Diplôme d'études superieurs* in 1936. The title of his dissertation was "Neo-Platonism and Christian Thought," a work, as his adviser noted, more noteworthy for its art than for its philosophy. This was as high as he could go in Algiers. For the *agrégation*, the highest degree, he would have had to attend a university in mainland France, a prospect totally out of the question given his financial means, the state of his health, and his current frame of mind.

It was also during this time (late 1934) that he secretly joined the Communist Party. He did so, as he wrote to Jean Grenier, because "I have such a strong desire to help reduce the sum of unhappiness and of bitterness which empoisons mankind."[1] But he left the Party in 1937, disappointed with its policies toward the Arabs and their claims of nationalism.

On June 16, 1934, Camus had married Simone Hié, a ravishing beauty, every young Algerian's pin-up girl, and the girlfriend of his friend Max-Pol Fouchet, whose friendship he thus lost for good. She became the object of his poems. For her he wrote "Melusina's Book," and from her he received his bitterest disappointment. Simone was a drug addict who stopped at nothing to get a fix. After a disastrous trip with her and a friend through France, the Czech Republic, and Italy, Camus returned to Algiers and separated from Simone. They were divorced in 1940. Simone died in 1970.

There followed for Camus a period of intense theater activity. He translated, adapted, and directed plays, and to earn money he tutored pupils. He lived with several like-minded friends in a rambling house, the Maison Fichu, the "House Above the World" chronicled in *A Happy Death.* The friends pooled their resources and managed, barely, to make ends meet. These days saw the first drafts of his plays *Caligula* and *The Misunderstanding.*

In May, 1937, his first book, *The Wrong Side and the Right Side*, appeared in a small edition. Later that year he moved to the French Savoy mountains for a rest necessitated by his ailing lungs. After a short trip to Italy, he returned to Algiers and a boring but much needed job as assistant at the Institut de Métérologie et de Physique du Globe. He left it later to become engaged in more decidedly literary activity as contributor to *Rivages* and *Alger Républicaine.* He finished the manuscript of *A Happy Death* but, unsure of it, he never published it. Instead, he finished *Nuptials* (1939) and began work on *The Stranger.*

The war began. Censorship forced the closing of *Alger Républicaine*, so Camus moved to Paris and began work at *Paris-Soir*. The Germans advanced, and Paris had to be evacuated. The staff of *Paris-Soir* moved to Clermont-Ferrand and then to Lyons. At Lyons, on December 3, 1940, Camus married Francine Faure, whom he had known for many years. She was a bright mathematician and an accomplished pianist, and she proved to be a strong, suffering woman, who endured her husband's triumphs, failures, loyalties and infidelities—especially with Maria Casarès.

Camus soon lost his job due to staff cuts, so he and Francine moved to Oran. She took a job as a substitute teacher, and he read manuscripts for Éditions Charlot, his first publisher. In his spare time he finished *The Myth of Sisyphus* and began work on *The Plague*. Both *The Myth of Sisyphus* and *The Stranger* were published in 1942.

Early that year Camus suffered another attack of tuberculosis. In August, he and Francine traveled to Le Panelier, a hamlet in the mountains south-west of Lyons. After seeing him settled and on the way to recovery, Francine returned to Algiers to look for a job. But in November the Allies landed in North Africa, and the Germans moved south, thus controlling all of France. Camus' return was barred. To support himself he took up work as reader for Gallimard, and eventually moved to Paris at the end of 1943. At this time he joined the staff of the underground newspaper *Combat*. Later the same year he met Sartre, whose friendship and company he treasured until 1957. During 1943-44 he published *Letters to a German Friend* and finished a revised version of *Caligula* as well as *The Misunderstanding*, which opened in mid-1944 to boos and hoots from the audience.

Then the Allies landed at Cherbourg. Paris was freed. Camus continued to write editorials for *Combat*, and they became the talk of Paris. By October, Francine had joined him, interrupting (at least for a time) his romantic idyll with Maria Casarès. Francine became pregnant. Their twin children, Jean and Catherine, were born in September, 1945. That month also saw the opening of *Caligula*, to mixed reviews.

The pace of Camus' life quickened. Embroilment in argument through editorials took time. The theater, his job at Gallimard, his family, his friends, hardly left him time for his own writings. Then came the tours—to Algiers in 1945, to the United States in 1946 (where he was enthusiastically received), to England in 1948, and to Latin America in 1949. Still he found time for *The Plague*, which was published in 1947, followed by the play, *State of Siege* (1948).

His health, again, imposed rest on him. This time there were new wonder-drugs that made recovery more definite. Then his political activities soured, both at *Combat* and with the very politicized writers of his generation. Still he wrote: *The Just Assassins* opened in December, 1950, with Maria Casarès as Dora. This was followed by the publication of *The Rebel* (1951) and *Summer* (1954). *Les Temps Modernes*, whose editor was Sartre, criticized *The Rebel* severely. Camus countered in kind, precipitating a retort by Sartre himself. Their friendship cracked, and the reverberations echoed throughout France.

In the meantime, the French-Algerian "problem" was growing. Camus found himself incapable of providing the leadership he would have desired. Extreme positions had been taken, and compromise was impossible. In the midst of this turmoil came his last novel, *The Fall* (1956), a merciless self-appraisal, followed by a collection of short stories, *Exile and the Kingdom* (1957). And then, the Nobel Prize for literature (1957).

Accepting the Prize at such a young age placed a high burden on him: he did not want to be seen as a writer whose best work lay behind him. He was forty-three and full of ideas, though suffering for some time from an incapacity to write a work of significance, a condition that necessitated the diverting of his energies, again, to the theater. He was already on the way to recovery and creation with his new project, *Le Premier Homme*, when he died in an automobile accident on January 4, 1960.

.oOo.

The point of departure is the absurd. The absurd burst into Camus' life at seventeen, when he was still in high school. He was full of life, full of visions. The local newspapers were replete with chronicles of his exploits as goalkeeper, even when his team lost. He enjoyed the sea with the sensual passion that made Algerians say they "indulged in a swim" rather than, tritely, that they "went for a swim."[2] He was at the top of his class academically. Suddenly, he coughed blood. Tuberculosis struck, and for the first time he contemplated the possibility of death. With Caligula he concluded, "Men die; and they are not happy."[3]

What is the absurd? It is, first of all, an experience. It is something one undergoes, like all experiences. One can think about it, conceptualize it. But that comes later. Above all, it is an experience, and one must make sure that no thought, no conceptualizations, no system or explanation ever obliterates the experience of the absurd.

The absurd is an experience of confrontation between one's longing for life, for meaning, for love, and the universe's indifference, opaqueness, and death; between the expectation of justice and the fact of injustice—between what we want and what we get. Metaphysically and socially, the absurd is a divorce. As with every divorce, the absurd is a matter of two parties. It is not the world that is absurd; nor we, humans; but the relationship that binds us to the world and the world to us. "The irrational [answer], the human nostalgia, and the absurd that is born of their encounter—these are the three characters in the drama."[4]

Sooner or later we all confront the absurd. But our answers to the question thus posed differ, and considerably. Some kill themselves, as if the mere elimination of a datum could solve the problem raised. Others pretend the question was never raised; or that it does not matter; or that there is an answer in heaven. Such efforts to wriggle out of the problem do not carry. Suicide, whether physical or philosophical, whether as denial of life or of light, is not an answer. It is simply a denial of experience, and that is the one thing we are forbidden to do if we are to be honest with ourselves.

The point, then, is to build a life without denying the data of experience or losing sight of it. "To realize the absurdity of life cannot be an end, but only a beginning," Camus wrote in *Alger Républicaine* (October 20, 1938). How does one move beyond the absurd without betraying it?

First, one must keep one's eyes open. Too much of life around us would have us close our eyes and deny the data of experience: promises of an after-life, or of a great society, affluence, power, pleasure, accomplishments; there are many types of smoke-screens, but they all have in common one thing, to cover up the evidence. "There are many ways of leaping, the essential being to leap."[5] Hence the antidote, lucidity, an intense, unclouded awareness that masks nothing. It is "the cold and implacable clarity one must endure in order to live."[6]

Secondly, we must approach actions with an openness that pre-judges nothing. Death is the standard. If both the saint and the sinner die, how are their deeds different? From the point of view of this life, who shall we say has lived more, and lived more humanly? Certainly, those who have lived the longest and the most. How does one live most humanly?

One must revolt. Without losing sight of the absurd, one must fight against anything and everything that would lessen the value of human life. The absurd imposes limits: one will never be able to rid human life of all pain and distress. But the humanness of human life lies precisely in the effort to diminish pain and enhance happiness. Those who do so Camus called "the true healers."[7] Like Cherea and Dr. Rieux, they are people in revolt against every injustice. Like Kalyayev, they love life, and they are rebels because they love life.[8] But being lucid they also realize that their achievements can be neither complete nor lasting. There will always be tyrants, and the threat of plague will always hang in the air. Hence their rebellion must be tempered by moderation. "If . . . rebellion could find a philosophy it would be a philosophy of limits, of calculated ignorance, and of risk."[9]

And so they strive, like Sisyphus, after an impossible which they know is beyond their reach, but in the seeking of which a truly human life may be lived. They look for a cure for this plague we all suffer, this bacillus we all carry, this misery of the absurd, yet they take care not to contaminate anyone in the process. They strive to be human while refusing to be gods; that is, they ask for things that depend on them alone.[10] As they pass by, one must imagine them happy.

.oOo.

The absurd is the link between people and the world. But it is not the only link. Camus defines happiness as "the simple harmony between a man and the life he leads."[11] The link of happiness, however, is conceived as harmony, while the absurd is a divorce. Happiness, therefore, unites what the absurd sunders. Further, happiness is a harmony that does not obliterate or deny the absurd. This means that the pursuit of happiness, like everything else, must take place in the context of the absurd. Camus chooses Sisyphus, the man condemned forever to roll a rock up a hill only to see it tumble down again, as the symbol of the pursuit of happiness in absurdity.

> One does not discover the absurd without being tempted to write a manual of happiness. "What! by such narrow ways—?" There is but one world, however. Happiness and the absurd are two sons of the same earth They are inseparable. It would be a mistake to say that happiness necessarily springs from the absurd discovery. It happens as well that the feeling of the absurd springs from happiness. "I conclude that all is well," says Oedipus [Sophocles, *Oedipus at Colonus*, line 1 ff.], and that remark is sacred. It echoes in the wild and limited universe of man. It teaches that all is not, has not been, exhausted. It drives out of this world a god who had come into it with dissatisfaction and a preference for futile sufferings. It makes of fate a human matter, which must be settled among men.
>
> . . . . . . . . .
>
> I leave Sisyphus at the foot of the mountain! One always finds one's burden again. But Sisyphus teaches the higher fidelity that negates the gods and raises rocks. He too concludes that all is well. This universe henceforth without a master seems to him neither sterile nor futile. Each atom of that stone, each mineral flake of that nightfilled mountain, in itself forms a world. The struggle itself toward the heights is enough to fill a man's heart. One must imagine Sisyphus happy.[12]

This lesson is difficult to learn because, according to Camus, many imagine that their happiness depends on the presence of certain conditions, such as money, time, health, etc. If these conditions are absent, they conclude that happiness cannot be obtained. But they err. "The mistake . . . lies in thinking . . . that there are conditions for happiness. Happiness either is or it isn't. It's the will to happiness which matters, a kind of vast ever present awareness."[13]

This will to happiness of Camus' is different from the Kantian categorical duty, which takes precedence over happiness. It is also different from the Nietzschean will to power which, again, precedes happiness. For Camus, both these positions subordinate happiness to other human endeavors, something he does not accept. Also, these views entail an absolutist position, "all or nothing"—perfect happiness or sense of duty/will to power—a position whose logic Camus repeatedly rejects as a violation of moderation. As Cherea tells Caligula, "What I want is to live, and to be happy. Neither, to my mind, is possible if one pushes the absurd to its logical conclusions."[14]

For Camus, true human happiness is the kind experienced on this earth, imperfect yet utterly enthralling. No heavenly happiness for him, no postponement of joy until a future time. "I am happy in this world," he writes in his *Notebooks*, "for my kingdom is of this world."[15] Describing it he writes:

> What is strange about finding on earth the unity Plotinus longed for? Unity expresses itself here in terms of sea and sky. The heart senses it through a certain taste of the flesh that constitutes its bitterness and greatness. I am learning that there is no superhuman happiness, no eternity outside the curve of the days. These ridiculous and essential assets, these relative truths are the only ones that move

me. I have not enough soul to understand the other, "ideal" ones. Not that we
should behave as beasts, but I can see no point in the happiness of angels. All I
know is that this sky will last longer than I shall. And what can I call eternity
except what will continue after my death?[16]

Happiness has many characteristics derived, or flowing, from Camus' definition. Happiness is a sensual, bodily feeling with a sense of health, of well-being,
and of sensory saturation. The passages abound, and most of Camus' early essays
express forcefully and alluringly this sensual characteristic of happiness.

> Under the morning sun, a great happiness hovers in space. . . . .
> Every beautiful thing has a natural pride in its own beauty, and today the
> world is allowing its pride to seep from every pore. Why, in its presence, should
> I deny the joy of living, as long as I know everything is not included in this joy?
> There is no shame in being happy.[17]

Another characteristic of happiness is that it is shared. This theme is played
throughout all of Camus' works—from *Caligula*, who wins only "the godlike
enlightenment of the solitary,"[18] to Jan, who realizes that "no one can be happy in
exile or estrangement,"[19] to D'Arrast who finds his place in the hut among the
poor.[20] The point is highlighted in *The Plague*. Rambert, the journalist who has
been quarantined in Oran against his wishes when the plague erupts, is trying to
escape unlawfully. Dr. Rieux and Tarrou know about it, but do not attempt to stop
him, because his fiancée is waiting for him outside. So Rambert's confession comes
to them as a surprise:

> "Doctor," Rambert said, "I'm not going. I want to stay with you."
> Tarrou made no movement; he went on driving. Rieux seemed unable to
> shake off his fatigue.
> "And what about her?" His voice was hardly audible.
> Rambert said he'd thought it over very carefully, and his views hadn't
> changed, but if he went away, he would feel ashamed of himself, and that would
> embarrass his relations with the woman he loved.
> Showing more animation, Rieux told him that was sheer nonsense; there was
> nothing shameful in preferring happiness. "Certainly," Rambert replied. "But it
> may be shameful to be happy by oneself."
> Tarrou, who had not spoken so far, now remarked, without turning his head,
> that if Rambert wished to take a share of other people's unhappiness, he'd have
> no time left for happiness. So the choice had to be made.
> "That's not it," Rambert rejoined. "Until now I always felt a stranger in this
> town, and that I'd no concern with you people. But now that I've seen what I have
> seen, I know that I belong here whether I want it or not. This business is
> everybody's business." When there was no reply from either of the others,
> Rambert seemed to grow annoyed. "But you know that as well as I do, damn it!
> Or else what are you up to in that hospital of yours? Have you made a definite
> choice and turned down happiness?"[21]

.oOo.

# Additional Reading

## Sources

Albert Camus, *Oeuvres Complètes*, ed. Roger Quilliot. 2 vols.; Paris: Bibliothèque de la
    Pléiade, Gallimard, 1962-1965.
————. *Youthful Writings*, ed. Paul Viallaneix. New York: Vintage, 1976.
————. *Lyrical and Critical Essays*. New York: Vintage, 1970
————. *A Happy Death*. New York: A. Knopf, 1972.
————. *The Stranger*. New York: Vintage, 1946.
————. *The Myth of Sisyphus*. New York: Vintage, 1955.
————. *Caligula and Three Other Plays*. New York: Vintage, 1958.
————. *The Plague*. New York: Modern Library, 1948.
————. *The Rebel*. New York: Vintage, 1956.
————. *The Fall*. New York: Vintage, 1956.
————. *Exile and the Kingdom*. New York: Vintage, 1957.
————. *Resistance, Rebellion, and Death*. New York: Modern Library, 1963.
————. *Notebooks*. 2 vols.; New York: Modern Library, 1965.
————. *American Journals*. New York: Paragon House, 1987.
————. *The First Man*. New York: 1995.

## Commentaries

Paul Archambault, *Camus' Hellenic Sources*. Chapel Hill: University of North Carolina
    Press, 1972.
Germaine Brée, *Camus*. New York: Harcourt, Brace, Jovanovich,    Inc., 1964.
————. ed., *Camus*. Englewood Cliffs, NJ: Prentice-Hall, Inc., 1962.
Edward L. Burke, "Camus and the Pursuit of Happiness," *Thought* XXXVII, (Fall, 1962),
    391-401.
Alfred Cordes, *The Descent of the Doves: Camus' Journey to the Spirit*. Washington, DC:
    University Press of America, 1980.
Donald Lazere, *The Unique Creation of Albert Camus*. New Haven: Yale University Press,
    1973.
Herbert Lottman, *Albert Camus*. New York: Doubleday, 1979.
Patrick McCarthy, *Camus*. New York, Random House, 1982.
Pierre Nguyen-Van-Huy, *La Métaphysique du Bonheur chez Albert Camus*. Neuchatel:
    Université de Fribourg, 1961.
Jean Onimus, *Albert Camus and Christianity*. Tuscaloosa: University of Alabama Press,

1970.

Roger Quilliot, *Sea and Prisons*. Alabama: University of Alabama Press, 1970.

James W. Woelfel, *Camus: A Theological Perspective*. Nashville: Abingdon, 1975.

## Notes

1. Lottman, *Albert Camus* (New York: Doubleday, 1979), 89.

2. *Nuptials*, "Summer in Algiers," in *Lyrical and Critical Essays* (New York: Vintage, 1970), 82.

3. "Caligula," in *Caligula and Three Other Plays* (New York: Vintage, 1958), 8.

4. *The Myth of Sisyphus* (New York: Vintage, 1955), 21.

5. Ibid., 31.

6. *The Rebel* (New York: Vintage, 1956), 85.

7. *The Plague* (New York: Modern Library, 1948), 230 and 278.

8. *The Just Assassins*, in *Caligula and Three Other Plays*, 243

9. *The Rebel*, 289.

10. Ibid., 271.

11. *Nuptials*, in *Lyrical and Critical Essays*, 101.

12. *The Myth of Sisyphus*, 90-91.

13. *Notebooks* (New York: Modern Library, 1965), Vol. I, 77.

14. "Caligula," in *Caligula and Three Other Plays*, 51-52.

15. *Notebooks,* Vol. I, 9.

16. *Nuptials*, in *Lyrical and Critical Essays*, 90-91.

17. Ibid., 68-70.

18. "Caligula," in *Caligula and Three Other Plays*, 72.

19. "The Misunderstanding," in *Caligula and Three Other Plays*, 87.

20. *Exile and the Kingdom* (New York: Vintage, 1957), 213.

21. *The Plague*, 188.

# EPILOGUE

It does not seem proper to end this book without some final word on happiness, some kind of colophon, or summary, of the ways in which happiness has been both lived and described. But how can one synthesize such disparate conceptions? Is not the very reason for the many conceptions of happiness that none of them, by itself, suffices to describe what happiness humans have enjoyed, in their single or collective lives, throughout the centuries? And who can say that the list of options is exhaustive, that we have said the last word on the possible ways of being happy?

Plutarch, in his life of Solon, recounts a conversation in which Croesus asked Solon if he had known a person happier than himself. When Solon struggled to recall the names of the happy people he had known, Croesus grew impatient, for none of the examples Solon could muster were reckoned happy because of their riches, an item which, Croesus thought, was of primary importance, and that, as the richest man then living, should have guaranteed him the title, "Happiest man on earth."

"What," asked Croesus angrily, "don't you reckon me among the happy at all?"

Solon replied: "Our humble wisdom forbids us to admire any one's happiness that may yet, in course of time, undergo change. So, to hail as happy any one that is still alive we think is as foolish as to count a wrestler victorious while he is still in the ring."

And shall I say the modes of happiness are all complete while the hopes of human life are still extended to the future like a rope over an abyss?

We are what we have been, and our conceptions of happiness do not preclude the blossoming of still unsown seeds. Humanity is, too, what shall be, when it shall be. And only then, if then, will it be possible to gather in one final formula the sum of all the happiness of the world. In the meantime, the following story may serve as an apt, if simple, conclusion to the book.

.oOo.

The world is full of strange happenings, and this one will surely seem the strangest of them all. But it *did* happen, a long, long time ago.

A young boy by the name of Babu Din was walking one sunny morning along the banks of the Sabarmati river in Ahmedabad, when he came upon an old brass lamp. He picked it up, held it to the sun, and began to brush the sand from it, when the lamp shook in his hands and a vapor flowed out of it, rose in the air, and condensed into a giant, weird-looking form. The boy realized it was a genie, and he was frightened, because genies are not always kind to strangers; but this genie was a friendly one, and, as was the custom, he instantly offered Babu Din the fulfillment of three wishes, no more, no less.

Babu Din did not have to think long to decide. He said: "Make me happy. I want to be happy."

"Ah," said the genie, "you have foolishly lost your first wish. I cannot grant it. Happiness means many different things to many different people. You would have had to choose which happiness you wanted for yourself, and then I could have granted your wish. Take care now, you have only two wishes left."

Now Babu Din realized that things would not be as easy as he had thought, so he took some time to think before he asked his second wish. At last he said: "Tell me what ways there are to be happy."

"Well," said the genie, "some think that being happy happens by sheer accident, like winning the lottery, so they believe they are happy only when something good happens to them. Some think that having pleasure is happiness, so they spend their lives avoiding pain. Some, with 'Alî, think that happiness consists in the good feeling that accompanies an inner sense of balance and piety. Some, on the other hand, like the mutakallimûn, believe that happiness is the peace that comes when pondering the secrets of Allah (blessed be his name!). Still others believe with 'Umar Khayyâm that happiness is to be found amidst the ecstasies of orgies and revelries. Some feel that happiness can be experienced only in paradise, in the delight the saints experience in the presence of Allah (blessed be he!). Still others experience happiness in their efforts to be what they want to be. Many, like the Khalîf, feel happy when surrounded by things, whether the rest of the world is rich or poor; and still others, like the sûfîs, think that happiness consists in self-control amidst the vicissitudes of life. These are the ways of happiness, young master, and I have told them to you in fulfillment of your second wish. Now you have only one wish left."

This time Babu Din spent a long while thinking, for he wanted his last wish to be really effective. He thought for so long that the genie grew impatient, and Babu Din was afraid he would leave without granting him his third wish.

At long last, Babu Din said: "You have told me that happiness is many things, and you have explained to me the various ways of being happy. Here is my third wish. Grant me the wisdom to know always which way to choose to be happy."

"You have chosen wisely," said the genie. "It shall be with you according to your wish." And as he bowed to Babu Din, his giant form grew dim till it dissolved in the thin air of the morning.

Babu Din's third wish was granted. He lived a very happy life all his days on earth, and when he died, his friends felt sure he was still happy in heaven, but of this they had no proof. Yet as he had tasted all the other ways of being happy the genie had described to him, they felt this one, too, must be his lot in paradise.

# INDEX